ALL GLORY TO ŚRĪ GURU AND GAURĀṄGA

ŚRĪMAD BHĀGAVATAM

of

KṚṢṆA-DVAIPĀYANA VYĀSA

यद् युज्यतेऽसुवसुकर्ममनोवचोभि-
देहात्मजादिषु नृभिस्तदसत् पृथक्त्वात् ।
तैरेव सद् भवति यत् क्रियतेऽपृथक्त्वात्
सर्वस्य तद् भवति मूलनिषेचनं यत् ॥

yad yujyate 'su-vasu-karma-mano-vacobhir
dehātmajādiṣu nṛbhis tad asat pṛthaktvāt
tair eva sad bhavati yat kriyate 'pṛthaktvāt
sarvasya tad bhavati mūla-niṣecanaṁ yat

(p. 24)

BOOKS by
His Divine Grace A. C. Bhaktivedanta Swami Prabhupāda

Bhagavad-gītā As It Is
Śrīmad-Bhāgavatam, Cantos 1–8 (24 Vols.)
Śrī Caitanya-caritāmṛta (17 Vols.)
Teachings of Lord Caitanya
The Nectar of Devotion
The Nectar of Instruction
Śrī Īśopaniṣad
Easy Journey to Other Planets
Kṛṣṇa Consciousness: The Topmost Yoga System
Kṛṣṇa, the Supreme Personality of Godhead (3 Vols.)
Perfect Questions, Perfect Answers
Dialectic Spiritualism—A Vedic View of Western Philosophy
Transcendental Teachings of Prahlād Mahārāja
Kṛṣṇa, the Reservoir of Pleasure
Life Comes from Life
The Perfection of Yoga
Beyond Birth and Death
On the Way to Kṛṣṇa
Rāja-vidyā: The King of Knowledge
Elevation to Kṛṣṇa Consciousness
Kṛṣṇa Consciousness: The Matchless Gift
Back to Godhead Magazine (Founder)

A complete catalogue is available upon request

The Bhaktivedanta Book Trust
3764 Watseka Avenue
Los Angeles, California 90034

ŚRĪMAD BHĀGAVATAM

Eighth Canto

"Withdrawal of the Cosmic Creations"

(Part Two—Chapters 9–16)

With the Original Sanskrit Text,
Its Roman Transliteration, Synonyms,
Translation and Elaborate Purports

by

His Divine Grace
A.C. Bhaktivedanta Swami Prabhupāda
Founder-*Ācārya* of the International Society for Krishna Consciousness

THE BHAKTIVEDANTA BOOK TRUST
New York · Los Angeles · London · Bombay

Readers interested in the subject matter of this book
are invited by the International Society for Krishna Consciousness
to correspond with its Secretary.

International Society for Krishna Consciousness
3764 Watseka Avenue
Los Angeles, California 90034

Library of Congress Catalogue Card Number: 73-169353
International Standard Book Number: 0-912776-91-9

First printing, 1976: 20,000 copies

Printed in the United States of America

Table of Contents

CHAPTER SIXTEEN
Executing the Payo-vrata Process of Worship

Preface

We must know the present need of human society. And what is that need? Human society is no longer bounded by geographical limits to particular countries or communities. Human society is broader than in the Middle Ages, and the world tendency is toward one state or one human society. The ideals of spiritual communism, according to *Śrīmad-Bhāgavatam*, are based more or less on the oneness of the entire human society, nay, on the entire energy of living beings. The need is felt by great thinkers to make this a successful ideology. *Śrīmad-Bhāgavatam* will fill this need in human society. It begins, therefore, with the aphorism of Vedānta philosophy (*janmādy asya yataḥ*) to establish the ideal of a common cause.

Human society, at the present moment, is not in the darkness of oblivion. It has made rapid progress in the field of material comforts, education and economic development throughout the entire world. But there is a pinprick somewhere in the social body at large, and therefore there are large-scale quarrels, even over less important issues. There is need of a clue as to how humanity can become one in peace, friendship and prosperity with a common cause. *Śrīmad-Bhāgavatam* will fill this need, for it is a cultural presentation for the re-spiritualization of the entire human society.

Śrīmad-Bhāgavatam should be introduced also in the schools and colleges, for it is recommended by the great student devotee Prahlāda Mahārāja in order to change the demonic face of society.

kaumāra ācaret prājño
dharmān bhāgavatān iha
durlabhaṁ mānuṣaṁ janma
tad apy adhruvam arthadam
(*Bhāg.* 7.6.1)

Disparity in human society is due to lack of principles in a godless civilization. There is God, or the Almighty One, from whom everything emanates, by whom everything is maintained and in whom everything is merged to rest. Material science has tried to find the ultimate source of creation very insufficiently, but it is a fact that there is one ultimate source of everything that be. This ultimate source is explained rationally and authoritatively in the beautiful *Bhāgavatam* or *Śrīmad-Bhāgavatam.*

Śrīmad-Bhāgavatam is the transcendental science not only for knowing the ultimate source of everything but also for knowing our relation with Him and our duty towards perfection of the human society on the basis of this perfect knowledge. It is powerful reading matter in the Sanskrit language, and it is now rendered into English elaborately so that simply by a careful reading one will know God perfectly well, so much so that the reader will be sufficiently educated to defend himself from the onslaught of atheists. Over and above this, the reader will be able to convert others to accept God as a concrete principle.

Śrīmad-Bhāgavatam begins with the definition of the ultimate source. It is a bona fide commentary on the *Vedānta-sūtra* by the same author, Śrīla Vyāsadeva, and gradually it develops into nine cantos up to the highest state of God realization. The only qualification one needs to study this great book of transcendental knowledge is to proceed step by step cautiously and not jump forward haphazardly as with an ordinary book. It should be gone through chapter by chapter, one after another. The reading matter is so arranged with its original Sanskrit text, its English transliteration, synonyms, translation and purports so that one is sure to become a God realized soul at the end of finishing the first nine cantos.

The Tenth Canto is distinct from the first nine cantos, because it deals directly with the transcendental activities of the Personality of Godhead Śrī Kṛṣṇa. One will be unable to capture the effects of the Tenth Canto without going through the first nine cantos. The book is complete in twelve cantos, each independent, but it is good for all to read them in small installments one after another.

I must admit my frailties in presenting *Śrīmad-Bhāgavatam,* but still I am hopeful of its good reception by the thinkers and leaders of society on the strength of the following statement of *Śrīmad-Bhāgavatam.*

tad-vāg-visargo janatāgha-viplavo
yasmin pratiślokam abaddhavaty api

nāmāny anantasya yaśo 'ṅkitāni yac
chṛṇvanti gāyanti gṛṇanti sādhavaḥ
(*Bhāg.* 1.5.11)

"On the other hand, that literature which is full with descriptions of the transcendental glories of the name, fame, form and pastimes of the unlimited Supreme Lord is a transcendental creation meant to bring about a revolution in the impious life of a misdirected civilization. Such transcendental literatures, even though irregularly composed, are heard, sung and accepted by purified men who are thoroughly honest."

Oṁ tat sat

A. C. Bhaktivedanta Swami

Introduction

"This *Bhāgavata Purāṇa* is as brilliant as the sun, and it has arisen just after the departure of Lord Kṛṣṇa to His own abode, accompanied by religion, knowledge, etc. Persons who have lost their vision due to the dense darkness of ignorance in the age of Kali shall get light from this *Purāṇa.*" (*Śrīmad-Bhāgavatam* 1.3.43)

The timeless wisdom of India is expressed in the *Vedas*, ancient Sanskrit texts that touch upon all fields of human knowledge. Originally preserved through oral tradition, the *Vedas* were first put into writing five thousand years ago by Śrīla Vyāsadeva, the "literary incarnation of God." After compiling the *Vedas*, Vyāsadeva set forth their essence in the aphorisms known as *Vedānta-sūtras. Śrīmad-Bhāgavatam* is Vyāsadeva's commentary on his own *Vedānta-sūtras.* It was written in the maturity of his spiritual life under the direction of Nārada Muni, his spiritual master. Referred to as "the ripened fruit of the tree of Vedic literature," *Śrīmad-Bhāgavatam* is the most complete and authoritative exposition of Vedic knowledge.

After compiling the *Bhāgavatam*, Vyāsa impressed the synopsis of it upon his son, the sage Śukadeva Gosvāmī. Śukadeva Gosvāmī subsequently recited the entire *Bhāgavatam* to Mahārāja Parīkṣit in an assembly of learned saints on the bank of the Ganges at Hastināpura (now Delhi). Mahārāja Parīkṣit was the emperor of the world and was a great *rājarṣi* (saintly king). Having received a warning that he would die within a week, he renounced his entire kingdom and retired to the bank of the Ganges to fast until death and receive spiritual enlightenment. The *Bhāgavatam* begins with Emperor Parīkṣit's sober inquiry to Śukadeva Gosvāmī: "You are the spiritual master of great saints and devotees. I am therefore begging you to show the way of perfection for all persons, and especially for one who is about to die. Please let me know what a man should hear, chant, remember and worship, and also what he should not do. Please explain all this to me."

Śukadeva Gosvāmī's answer to this question, and numerous other questions posed by Mahārāja Parīkṣit, concerning everything from the nature of the self to the origin of the universe, held the assembled sages in rapt attention continuously for the seven days leading to the King's death. The sage Sūta Gosvāmī, who was present on the bank of the Ganges when Śukadeva Gosvāmī first recited *Śrīmad-Bhāgavatam*, later repeated the *Bhāgavatam* before a gathering of sages in the forest of Naimiṣāraṇya. Those sages, concerned about the spiritual welfare of the people in general, had gathered to perform a long, continuous chain of sacrifices to counteract the degrading influence of the incipient age of Kali. In response to the sages' request that he speak the essence of Vedic wisdom, Sūta Gosvāmī repeated from memory the entire eighteen thousand verses of *Śrīmad-Bhāgavatam*, as spoken by Śukadeva Gosvāmī to Mahārāja Parīkṣit.

The reader of *Śrīmad-Bhāgavatam* hears Sūta Gosvāmī relate the questions of Mahārāja Parīkṣit and the answers of Śukadeva Gosvāmī. Also, Sūta Gosvāmī sometimes responds directly to questions put by Śaunaka Ṛṣi, the spokesman for the sages gathered at Naimiṣāraṇya. One therefore simultaneously hears two dialogues: one between Mahārāja Parīkṣit and Śukadeva Gosvāmī on the bank of the Ganges, and another at Naimiṣāraṇya between Sūta Gosvāmī and the sages at Naimiṣāraṇya Forest, headed by Śaunaka Ṛṣi. Furthermore, while instructing King Parīkṣit, Śukadeva Gosvāmī often relates historical episodes and gives accounts of lengthy philosophical discussions between such great souls as the saint Maitreya and his disciple Vidura. With this understanding of the history of the *Bhāgavatam*, the reader will easily be able to follow its intermingling of dialogues and events from various sources. Since philosophical wisdom, not chronological order, is most important in the text, one need only be attentive to the subject matter of *Śrīmad-Bhāgavatam* to appreciate fully its profound message.

The translator of this edition compares the *Bhāgavatam* to sugar candy—wherever you taste it, you will find it equally sweet and relishable. Therefore, to taste the sweetness of the *Bhāgavatam*, one may begin by reading any of its volumes. After such an introductory taste, however, the serious reader is best advised to go back to Volume One of the First Canto and then proceed through the *Bhāgavatam*, volume after volume, in its natural order.

This edition of the *Bhāgavatam* is the first complete English translation of this important text with an elaborate commentary, and it is the first widely available to the English-speaking public. It is the product of the scholarly and devotional effort of His Divine Grace A. C. Bhaktivedanta Swami Prabhupāda, the world's most distinguished teacher of Indian religious and philosophical thought. His consummate Sanskrit scholarship and intimate familiarity with Vedic culture and thought as well as the modern way of life combine to reveal to the West a magnificent exposition of this important classic.

Readers will find this work of value for many reasons. For those interested in the classical roots of Indian civilization, it serves as a vast reservoir of detailed information on virtually every one of its aspects. For students of comparative philosophy and religion, the *Bhāgavatam* offers a penetrating view into the meaning of India's profound spiritual heritage. To sociologists and anthropologists, the *Bhāgavatam* reveals the practical workings of a peaceful and scientifically organized Vedic culture, whose institutions were integrated on the basis of a highly developed spiritual world view. Students of literature will discover the *Bhāgavatam* to be a masterpiece of majestic poetry. For students of psychology, the text provides important perspectives on the nature of consciousness, human behavior and the philosophical study of identity. Finally, to those seeking spiritual insight, the *Bhāgavatam* offers simple and practical guidance for attainment of the highest self-knowledge and realization of the Absolute Truth. The entire multivolume text, presented by the Bhaktivedanta Book Trust, promises to occupy a significant place in the intellectual, cultural and spiritual life of modern man for a long time to come.

—The Publishers

His Divine Grace
A. C. Bhaktivedanta Swami Prabhupāda
Founder-Ācārya of the International Society for Krishna Consciousness

PLATE ONE

Having taken possession of the container of nectar, the Supreme Personality of Godhead, in the beguiling form of Mohinī, smiled slightly and said, "My dear demons, if you accept whatever I may do, whether honest or dishonest, then I can take responsibility for dividing the nectar among you." Because the chiefs of the demons were not very expert in deciding things, upon hearing the sweet words of Mohinī-mūrti they immediately assented. Thus Mohinī-mūrti, wearing a most beautiful sari and tinkling ankle bells, entered the lavishly decorated arena. She walked very slowly because of Her big, low hips, and Her eyes moved restlessly due to youthful pride. Her breasts were like water jugs, Her thighs resembled the trunks of elephants and She carried a waterpot in Her hand. Her attractive nose and cheeks and Her ears, adorned with golden earrings, made Her face very beautiful. As She moved, Her sari's border on Her breasts moved slightly aside. When the demigods and demons saw these beautiful features of Mohinī-mūrti, who was glancing at them and slightly smiling, they were all completely enchanted. Having thus bewildered the demons with Her sweet words and charming beauty, Mohinī-mūrti fulfilled Her plan by distributing all the nectar to the demigods, freeing them from invalidity, old age and death. *(pp. 11–17)*

PLATE TWO

Rāhu, the demon who causes eclipses of the sun and moon, covered himself with the dress of a demigod and thus entered the assembly of the demigods and drank nectar without being detected by anyone, even by the Supreme Personality of Godhead. The moon and the sun, however, because of permanent animosity toward Rāhu, understood the situation. Thus Rāhu was detected. Then the Supreme Lord, Hari (Mohinī), using His disc, which was sharp like a razor, at once cut off Rāhu's head. When Rāhu's head was severed from his body, his body immediately died, but his head, having been touched by the nectar, became immortal. *(pp. 20–21)*

PLATE THREE

When the demigods could find no way to counteract the activities of the demons, they wholeheartedly meditated upon Lord Viṣṇu, the Supreme Personality of Godhead and the creator of the universe. Immediately the Lord became visible to the demigods. With eyes resembling the petals of a newly blossomed lotus, He appeared before them sitting on the back of Garuḍa, spreading His lotus feet over Garuḍa's shoulders. He was dressed in yellow and decorated with the Kaustubha gem, an invaluable helmet and brilliant earrings. He was holding various weapons in His eight hands. As the dangers of a dream cease when the dreamer awakens, the illusions created by the jugglery of the demons were vanquished by the transcendental prowess of Lord Viṣṇu as soon as He entered the battlefield. But the demons were undaunted. Suddenly, the demon Kālanemi, seeing the Supreme Lord on the battlefield, took up his trident and prepared to discharge it at Garuḍa's head. *(pp. 58–61)*

PLATE FOUR

After hearing how the Supreme Personality of Godhead, Hari, had appeared in the form of a woman, captivated the demons and enabled the demigods to drink nectar, Lord Śiva went to the place where Madhusūdana, the Lord, resides. Accompanied by his wife, Umā, Lord Śiva went there to see the Lord's form of a woman. The Supreme Personality of Godhead welcomed Lord Śiva and Umā with great respect, and after being seated comfortably, Lord Śiva duly worshiped the Lord and smilingly spoke as follows: "My Lord, I have seen all kinds of incarnations You have exhibited by Your transcendental qualities, but I have never seen Your form of a beautiful young woman. My Lord, please show me that form of Yours, which You showed to the demons to captivate them completely and in this way enable the demigods to drink nectar. I am very eager to see that form." When Lord Viṣṇu heard Śiva's request, He smiled with gravity and replied as follows: "O Śiva, you have pleased Me by your worship, and now I shall show you My form of a beautiful woman, which is very much appreciated by those who are lusty. Since you want to see that form, I shall now reveal it in your presence." *(pp. 98–119)*

PLATE FIVE

Those who are known as the impersonalist Vedāntists regard Kṛṣṇa as the impersonal Brahman. Others, known as Mīmāṁsaka philosophers, regard Him as religion. The Sāṅkhya philosophers regard Him as the transcendental person who is beyond *prakṛti* and *puruṣa* and who is the controller of even the demigods. Although these realizations are all partially true, it is only followers of the codes of devotional service known as the Pañcarātras who can know Kṛṣṇa completely—as the beloved cowherd boy of Vṛndāvana, who is always engaging in wonderful pastimes with His dear devotees, and whose unparalleled beauty attracts everyone in the three worlds. *(pp. 110–111)*

PLATE SIX

Desiring to conquer Indra, the King of heaven, Bali Mahārāja performed a special ritualistic ceremony called Visvajit. When ghee (clarified butter) was offered in the fire of sacrifice, there appeared from the fire a celestial chariot covered with gold and silk. There also appeared yellow horses like those of Indra, a flag marked with a lion, a gilded bow, two quivers of infallible arrows and celestial armor. Then Bali Mahārāja's grandfather Prahlāda Mahārāja offered Bali a garland of flowers that would never fade, and Śukrācārya gave him a conchshell. *(pp. 186–188)*

PLATE SEVEN

When Bali Mahārāja assembled his own soldiers and the demon chiefs, who were equal to him in strength, opulence and beauty, they appeared as if they would swallow the sky and burn all directions with their vision. After thus gathering the demoniac soldiers, Bali Mahārāja departed for the opulent capital of Indra. Indeed, he seemed to make the entire surface of the world tremble. Upon reaching the abode of Indra, Bali Mahārāja assembled his soldiers outside the city's walls and sounded the conchshell given him by his spiritual master, Śukrācārya, thus creating a fearful situation for the women protected by Indra. Seeing Bali's indefatigable endeavor and understanding his motive, King Indra was struck with wonder. *(pp. 190–199)*

CHAPTER NINE

The Lord Incarnates as Mohinī-mūrti

This chapter describes how the demons, being enchanted by the beauty of the Mohinī form, agreed to hand over the container of nectar to Mohinīdevī, who tactfully delivered it to the demigods.

When the demons got possession of the container of nectar, an extraordinarily beautiful young woman appeared before them. All the demons became captivated by the young woman's beauty and became attached to Her. Now, because the demons were fighting among themselves to possess the nectar, they selected this beautiful woman as a mediator to settle their quarrel. Taking advantage of their weakness in this regard, Mohinī, the incarnation of the Supreme Personality of Godhead, got the demons to promise that whatever decision She might give, they would not refuse to accept it. When the demons made this promise, the beautiful woman, Mohinī-mūrti, had the demigods and demons sit in different lines so that She could distribute the nectar. She knew that the demons were quite unfit to drink the nectar. Therefore, by cheating them She distributed all the nectar to the demigods. When the demons saw this cheating of Mohinī-mūrti, they remained silent. But one demon, named Rāhu, dressed himself like a demigod and sat down in the line of the demigods. He sat beside the sun and the moon. When the Supreme Personality of Godhead understood how Rāhu was cheating, He immediately cut off the demon's head. Rāhu, however, had already tasted the nectar, and therefore although his head was severed, he remained alive. After the demigods finished drinking the nectar, the Supreme Personality of Godhead assumed His own form. Śukadeva Gosvāmī ends this chapter by describing how powerful is the chanting of the holy names, pastimes and paraphernalia of the Supreme Personality of Godhead.

TEXT 1

श्रीशुक उवाच

तेऽन्योन्यतोऽसुराः पात्रं हरन्तस्त्यक्तसौहृदाः ।
क्षिपन्तो दस्युधर्माण आयान्तीं ददृशुः स्त्रियम् ॥ १ ॥

śrī-śuka uvāca
te 'nyonyato 'surāḥ pātraṁ
harantas tyakta-sauhṛdāḥ
kṣipanto dasyu-dharmāṇa
āyāntīṁ dadṛśuḥ striyam

śrī-śukaḥ uvāca—Śrī Śukadeva Gosvāmī said; *te*—the demons; *anyonyataḥ*—among themselves; *asurāḥ*—the demons; *pātram*—the container of nectar; *harantaḥ*—snatching from one another; *tyakta-sauhṛdāḥ*—became inimical toward one another; *kṣipantaḥ*—sometimes throwing; *dasyu-dharmāṇaḥ*—sometimes snatching like robbers; *āyāntīm*—coming forward; *dadṛśuḥ*—saw; *striyam*—a very beautiful and attractive woman.

TRANSLATION

Śukadeva Gosvāmī said: Thereafter, the demons became inimical toward one another. Throwing and snatching the container of nectar, they gave up their friendly relationship. Meanwhile, they saw a very beautiful young woman coming forward toward them.

TEXT 2

अहो रूपमहो धाम अहो अस्या नवं वयः ।
इति ते तामभिद्रुत्य पप्रच्छुर्जातहृच्छयाः ॥ २ ॥

aho rūpam aho dhāma
aho asyā navaṁ vayaḥ
iti te tām abhidrutya
papracchur jāta-hṛc-chayāḥ

aho—how wonderful; *rūpam*—Her beauty; *aho*—how wonderful; *dhāma*—Her bodily luster; *aho*—how wonderful; *asyāḥ*—of Her; *navam*—new; *vayaḥ*—beautiful age; *iti*—in this way; *te*—those demons; *tām*—unto the beautiful woman; *abhidrutya*—going before Her hastily; *papracchuḥ*—inquired from Her; *jāta-hṛt-śayāḥ*—their hearts being filled with lust to enjoy Her.

TRANSLATION

Upon seeing the beautiful woman, the demons said, "Alas, how wonderful is Her beauty, how wonderful the luster of Her body, and how wonderful the beauty of Her youthful age!" Speaking in this way, they quickly approached Her, full of lusty desires to enjoy Her, and began to inquire from Her in many ways.

TEXT 3

का त्वं कञ्जपलाशाक्षि कुतो वा किं चिकीर्षसि ।
कस्यासि वद वामोरु मथ्नतीव मनांसि नः ॥ ३ ॥

kā tvaṁ kañja-palāśākṣi
kuto vā kiṁ cikīrṣasi
kasyāsi vada vāmoru
mathnatīva manāṁsi naḥ

kā—who; *tvam*—are You; *kañja-palāśa-akṣi*—having eyes like the petals of a lotus; *kutaḥ*—from where; *vā*—either; *kim cikīrṣasi*—what is the purpose for which You have come here; *kasya*—of whom; *asi*—do You belong; *vada*—kindly tell us; *vāma-ūru*—O You whose thighs are extraordinarily beautiful; *mathnatī*—agitating; *iva*—like; *manāṁsi*—within our minds; *naḥ*—our.

TRANSLATION

O wonderfully beautiful girl, You have such nice eyes, resembling the petals of a lotus flower. Who are You? Where do You come from? What is Your purpose in coming here, and to whom do You belong? O You whose thighs are extraordinarily beautiful, our minds are becoming agitated simply because of seeing You.

PURPORT

The demons inquired from the wonderfully beautiful girl, "To whom do You belong?" A woman is supposed to belong to her father before her marriage, to her husband after her marriage, and to her grown sons in her old age. In regard to this inquiry, Śrīla Viśvanātha Cakravartī Ṭhākura says that the question "To whom do You belong?" means "Whose daughter are You?" Since the demons could understand that the beautiful girl was still unmarried, every one of them desired to marry Her. Thus they inquired, "Whose daughter are You?"

TEXT 4

न वयं त्वामरैर्दैत्यैः सिद्धगन्धर्वचारणैः ।
नास्पृष्टपूर्वां जानीमो लोकेशैश्च कुतो नृभिः ॥ ४ ॥

na vayaṁ tvāmarair daityaiḥ
siddha-gandharva-cāraṇaiḥ
nāspṛṣṭa-pūrvāṁ jānīmo
lokeśaiś ca kuto nṛbhiḥ

na—it is not; *vayam*—we; *tvā*—unto You; *amaraiḥ*—by the demigods; *daityaiḥ*—by the demons; *siddha*—by the Siddhas; *gandharva*—by the Gandharvas; *cāraṇaiḥ*—and by the Cāraṇas; *na*—not; *aspṛṣṭa-pūrvām*—never enjoyed or touched by anyone; *jānīmaḥ*—know exactly; *loka-īśaiḥ*—by the various directors of the universe; *ca*—also; *kutaḥ*—what to speak of; *nṛbhiḥ*—by human society.

TRANSLATION

What to speak of human beings, even the demigods, demons, Siddhas, Gandharvas, Cāraṇas and the various directors of the universe, the Prajāpatis, have never touched You before. It is not that we are unable to understand Your identity.

PURPORT

Even the *asuras* observed the etiquette that no one should address a married woman with lust. The great analyst Cāṇakya Paṇḍita says, *mātṛvat para-dāreṣu:* one should consider another's wife to be one's mother. The *asuras,* the demons, took it for granted that the beautiful young woman, Mohinī-mūrti, who had arrived before them, was certainly not married. Therefore they assumed that no one in the world, including the demigods, the Gandharvas, the Cāraṇas and the Siddhas, had ever touched Her. The demons knew that the young girl was unmarried, and therefore they dared to address Her. They supposed that the young girl, Mohinī-mūrti, had come there to find a husband among all those present (the Daityas, the demigods, the Gandharvas and so on).

TEXT 5

नूनं त्वं विधिना सुभ्रूः प्रेषितासि शरीरिणाम् ।
सर्वेन्द्रियमनःप्रीतिं विधातुं सघृणेन किम् ॥ ५ ॥

nūnaṁ tvaṁ vidhinā subhrūḥ
preṣitāsi śarīriṇām
sarvendriya-manaḥ prītiṁ
vidhātuṁ saghṛṇena kim

nūnam—indeed; *tvam*—You; *vidhinā*—by Providence; *su-bhrūḥ*—O You with the beautiful eyebrows; *preṣitā*—sent; *asi*—certainly You are so; *śarīriṇām*—of all embodied living entities; *sarva*—all; *indriya*—of the senses; *manaḥ*—and of the mind; *prītim*—what is pleasing; *vidhātum*—to administer; *sa-ghṛṇena*—by Your causeless mercy; *kim*—whether.

TRANSLATION

O beautiful girl with beautiful eyebrows, certainly Providence, by His causeless mercy, has sent You to please the senses and minds of all of us. Is this not a fact?

TEXT 6

सा त्वं नः स्पर्धमानानामेकवस्तुनि मानिनि ।
ज्ञातीनां बद्धवैराणां शं विधत्स्व सुमध्यमे ॥ ६ ॥

sā tvaṁ naḥ spardhamānānām
eka-vastuni mānini
jñātīnāṁ baddha-vairāṇāṁ
śaṁ vidhatsva sumadhyame

sā—as such You are; *tvam*—Your good self; *naḥ*—of all of us demons; *spardhamānānām*—of those who are becoming increasingly inimical; *eka-vastuni*—in one subject matter (the container of nectar); *mānini*—O You who are most beautiful in Your prestigious position; *jñātīnām*—among our family members; *baddha-vairāṇām*—increasingly becoming enemies; *śam*—auspiciousness; *vidhatsva*—must execute; *su-madhyame*—O beautiful thin-waisted woman.

TRANSLATION

We are now all engaged in enmity among ourselves because of this one subject matter—the container of nectar. Although we have been born in the same family, we are becoming increasingly inimical. O thin-waisted woman, who are so beautiful in Your prestigious position, we therefore request You to favor us by settling our dispute.

PURPORT

The demons understood that the beautiful woman had attracted the attention of them all. Therefore they unanimously requested Her to become the arbiter to settle their dispute.

TEXT 7

वयं कश्यपदायादा भ्रातरः कृतपौरुषाः ।
विभजस्व यथान्यायं नैव भेदो यथा भवेत् ॥ ७ ॥

vayaṁ kaśyapa-dāyādā
bhrātaraḥ kṛta-pauruṣāḥ
vibhajasva yathā-nyāyaṁ
naiva bhedo yathā bhavet

vayam—all of us; *kaśyapa-dāyādāḥ*—descendants of Kaśyapa Muni; *bhrātaraḥ*—we are all brothers; *kṛta-pauruṣāḥ*—who are all able and competent; *vibhajasva*—just divide; *yathā-nyāyam*—according to law; *na*—not; *eva*—certainly; *bhedaḥ*—partiality; *yathā*—as; *bhavet*—should so become.

TRANSLATION

All of us, both demons and demigods, have been born of the same father, Kaśyapa, and thus we are related as brothers. But now we are exhibiting our personal prowess in dissension. Therefore we request You to settle our dispute and divide the nectar equally among us.

TEXT 8

इत्युपामन्त्रितो दैत्यैर्मायायोषिद्वपुर्हरिः ।
प्रहस्य रुचिरापाङ्गैर्निरीक्षन्निदमब्रवीत् ॥ ८ ॥

ity upāmantrito daityair
māyā-yoṣid-vapur hariḥ
prahasya rucirāpāṅgair
nirīkṣann idam abravīt

iti—thus; *upāmantritaḥ*—being fervently requested; *daityaiḥ*—by the demons; *māyā-yoṣit*—the illusory woman; *vapuḥ hariḥ*—the incarnation of the Supreme Personality of Godhead; *prahasya*—smiling; *rucira*—beautiful; *apāṅgaiḥ*—by exhibiting attractive feminine features; *nirīkṣan*—looking at them; *idam*—these words; *abravīt*—said.

TRANSLATION

Having thus been requested by the demons, the Supreme Personality of Godhead, who had assumed the form of a beautiful woman, began to smile. Looking at them with attractive feminine gestures, She spoke as follows.

TEXT 9

श्रीभगवानुवाच
कथं कश्यपदायादाः पुंश्चल्यां मयि सङ्गताः ।
विश्वासं पण्डितो जातु कामिनीषु न याति हि ॥ ९ ॥

śrī-bhagavān uvāca
kathaṁ kaśyapa-dāyādāḥ
puṁścalyāṁ mayi saṅgatāḥ

viśvāsaṁ paṇḍito jātu
kāminīṣu na yāti hi

śrī-bhagavān uvāca—the Supreme Personality of Godhead in the form of Mohinī-mūrti said; *katham*—how is it so; *kaśyapa-dāyādāḥ*—you are all descendants of Kaśyapa Muni; *puṁścalyām*—unto a prostitute who agitates the minds of men; *mayi*—unto Me; *saṅgatāḥ*—you come in My association; *viśvāsam*—faith; *paṇḍitaḥ*—those who are learned; *jātu*—at any time; *kāminīṣu*—unto a woman; *na*—never; *yāti*—takes place; *hi*—indeed.

TRANSLATION

The Supreme Personality of Godhead, in the form of Mohinī, told the demons: O sons of Kaśyapa Muni, I am only a prostitute. How is it that you have so much faith in Me? A learned person never puts his faith in a woman.

PURPORT

Cāṇakya Paṇḍita, the great politician and moral instructor, said, *viśvāso naiva kartavyaḥ strīṣu rāja-kuleṣu ca:* "Never put your faith in a woman or a politician." Thus the Supreme Personality of Godhead, who was pretending to be a woman, warned the demons against putting so much faith in Her, for She had appeared as an attractive woman ultimately to cheat them. Indirectly disclosing the purpose for which She had appeared before them, She said to the sons of Kaśyapa, "How is this? You were all born of a great *ṛṣi*, yet you are putting your faith in a woman who is loitering here and there like a prostitute, unprotected by father or husband. Women in general should not be trusted, and what to speak of a woman loitering like a prostitute?" The word *kāminī* is significant in this connection. Women, especially beautiful young women, invoke the dormant lusty desires of a man. Therefore, according to *Manu-saṁhitā*, every woman should be protected, either by her husband, by her father or by her grown sons. Without such protection, a woman will be exploited. Indeed, women like to be exploited by men. As soon as a woman is exploited by a man, she becomes a common prostitute. This is explained by Mohinī-mūrti, the Supreme Personality of Godhead.

TEXT 10

सालावृकाणां स्त्रीणां च स्वैरिणीनां सुरद्विषः ।
सख्यान्याहुरनित्यानि नूत्नं नूत्नं विचिन्वताम् ॥१०॥

sālāvṛkāṇāṁ strīṇāṁ ca
svairiṇīnāṁ sura-dviṣaḥ
sakhyāny āhur anityāni
nūtnaṁ nūtnaṁ vicinvatām

sālāvṛkāṇām—of monkeys, jackals and dogs; *strīṇām ca*—and of women; *svairiṇīnām*—especially women who are independent; *sura-dviṣaḥ*—O demons; *sakhyāni*—friendship; *āhuḥ*—it is said; *anityāni*—temporary; *nūtnam*—new friends; *nūtnam*—new friends; *vicinvatām*—all of whom are thinking.

TRANSLATION

O demons, as monkeys, jackals and dogs are unsteady in their sexual relationships and want newer and newer friends every day, women who live independently seek new friends daily. Friendship with such a woman is never permanent. This is the opinion of learned scholars.

TEXT 11

श्रीशुक उवाच
इति ते क्ष्वेलितैस्तस्या आश्वस्तमनसोऽसुराः ।
जहसुर्भावगम्भीरं ददुश्चामृतभाजनम् ॥११॥

śrī-śuka uvāca
iti te kṣvelitais tasyā
āśvasta-manaso 'surāḥ
jahasur bhāva-gambhīraṁ
daduś cāmṛta-bhājanam

śrī-śukaḥ uvāca—Śrī Śukadeva Gosvāmī said; *iti*—thus; *te*—those demons; *kṣvelitaiḥ*—by speaking as if jokingly; *tasyāḥ*—of Mohinī-mūrti; *āśvasta*—grateful, with faith; *manasaḥ*—their minds; *asurāḥ*—all the demons; *jahasuḥ*—laughed; *bhāva-gambhīram*—although

Mohinī-mūrti was full of gravity; *daduḥ*—delivered; *ca*—also; *amṛta-bhājanam*—the container of nectar.

TRANSLATION

Śrī Śukadeva Gosvāmī continued: After the demons heard the words of Mohinī-mūrti, who had spoken as if jokingly, they were all very confident. They laughed with gravity, and ultimately they delivered the container of nectar into Her hands.

PURPORT

The Personality of Godhead in His form of Mohinī was certainly not joking but talking seriously, with gravity. The demons, however, being captivated by Mohinī-mūrti's bodily features, took Her words as a joke and confidently delivered the container of nectar into Her hands. Thus Mohinī-mūrti resembles Lord Buddha, who appeared *sammohāya sura-dviṣām*—to cheat the *asuras*. The word *sura-dviṣām* refers to those who are envious of the demigods or devotees. Sometimes an incarnation of the Supreme Personality of Godhead cheats the atheists. Thus we see here that although Mohinī-mūrti was speaking factually to the *asuras*, the *asuras* took Her words to be facetious. Indeed, they were so confident of Mohinī-mūrti's honesty that they immediately delivered the container of nectar into Her hands, as if they would allow Her to do with the nectar whatever She liked, whether She distributed it, threw it away or drank it Herself without giving it to them.

TEXT 12

ततो गृहीत्वामृतभाजनं हरि-
र्बभाष ईषत्स्मितशोभया गिरा ।
यद्यभ्युपेतं क्व च साध्वसाधु वा
कृतं मया वो विभजे सुधामिमाम् ॥१२॥

tato gṛhītvāmṛta-bhājanaṁ harir
babhāṣa īṣat-smita-śobhayā girā
yady abhyupetaṁ kva ca sādhv asādhu vā
kṛtaṁ mayā vo vibhaje sudhām imām

tataḥ—thereafter; *gṛhītvā*—taking possession of; *amṛta-bhājanam*—the pot containing the nectar; *hariḥ*—the Supreme Personality of Godhead, Hari, in the form of Mohinī; *babhāṣa*—spoke; *īṣat*—slightly; *smita-śobhayā girā*—with smiling beauty and by words; *yadi*—if; *abhyupetam*—promised to be accepted; *kva ca*—whatever it may be; *sādhu asādhu vā*—whether honest or dishonest; *kṛtam mayā*—is done by Me; *vaḥ*—unto you; *vibhaje*—I shall give you the proper share; *sudhām*—nectar; *imām*—this.

TRANSLATION

Thereafter, the Supreme Personality of Godhead, having taken possession of the container of nectar, smiled slightly and spoke in attractive words. She said: My dear demons, if you accept whatever I may do, whether honest or dishonest, then I can take responsibility for dividing the nectar among you.

PURPORT

The Supreme Personality of Godhead cannot abide by anyone's dictation. Whatever He does is absolute. The demons, of course, were deluded by the illusory potency of the Supreme Personality of Godhead, and thus Mohinī-mūrti got them to promise that whatever She would do they would accept.

TEXT 13

इत्यभिव्याहृतं तस्या आकर्ण्यासुरपुङ्गवाः ।
अप्रमाणविदस्तस्यास्तत् तथेत्यन्वमंसत ॥१३॥

ity abhivyāhṛtaṁ tasyā
ākarṇyāsura-puṅgavāḥ
apramāṇa-vidas tasyās
tat tathety anvamaṁsata

iti—thus; *abhivyāhṛtam*—the words that were spoken; *tasyāḥ*—Her; *ākarṇya*—after hearing; *asura-puṅgavāḥ*—the chiefs of the demons; *apramāṇa-vidaḥ*—because they were all foolish; *tasyāḥ*—of Her; *tat*—

those words; *tathā*—let it be so; *iti*—thus; *anvamaṁsata*—agreed to accept.

TRANSLATION

The chiefs of the demons were not very expert in deciding things. Upon hearing the sweet words of Mohinī-mūrti, they immediately assented. "Yes," they answered. "What You have said is all right." Thus the demons agreed to accept Her decision.

TEXTS 14–15

अथोपोष्य कृतस्नाना हुत्वा च हविषानलम् ।
दत्त्वा गोविप्रभूतेभ्यः कृतस्वस्त्ययना द्विजैः ॥१४॥
यथोपजोषं वासांसि परिधायाहतानि ते ।
कुशेषु प्राविशन्सर्वे प्रागग्रेष्वभिभूषिताः ॥१५॥

athopoṣya kṛta-snānā
hutvā ca haviṣānalam
dattvā go-vipra-bhūtebhyaḥ
kṛta-svastyayanā dvijaiḥ

yathopajoṣaṁ vāsāṁsi
paridhāyāhatāni te
kuśeṣu prāviśan sarve
prāg-agreṣv abhibhūṣitāḥ

atha—thereafter; *upoṣya*—observing a fast; *kṛta-snānāḥ*—performing bathing; *hutvā*—offering oblations; *ca*—also; *haviṣā*—with clarified butter; *analam*—into the fire; *dattvā*—giving in charity; *go-vipra-bhūtebhyaḥ*—unto the cows, *brāhmaṇas* and living beings in general; *kṛta-svastyayanāḥ*—performing ritualistic ceremonies; *dvijaiḥ*—as dictated by the *brāhmaṇas; yathā-upajoṣam*—according to one's taste; *vāsāṁsi*—garments; *paridhāya*—putting on; *āhatāni*—first-class and new; *te*—all of them; *kuśeṣu*—on seats made of *kuśa* grass; *prāviśan*—sitting on them; *sarve*—all of them; *prāk-agreṣu*—facing east; *abhibhūṣitāḥ*—properly decorated with ornaments.

TRANSLATION

The demigods and demons then observed a fast. After bathing, they offered clarified butter and oblations into the fire and gave charity to the cows and to the brāhmaṇas and members of the other orders of society, namely the kṣatriyas, vaiśyas and śūdras, who were all rewarded as they deserved. Thereafter, the demigods and demons performed ritualistic ceremonies under the directions of the brāhmaṇas. Then they dressed themselves with new garments according to their own choice, decorated their bodies with ornaments, and sat facing east on seats made of kuśa grass.

PURPORT

The *Vedas* enjoin that for every ritualistic ceremony one must first become clean by bathing either in the water of the Ganges or Yamunā or in the sea. Then one may perform the ritualistic ceremony and offer clarified butter into the fire. In this verse the words *paridhāya āhatāni* are especially significant. A *sannyāsī* or a person about to perform a ritualistic ceremony should not dress himself in clothing sewn with a needle.

TEXTS 16–17

प्राङ्मुखेषूपविष्टेषु सुरेषु दितिजेषु च ।
धूपामोदितशालायां जुष्टायां माल्यदीपकैः ॥१६॥
तस्यां नरेन्द्र करभोरुरुशद्दुकूल-
श्रोणीतटालसगतिर्मदविह्वलाक्षी ।
सा कूजती कनकनूपुरशिञ्जितेन
कुम्भस्तनी कलसपाणिरथाविवेश ॥१७॥

prāṅ-mukheṣūpaviṣṭeṣu
sureṣu ditijeṣu ca
dhūpāmodita-śālāyāṁ
juṣṭāyāṁ mālya-dīpakaiḥ

tasyāṁ narendra karabhorur uśad-dukūla-
śroṇī-taṭālasa-gatir mada-vihvalākṣī

sā kūjatī kanaka-nūpura-śiñjitena
kumbha-stanī kalasa-pāṇir athāviveśa

prāk-mukheṣu—facing east; *upaviṣṭeṣu*—were sitting on their respective seats; *sureṣu*—all the demigods; *diti-jeṣu*—the demons; *ca*—also; *dhūpa-āmodita-śālāyām*—in the arena, which was full of the smoke of incense; *juṣṭāyām*—fully decorated; *mālya-dīpakaiḥ*—with flower garlands and lamps; *tasyām*—in that arena; *nara-indra*—O King; *karabha-ūruḥ*—having thighs resembling the trunks of elephants; *uśat-dukūla*—dressed with a very beautiful sari; *śroṇī-taṭa*—because of big hips; *alasa-gatiḥ*—stepping very slowly; *mada-vihvala-akṣī*—whose eyes were restless because of youthful pride; *sā*—She; *kūjatī*—tinkling; *kanaka-nūpura*—of golden ankle bells; *śiñjitena*—with the sound; *kumbha-stanī*—a woman whose breasts were like water jugs; *kalasa-pāṇiḥ*—holding a waterpot in Her hand; *atha*—thus; *āviveśa*—entered the arena.

TRANSLATION

O King, as the demigods and demons sat facing east in an arena fully decorated with flower garlands and lamps and fragrant with the smoke of incense, that woman, dressed in a most beautiful sari, Her ankle bells tinkling, entered the arena, walking very slowly because of Her big, low hips. Her eyes were restless due to youthful pride, Her breasts were like water jugs, Her thighs resembled the trunks of elephants, and She carried a waterpot in Her hand.

TEXT 18

तां श्रीसखीं कनककुण्डलचारुकर्ण-
नासाकपोलवदनां परदेवताख्याम् ।
संवीक्ष्य संमुमुहुरुत्स्मितवीक्षणेन
देवासुरा विगलितस्तनपट्टिकान्ताम् ॥१८॥

tāṁ śrī-sakhīṁ kanaka-kuṇḍala-cāru-karṇa-
nāsā-kapola-vadanāṁ para-devatākhyām
saṁvīkṣya sammumuhur utsmita-vīkṣaṇena
devāsurā vigalita-stana-paṭṭikāntām

tām—unto Her; *śrī-sakhīm*—appearing like a personal associate of the goddess of fortune; *kanaka-kuṇḍala*—with golden earrings; *cāru*—very beautiful; *karṇa*—ears; *nāsā*—nose; *kapola*—cheeks; *vadanām*—face; *para-devatā-ākhyām*—the Supreme Lord, the Personality of Godhead, appearing in that form; *saṁvīkṣya*—looking at Her; *sammumuhuḥ*—all of them became enchanted; *utsmita*—slightly smiling; *vīkṣaṇena*—glancing over them; *deva-asurāḥ*—all the demigods and demons; *vigalita-stana-paṭṭika-antām*—the border of the sari on the breasts moved slightly.

TRANSLATION

Her attractive nose and cheeks and Her ears, adorned with golden earrings, made Her face very beautiful. As She moved, Her sari's border on Her breasts moved slightly aside. When the demigods and demons saw these beautiful features of Mohinī-mūrti, who was glancing at them and slightly smiling, they were all completely enchanted.

PURPORT

Śrīla Viśvanātha Cakravartī Ṭhākura remarks here that Mohinī-mūrti is the Supreme Personality of Godhead in a feminine form and that the goddess of fortune is Her associate. This form assumed by the Personality of Godhead challenged the goddess of fortune. The goddess of fortune is beautiful, but if the Lord accepts the form of a woman, He surpasses the goddess of fortune in beauty. It is not that the goddess of fortune, being female, is the most beautiful. The Lord is so beautiful that He can excel any beautiful goddess of fortune by assuming a female form.

TEXT 19

असुराणां सुधादानं सर्पाणामिव दुर्नयम् ।
मत्वा जातिनृशंसानां न तां व्यभजदच्युतः ॥१९॥

asurāṇāṁ sudhā-dānaṁ
sarpāṇām iva durnayam
matvā jāti-nṛśaṁsānāṁ
na tāṁ vyabhajad acyutaḥ

asurāṇām—of the demons; *sudhā-dānam*—giving of the nectar; *sarpāṇām*—of snakes; *iva*—like; *durnayam*—miscalculation; *matvā*—thinking like that; *jāti-nṛśaṁsānām*—of those who are by nature very envious; *na*—not; *tām*—the nectar; *vyabhajat*—delivered the share; *acyutaḥ*—the Supreme Personality of Godhead, who never falls down.

TRANSLATION

Demons are by nature crooked like snakes. Therefore, to distribute a share of the nectar to them was not at all feasible, since this would be as dangerous as supplying milk to a snake. Considering this, the Supreme Personality of Godhead, who never falls down, did not deliver a share of nectar to the demons.

PURPORT

It is said, *sarpaḥ krūraḥ khalaḥ krūraḥ sarpāt krūrataraḥ khalaḥ:* "The snake is very crooked and envious, and so also is a person like a demon." *Mantrauṣadhi-vaśaḥ sarpaḥ khalaḥ kena nivāryate:* "One can bring a snake under control with *mantras,* herbs and drugs, but an envious and crooked person cannot be brought under control by any means." Considering this logic, the Supreme Personality of Godhead thought it unwise to distribute nectar to the demons.

TEXT 20

कल्पयित्वा पृथक् पङ्क्तीरुभयेषां जगत्पतिः ।
तांश्चोपवेशयामास स्वेषु स्वेषु च पङ्क्तिषु ॥२०॥

kalpayitvā pṛthak paṅktīr
ubhayeṣāṁ jagat-patiḥ
tāṁś copaveśayām āsa
sveṣu sveṣu ca paṅktiṣu

kalpayitvā—after arranging; *pṛthak paṅktīḥ*—different seats; *ubhayeṣām*—of both the demigods and the demons; *jagat-patiḥ*—the master of the universe; *tān*—all of them; *ca*—and; *upaveśayām āsa*—

seated; *sveṣu sveṣu*—in their own places; *ca*—also; *paṅktiṣu*—all in order.

TRANSLATION

The Supreme Personality of Godhead as Mohinī-mūrti, the master of the universe, arranged separate lines of sitting places and seated the demigods and demons according to their positions.

TEXT 21

दैत्यान्गृहीतकलसो वञ्चयन्नुपसञ्चरैः ।
दूरस्थान् पाययामास जरामृत्युहरां सुधाम् ॥२१॥

daityān gṛhīta-kalaso
vañcayann upasañcaraiḥ
dūra-sthān pāyayām āsa
jarā-mṛtyu-harāṁ sudhām

daityān—the demons; *gṛhīta-kalasaḥ*—the Lord, who bore the container of nectar; *vañcayan*—by cheating; *upasañcaraiḥ*—with sweet words; *dūra-sthān*—the demigods, who were sitting at a distant place; *pāyayām āsa*—made them drink; *jarā-mṛtyu-harām*—which can counteract invalidity, old age and death; *sudhām*—such nectar.

TRANSLATION

Taking the container of nectar in Her hands, She first approached the demons, satisfied them with sweet words and thus cheated them of their share of the nectar. Then She administered the nectar to the demigods, who were sitting at a distant place, to make them free from invalidity, old age and death.

PURPORT

Mohinī-mūrti, the Personality of Godhead, gave the demigods seats at a distance. Then She approached the demons and spoke with them very graciously, so that they thought themselves very fortunate to talk with Her. Since Mohinī-mūrti had seated the demigods at a distant place, the demons thought that the demigods would get only a little of the nectar and that Mohinī-mūrti was so pleased with the demons that She would give the demons all the nectar. The words *vañcayann upasañcaraiḥ* indicate that the Lord's whole policy was to cheat the demons simply by speaking sweet words. The Lord's intention was to distribute the nectar only to the demigods.

TEXT 22

ते पालयन्तः समयमसुराः स्वकृतं नृप ।
तूष्णीमासन्कृतस्नेहाः स्त्रीविवादजुगुप्सया ॥२२॥

te pālayantaḥ samayam
asurāḥ sva-kṛtaṁ nṛpa
tūṣṇīm āsan kṛta-snehāḥ
strī-vivāda-jugupsayā

te—the demons; *pālayantaḥ*—keeping in order; *samayam*—equilibrium; *asurāḥ*—the demons; *sva-kṛtam*—made by them; *nṛpa*—O King; *tūṣṇīm āsan*—remained silent; *kṛta-snehāḥ*—because of having developed attachment to Mohinī-mūrti; *strī-vivāda*—disagreeing with a woman; *jugupsayā*—because of thinking such an action as abominable.

TRANSLATION

O King, since the demons had promised to accept whatever the woman did, whether just or unjust, now, to keep this promise, to show their equilibrium and to save themselves from fighting with a woman, they remained silent.

TEXT 23

तस्यां कृतातिप्रणयाः प्रणयापायकातराः ।
बहुमानेन चाबद्धा नोचुः किञ्चन विप्रियम् ॥२३॥

tasyāṁ kṛtātipraṇayāḥ
praṇayāpāya-kātarāḥ
bahu-mānena cābaddhā
nocuḥ kiñcana vipriyam

tasyām—of Mohinī-mūrti; *kṛta-ati-praṇayāḥ*—because of staunch friendship; *praṇaya-apāya-kātarāḥ*—being afraid that their friendship with Her would be broken; *bahu-mānena*—by great respect and honor; *ca*—also; *ābaddhāḥ*—being too attached to Her; *na*—not; *ūcuḥ*—they said; *kiñcana*—even the slightest thing; *vipriyam*—by which Mohinī-mūrti might be displeased with them.

TRANSLATION

The demons had developed affection for Mohinī-mūrti and a kind of faith in Her, and they were afraid of disturbing their relationship. Therefore they showed respect and honor to Her words and did not say anything that might disturb their friendship with Her.

PURPORT

The demons were so captivated by the tricks and friendly words of Mohinī-mūrti that although the demigods were served first, the demons were pacified merely by sweet words. The Lord said to the demons, "The demigods are very miserly and are excessively anxious to take the nectar first. So let them have it first. Since you are not like them you can wait a little longer. You are all heroes and are so pleased with Me. It is better for you to wait until after the demigods drink."

TEXT 24

देवलिङ्गप्रतिच्छन्नः स्वर्भानुर्देवसंसदि ।
प्रविष्टः सोममपिबच्चन्द्रार्काभ्यां च सूचितः ॥२४॥

deva-liṅga-praticchannaḥ
svarbhānur deva-saṁsadi
praviṣṭaḥ somam apibac
candrārkābhyāṁ ca sūcitaḥ

deva-liṅga-praticchannaḥ—covering himself with the dress of a demigod; *svarbhānuḥ*—Rāhu (who attacks and eclipses the sun and moon); *deva-saṁsadi*—in the group of the demigods; *praviṣṭaḥ*—having entered; *somam*—the nectar; *apibat*—drank; *candra-arkābhyām*—by both the moon and the sun; *ca*—and; *sūcitaḥ*—was pointed out.

TRANSLATION

Rāhu, the demon who causes eclipses of the sun and moon, covered himself with the dress of a demigod and thus entered the assembly of the demigods and drank nectar without being detected by anyone, even by the Supreme Personality of Godhead. The moon and the sun, however, because of permanent animosity toward Rāhu, understood the situation. Thus Rāhu was detected.

PURPORT

The Supreme Personality of Godhead, Mohinī-mūrti, was able to bewilder all the demons, but Rāhu was so clever that he was not bewildered. Rāhu could understand that Mohinī-mūrti was cheating the demons, and therefore he changed his dress, disguised himself as a demigod, and sat down in the assembly of the demigods. Here one may ask why the Supreme Personality of Godhead could not detect Rāhu. The reason is that the Lord wanted to show the effects of drinking nectar. This will be revealed in the following verses. The moon and sun, however, were always alert in regard to Rāhu. Thus when Rāhu entered the assembly of the demigods, the moon and sun immediately detected him, and then the Supreme Personality of Godhead also became aware of him.

TEXT 25

चक्रेण क्षुरधारेण जहार पिबतः शिरः ।
हरिस्तस्य कबन्धस्तु सुधयाप्लावितोऽपतत् ॥२५॥

cakreṇa kṣura-dhāreṇa
jahāra pibataḥ śiraḥ
haris tasya kabandhas tu
sudhayāplāvito 'patat

cakreṇa—by the disc; *kṣura-dhāreṇa*—which was sharp like a razor; *jahāra*—cut off; *pibataḥ*—while drinking nectar; *śiraḥ*—the head; *hariḥ*—the Supreme Personality of Godhead; *tasya*—of that Rāhu; *kabandhaḥ tu*—but the headless body; *sudhayā*—by the nectar; *aplāvitaḥ*—without being touched; *apatat*—immediately fell dead.

TRANSLATION

The Supreme Personality of Godhead, Hari, using His disc, which was sharp like a razor, at once cut off Rāhu's head. When Rāhu's head was severed from his body, the body, being untouched by the nectar, could not survive.

PURPORT

When the Personality of Godhead, Mohinī-mūrti, severed Rāhu's head from his body, the head remained alive although the body died. Rāhu had been drinking nectar through his mouth, and before the nectar entered his body, his head was cut off. Thus Rāhu's head remained alive whereas the body died. This wonderful act performed by the Lord was meant to show that nectar is miraculous ambrosia.

TEXT 26

शिरस्त्वमरतां नीतमजो ग्रहमचीक्लृपत् ।
यस्तु पर्वणि चन्द्रार्कावभिधावति वैरधीः ॥२६॥

śiras tv amaratāṁ nītam
ajo graham acīkḷpat
yas tu parvaṇi candrārkāv
abhidhāvati vaira-dhīḥ

śiraḥ—the head; *tu*—of course; *amaratām*—immortality; *nītam*—having obtained; *ajaḥ*—Lord Brahmā; *graham*—as one of the planets; *acīkḷpat*—recognized; *yaḥ*—the same Rāhu; *tu*—indeed; *parvaṇi*—during the periods of the full moon and dark moon; *candra-arkau*—both the moon and the sun; *abhidhāvati*—chases; *vaira-dhīḥ*—because of animosity.

TRANSLATION

Rāhu's head, however, having been touched by the nectar, became immortal. Thus Lord Brahmā accepted Rāhu's head as one of the planets. Since Rāhu is an eternal enemy of the moon and the sun, he always tries to attack them on the nights of the full moon and the dark moon.

PURPORT

Since Rāhu had become immortal, Lord Brahmā accepted him as one of the *grahas*, or planets, like the moon and the sun. Rāhu, however, being an eternal enemy of the moon and sun, attacks them periodically during the nights of the full moon and the dark moon.

TEXT 27

पीतप्रायेऽमृते देवैर्भगवान् लोकभावनः ।
पश्यतामसुरेन्द्राणां स्वं रूपं जगृहे हरिः ॥२७॥

pīta-prāye 'mṛte devair
bhagavān loka-bhāvanaḥ
paśyatām asurendrāṇāṁ
svaṁ rūpaṁ jagṛhe hariḥ

pīta-prāye—when almost finished being drunk; *amṛte*—the nectar; *devaiḥ*—by the demigods; *bhagavān*—the Supreme Personality of Godhead as Mohinī-mūrti; *loka-bhāvanaḥ*—the maintainer and well-wisher of the three worlds; *paśyatām*—in the presence of; *asura-indrāṇām*—all the demons, with their chiefs; *svam*—own; *rūpam*—form; *jagṛhe*—manifested; *hariḥ*—the Supreme Personality of Godhead.

TRANSLATION

The Supreme Personality of Godhead is the best friend and well-wisher of the three worlds. Thus when the demigods had almost finished drinking the nectar, the Lord, in the presence of all the demons, disclosed His original form.

TEXT 28

एवं सुरासुरगणाः समदेशकाल-
हेत्वर्थकर्ममतयोऽपि फले विकल्पाः ।
तत्रामृतं सुरगणाः फलमञ्जसापु-
र्यत्पादपङ्कजरजःश्रयणान्न दैत्याः ॥२८॥

evaṁ surāsura-gaṇāḥ sama-deśa-kāla-
hetv-artha-karma-matayo 'pi phale vikalpāḥ
tatrāmṛtaṁ sura-gaṇāḥ phalam añjasāpur
yat-pāda-paṅkaja-rajaḥ-śrayaṇān na daityāḥ

evam—thus; *sura*—the demigods; *asura-gaṇāḥ*—and the demons; *sama*—equal; *deśa*—place; *kāla*—time; *hetu*—cause; *artha*—objective; *karma*—activities; *matayaḥ*—ambition; *api*—although one; *phale*—in the result; *vikalpāḥ*—not equal; *tatra*—thereupon; *amṛtam*—nectar; *sura-gaṇāḥ*—the demigods; *phalam*—the result; *añjasā*—easily, totally or directly; *āpuḥ*—achieved; *yat*—because of; *pāda-paṅkaja*—of the lotus feet of the Supreme Personality of Godhead; *rajaḥ*—of the saffron dust; *śrayaṇāt*—because of receiving benedictions or taking shelter; *na*—not; *daityāḥ*—the demons.

TRANSLATION

The place, the time, the cause, the purpose, the activity and the ambition were all the same for both the demigods and the demons, but the demigods achieved one result and the demons another. Because the demigods are always under the shelter of the dust of the Lord's lotus feet, they could very easily drink the nectar and get its result. The demons, however, not having sought shelter at the lotus feet of the Lord, were unable to achieve the result they desired.

PURPORT

In *Bhagavad-gītā* (4.11) it is said, *ye yathā māṁ prapadyante tāṁs tathaiva bhajāmy aham:* the Supreme Personality of Godhead is the supreme judge who rewards or punishes different persons according to their surrender unto His lotus feet. Therefore it can actually be seen that although *karmīs* and *bhaktas* may work in the same place, at the same time, with the same energy and with the same ambition, they achieve different results. The *karmīs* transmigrate through different bodies in the cycle of birth and death, sometimes going upward and sometimes downward, thus suffering the results of their actions in the *karma-cakra*, the cycle of birth and death. The devotees, however, because of fully surrendering at the lotus feet of the Lord, are never baffled in their attempts. Although externally they work almost like the *karmīs*, the devotees go back home, back to Godhead, and achieve success in every effort. The demons or atheists have faith in their own endeavors, but although they work very hard day and night, they cannot get any more than their destiny. The devotees, however, can surpass the reactions of *karma* and achieve wonderful results, even without effort. It is also said, *phalena paricīyate:* one's success or defeat in any activity is understood by its result. There are many *karmīs* in the dress of devotees, but the Supreme Personality of Godhead can detect their purpose. The *karmīs* want to use the property of the Lord for their selfish sense gratification, but a devotee endeavors to use the Lord's property for God's service. Therefore a devotee is always distinct from the *karmīs*, although the *karmīs* may dress like devotees. As confirmed in *Bhagavad-gītā* (3.9), *yajñārthāt karmaṇo 'nyatra loko 'yaṁ karma-bandhanaḥ.* One who works for Lord Viṣṇu is free from this material world, and after giving up his body he goes back home, back to Godhead. A *karmī*, however, although externally working like a devotee, is entangled in his nondevotional activity, and thus he suffers the tribulations of material existence. Thus from the results achieved by the *karmīs* and devotees, one can understand the presence of the Supreme Personality of Godhead, who acts differently for the *karmīs* and *jñānīs* than for the devotees. The author of *Śrī Caitanya-caritāmṛta* therefore says:

kṛṣṇa-bhakta——niṣkāma, ataeva 'śānta'
bhukti-mukti-siddhi-kāmī——sakali 'aśānta'

The *karmīs* who desire sense gratification, the *jñānīs* who aspire for the liberation of merging into the existence of the Supreme, and the *yogīs* who seek material success in mystic power are all restless, and ultimately they are baffled. But the devotee, who does not expect any personal benefit and whose only ambition is to spread the glories of the Supreme Personality of Godhead, is blessed with all the auspicious results of *bhakti-yoga*, without hard labor.

TEXT 29

यद् युज्यतेऽसुवसुकर्ममनोवचोभि-
र्देहात्मजादिषु नृभिस्तदसत् पृथक्त्वात् ।

तैरेव सद् भवति यत् क्रियतेऽपृथक्त्वात्
सर्वस्य तद् भवति मूलनिषेचनं यत् ॥२९॥

yad yujyate 'su-vasu-karma-mano-vacobhir
dehātmajādiṣu nṛbhis tad asat pṛthaktvāt
tair eva sad bhavati yat kriyate 'pṛthaktvāt
sarvasya tad bhavati mūla-niṣecanaṁ yat

yat—whatever; *yujyate*—is performed; *asu*—for the protection of one's life; *vasu*—protection of wealth; *karma*—activities; *manaḥ*—by the acts of the mind; *vacobhiḥ*—by the acts of words; *deha-ātma-ja-ādiṣu*—for the sake of one's personal body or family, etc., with reference to the body; *nṛbhiḥ*—by the human beings; *tat*—that; *asat*—impermanent, transient; *pṛthaktvāt*—because of separation from the Supreme Personality of Godhead; *taiḥ*—by the same activities; *eva*—indeed; *sat bhavati*—becomes factual and permanent; *yat*—which; *kriyate*—is performed; *apṛthaktvāt*—because of nonseparation; *sarvasya*—for everyone; *tat bhavati*—becomes beneficial; *mūla-niṣecanam*—exactly like pouring water on the root of a tree; *yat*—which.

TRANSLATION

In human society there are various activities performed for the protection of one's wealth and life by one's words, one's mind and one's actions, but they are all performed for one's personal or extended sense gratification with reference to the body. All these activities are baffled because of being separate from devotional service. But when the same activities are performed for the satisfaction of the Lord, the beneficial results are distributed to everyone, just as water poured on the root of a tree is distributed throughout the entire tree.

PURPORT

This is the distinction between materialistic activities and activities performed in Kṛṣṇa consciousness. The entire world is active, and this includes the *karmīs*, the *jñānīs*, the *yogīs* and the *bhaktas*. However, all activities except those of the *bhaktas*, the devotees, end in bafflement and a waste of time and energy. *Moghāśā mogha-karmāṇo mogha-jñānā vicetasaḥ:* if one is not a devotee, his hopes, his activities and his knowledge are all baffled. A nondevotee works for his personal sense gratification or for the sense gratification of his family, society, community or nation, but because all such activities are separate from the Supreme Personality of Godhead, they are considered *asat.* The word *asat* means bad or temporary, and *sat* means permanent and good. Activities performed for the satisfaction of Kṛṣṇa are permanent and good, but *asat* activity, although sometimes celebrated as philanthropy, altruism, nationalism, this "ism" or that "ism," will never produce any permanent result and is therefore all bad. Even a little work done in Kṛṣṇa consciousness is a permanent asset and is all-good because it is done for Kṛṣṇa, the all-good Supreme Personality of Godhead, who is everyone's friend (*suhṛdaṁ sarva-bhūtānām*). The Supreme Personality of Godhead is the only enjoyer and proprietor of everything (*bhoktāraṁ yajña-tapasāṁ sarva-loka-maheśvaram*). Therefore any activity performed for the Supreme Lord is permanent. As a result of such activities, the performer is immediately recognized. *Na ca tasmān manuṣyeṣu kaścin me priya-kṛttamaḥ.* Such a devotee, because of full knowledge of the Supreme Personality of Godhead, is immediately transcendental, although he may superficially appear to be engaged in materialistic activities. The only distinction between materialistic activity and spiritual activity is that material activity is performed only to satisfy one's own senses whereas spiritual activity is meant to satisfy the transcendental senses of the Supreme Personality of Godhead. By spiritual activity everyone factually benefits, whereas by materialistic activity no one benefits and instead one becomes entangled in the laws of *karma.*

Thus ends the Bhaktivedanta purports of the Eighth Canto, Ninth Chapter, of the Śrīmad-Bhāgavatam, *entitled "The Lord Incarnates as Mohinī-mūrti."*

CHAPTER TEN

The Battle Between the Demigods and the Demons

The summary of Chapter Ten is as follows. Because of envy, the fight between the demons and the demigods continued. When the demigods were almost defeated by demoniac maneuvers and became morose, Lord Viṣṇu appeared among them.

Both the demigods and the demons are expert in activities involving the material energy, but the demigods are devotees of the Lord, whereas the demons are just the opposite. The demigods and demons churned the ocean of milk to get nectar from it, but the demons, not being devotees of the Lord, could derive no profit. After feeding nectar to the demigods, Lord Viṣṇu returned to His abode on the back of Garuḍa, but the demons, being most aggrieved, again declared war against the demigods. Bali Mahārāja, the son of Virocana, became the commander in chief of the demons. In the beginning of the battle, the demigods prepared to defeat the demons. Indra, King of heaven, fought with Bali, and other demigods, like Vāyu, Agni and Varuṇa, fought against other leaders of the demons. In this fight the demons were defeated, and to save themselves from death they began to manifest many illusions through material maneuvers, killing many soldiers on the side of the demigods. The demigods, finding no other recourse, surrendered again to the Supreme Personality of Godhead, Viṣṇu, who then appeared and counteracted all the illusions presented by the jugglery of the demons. Heroes among the demons such as Kālanemi, Mālī, Sumālī and Mālyavān fought the Supreme Personality of Godhead and were all killed by the Lord. The demigods were thus freed from all dangers.

TEXT 1

श्रीशुक उवाच
इति दानवदैतेया नाविन्दन्नमृतं नृप ।
युक्ताः कर्मणि यत्ताश्च वासुदेवपराङ्मुखाः ॥ १ ॥

śrī-śuka uvāca
iti dānava-daiteyā
nāvindann amṛtaṁ nṛpa
yuktāḥ karmaṇi yattāś ca
vāsudeva-parāṅmukhāḥ

śrī-śukaḥ uvāca—Śrī Śukadeva Gosvāmī said; *iti*—thus; *dānava-daiteyāḥ*—the *asuras* and the demons; *na*—not; *avindan*—achieved (the desired result); *amṛtam*—nectar; *nṛpa*—O King; *yuktāḥ*—all being combined; *karmaṇi*—in the churning; *yattāḥ*—engaged with full attention and effort; *ca*—and; *vāsudeva*—of the Supreme Personality of Godhead, Kṛṣṇa; *parāṅmukhāḥ*—because of being nondevotees.

TRANSLATION

Śukadeva Gosvāmī said: O King, the demons and Daityas all engaged with full attention and effort in churning the ocean, but because they were not devotees of Vāsudeva, the Supreme Personality of Godhead, Kṛṣṇa, they were not able to drink the nectar.

TEXT 2

साधयित्वामृतं राजन्पाययित्वा स्वकान्सुरान् ।
पश्यतां सर्वभूतानां ययौ गरुडवाहनः ॥ २ ॥

sādhayitvāmṛtaṁ rājan
pāyayitvā svakān surān
paśyatāṁ sarva-bhūtānāṁ
yayau garuḍa-vāhanaḥ

sādhayitvā—after executing; *amṛtam*—generation of the nectar; *rājan*—O King; *pāyayitvā*—and feeding; *svakān*—to His own devotees; *surān*—to the demigods; *paśyatām*—in the presence of; *sarva-bhūtānām*—all living entities; *yayau*—went away; *garuḍa-vāhanaḥ*—the Supreme Personality of Godhead, carried by Garuḍa.

TRANSLATION

O King, after the Supreme Personality of Godhead had brought to completion the affairs of churning the ocean and feeding the

nectar to the demigods, who are His dear devotees, He left the presence of them all and was carried by Garuḍa to His own abode.

TEXT 3

सपत्नानां परामृद्धिं दृष्ट्वा ते दितिनन्दनाः ।
अमृष्यमाणा उत्पेतुर्देवान्प्रत्युद्यतायुधाः ॥ ३ ॥

sapatnānāṁ parām ṛddhiṁ
dṛṣṭvā te diti-nandanāḥ
amṛṣyamāṇā utpetur
devān pratyudyatāyudhāḥ

sapatnānām—of their rivals, the demigods; *param*—the best; *ṛddhim*—opulence; *dṛṣṭvā*—observing; *te*—all of them; *diti-nandanāḥ*—the sons of Diti, the Daityas; *amṛṣyamāṇāḥ*—being intolerant; *utpetuḥ*—ran toward (just to create a disturbance); *devān*—the demigods; *pratyudyata-āyudhāḥ*—their weapons raised.

TRANSLATION

Seeing the victory of the demigods, the demons became intolerant of their superior opulence. Thus they began to march toward the demigods with raised weapons.

TEXT 4

ततः सुरगणाः सर्वे सुधया पीतयैधिताः ।
प्रतिसंयुयुधुः शस्त्रैर्नारायणपदाश्रयाः ॥ ४ ॥

tataḥ sura-gaṇāḥ sarve
sudhayā pītayaidhitāḥ
pratisaṁyuyudhuḥ śastrair
nārāyaṇa-padāśrayāḥ

tataḥ—thereafter; *sura-gaṇāḥ*—the demigods; *sarve*—all of them; *sudhayā*—by the nectar; *pītayā*—which had been drunk; *edhitāḥ*—being enlivened by such drinking; *pratisaṁyuyudhuḥ*—they counterattacked the demons; *śastraiḥ*—by regular weapons; *nārāyaṇa-pada-āśrayāḥ*—their real weapon being shelter at the lotus feet of Nārāyaṇa.

TRANSLATION

Thereafter, being enlivened because of drinking the nectar, the demigods, who are always at the shelter of the lotus feet of Nārāyaṇa, used their various weapons to counterattack the demons in a fighting spirit.

TEXT 5

तत्र दैवासुरो नाम रणः परमदारुणः ।
रोधस्युदन्वतो राजंस्तुमुलो रोमहर्षणः ॥ ५ ॥

tatra daivāsuro nāma
raṇaḥ parama-dāruṇaḥ
rodhasy udanvato rājaṁs
tumulo roma-harṣaṇaḥ

tatra—there (at the beach of the ocean of milk); *daiva*—the demigods; *asuraḥ*—the demons; *nāma*—as they are celebrated; *raṇaḥ*—fighting; *parama*—very much; *dāruṇaḥ*—fierce; *rodhasi*—on the beach of the sea; *udanvataḥ*—of the ocean of milk; *rājan*—O King; *tumulaḥ*—tumultuous; *roma-harṣaṇaḥ*—hair standing on the body.

TRANSLATION

O King, a fierce battle on the beach of the ocean of milk ensued between the demigods and the demons. The fighting was so terrible that simply hearing about it would make the hair on one's body stand on end.

TEXT 6

तत्रान्योन्यं सपत्नास्ते संरब्धमनसो रणे ।
समासाद्यासिभिर्बाणैर्निजघ्नुर्विविधायुधैः ॥ ६ ॥

tatrānyonyaṁ sapatnās te
saṁrabdha-manaso raṇe

samāsādyāsibhir bāṇair
nijaghnur vividhāyudhaiḥ

tatra—thereupon; *anyonyam*—one another; *sapatnāḥ*—all of them becoming fighters; *te*—they; *saṁrabdha*—very angry; *manasaḥ*—within their minds; *raṇe*—in that battle; *samāsādya*—getting the opportunity to fight between themselves; *asibhiḥ*—with swords; *bāṇaiḥ*—with arrows; *nijaghnuḥ*—began to beat one another; *vividha-āyudhaiḥ*—with varieties of weapons.

TRANSLATION

Both parties in that fight were extremely angry at heart, and in enmity they beat one another with swords, arrows and varieties of other weapons.

PURPORT

There are always two kinds of men in this universe, not only on this planet but also in higher planetary systems. All the kings dominating planets like the sun and moon also have enemies like Rāhu. It is because of occasional attacks upon the sun and moon by Rāhu that eclipses take place. The fighting between the demons and demigods is perpetual; it cannot be stopped unless intelligent persons from both sides take to Kṛṣṇa consciousness.

TEXT 7

शङ्खतूर्यमृदङ्गानां भेरीडमरिणां महान् ।
हस्त्यश्वरथपत्तीनां नदतां निस्वनोऽभवत् ॥ ७ ॥

śaṅkha-tūrya-mṛdaṅgānāṁ
bherī-ḍamariṇāṁ mahān
hasty-aśva-ratha-pattīnāṁ
nadatāṁ nisvano 'bhavat

śaṅkha—of conchshells; *tūrya*—of big bugles; *mṛdaṅgānām*—and of drums; *bherī*—of bugles; *ḍamariṇām*—of kettledrums; *mahān*—great and tumultuous; *hasti*—of elephants; *aśva*—of horses; *ratha-pattīnām*—of fighters on chariots or on the ground; *nadatām*—all of them making sounds together; *nisvanaḥ*—a tumultuous sound; *abhavat*—so became.

TRANSLATION

The sounds of the conchshells, bugles, drums, bherīs and ḍamarīs [kettledrums], as well as the sounds made by the elephants, horses and soldiers, who were both on chariots and on foot, were tumultuous.

TEXT 8

रथिनो रथिभिस्तत्र पत्तिभिः सह पत्तयः ।
हया हयैरिभाश्चेभैः समसज्जन्त संयुगे ॥ ८ ॥

rathino rathibhis tatra
pattibhiḥ saha pattayaḥ
hayā hayair ibhāś cebhaiḥ
samasajjanta saṁyuge

rathinaḥ—fighters on chariots; *rathibhiḥ*—with the charioteers of the enemy; *tatra*—in the battlefield; *pattibhiḥ*—with the infantry soldiers; *saha*—with; *pattayaḥ*—the infantry of the enemy soldiers; *hayāḥ*—the horses; *hayaiḥ*—with the enemy's soldiers; *ibhāḥ*—the soldiers fighting on the backs of elephants; *ca*—and; *ibhaiḥ*—with the enemy's soldiers on the backs of elephants; *samasajjanta*—began to fight together on an equal level; *saṁyuge*—on the battlefield.

TRANSLATION

On that battlefield, the charioteers fought with the opposing charioteers, the infantry soldiers with the opposing infantry, the soldiers on horseback with the opposing soldiers on horseback, and the soldiers on the backs of elephants with the enemy soldiers on elephants. In this way, the fighting took place between equals.

TEXT 9

उष्ट्रैः केचिदिभैः केचिदपरे युयुधुः खरैः ।
केचिद् गौरमुखैर्ऋक्षैर्द्वीपिभिर्हरिभिर्भटाः ॥ ९ ॥

uṣṭraiḥ kecid ibhaiḥ kecid
apare yuyudhuḥ kharaiḥ
kecid gaura-mukhair ṛkṣair
dvīpibhir haribhir bhaṭāḥ

uṣṭraiḥ—on the backs of camels; *kecit*—some persons; *ibhaiḥ*—on the backs of elephants; *kecit*—some persons; *apare*—others; *yuyudhuḥ*—engaged in fighting; *kharaiḥ*—on the backs of asses; *kecit*—some persons; *gaura-mukhaiḥ*—on white-faced monkeys; *ṛkṣaiḥ*—on red-faced monkeys; *dvīpibhiḥ*—on the backs of tigers; *haribhiḥ*—on the backs of lions; *bhaṭāḥ*—all the soldiers engaged in this way.

TRANSLATION

Some soldiers fought on the backs of camels, some on the backs of elephants, some on asses, some on white-faced and red-faced monkeys, some on tigers and some on lions. In this way, they all engaged in fighting.

TEXTS 10–12

गृध्रैः कङ्कैर्बकैरन्ये श्येनभासैस्तिमिङ्गिलैः ।
शरभैर्महिषैः खड्गैर्गोवृषैर्गवयारुणैः ॥१०॥
शिवाभिराखुभिः केचित् कृकलासैः शशैर्नरैः ।
बस्तैरेके कृष्णसारैर्हंसैरन्ये च सूकरैः ॥११॥
अन्ये जलस्थलखगैः सत्त्वैर्विकृतविग्रहैः ।
सेनयोरुभयो राजन्विविशुस्तेऽग्रतोऽग्रतः ॥१२॥

gṛdhraiḥ kaṅkair bakair anye
śyena-bhāsais timiṅgilaiḥ
śarabhair mahiṣaiḥ khaḍgair
go-vṛṣair gavayāruṇaiḥ

śivābhir ākhubhiḥ kecit
kṛkalāsaiḥ śaśair naraiḥ

bastair eke kṛṣṇa-sārair
haṁsair anye ca sūkaraiḥ

anye jala-sthala-khagaiḥ
sattvair vikṛta-vigrahaiḥ
senayor ubhayo rājan
viviśus te 'grato 'grataḥ

gṛdhraiḥ—on the backs of vultures; *kaṅkaiḥ*—on the backs of eagles; *bakaiḥ*—on the backs of ducks; *anye*—others; *śyena*—on the backs of hawks; *bhāsaiḥ*—on the backs of *bhāsas; timiṅgilaiḥ*—on the backs of big fish known as *timiṅgilas; śarabhaiḥ*—on the backs of *śarabhas; mahiṣaiḥ*—on the backs of buffalo; *khaḍgaiḥ*—on the backs of rhinoceroses; *go*—on the backs of cows; *vṛṣaiḥ*—on the backs of bulls; *gavaya-aruṇaiḥ*—on the backs of *gavayas* and *aruṇas; śivābhiḥ*—on the backs of jackals; *ākhubhiḥ*—on the backs of big rats; *kecit*—some persons; *kṛkalāsaiḥ*—on the backs of big lizards; *śaśaiḥ*—on the backs of big rabbits; *naraiḥ*—on the backs of human beings; *bastaiḥ*—on the backs of goats; *eke*—some; *kṛṣṇa-sāraiḥ*—on the backs of black deer; *haṁsaiḥ*—on the backs of swans; *anye*—others; *ca*—also; *sūkaraiḥ*—on the backs of boars; *anye*—others; *jala-sthala-khagaiḥ*—animals moving on the water, on land and in the sky; *sattvaiḥ*—by creatures being used as vehicles; *vikṛta*—are deformed; *vigrahaiḥ*—by such animals whose bodies; *senayoḥ*—of the two parties of soldiers; *ubhayoḥ*—of both; *rājan*—O King; *viviśuḥ*—entered; *te*—all of them; *agrataḥ agrataḥ*—going forward face to face.

TRANSLATION

O King, some soldiers fought on the backs of vultures, eagles, ducks, hawks and bhāsa birds. Some fought on the backs of timiṅgilas, which can devour huge whales, some on the backs of śarabhas, and some on buffalo, rhinoceroses, cows, bulls, jungle cows and aruṇas. Others fought on the backs of jackals, rats, lizards, rabbits, human beings, goats, black deer, swans and boars. In this way, mounted on animals of the water, land and sky, including animals with deformed bodies, both armies faced each other and went forward.

TEXTS 13–15

चित्रध्वजपटै राजन्नातपत्रैः सितामलैः ।
महाधनैर्वज्रदण्डैर्व्यजनैर्बार्हचामरैः ॥१३॥
वातोद्धूतोत्तरोष्णीषैरर्चिर्भिर्वर्मभूषणैः ।
स्फुरद्भिर्विशदैः शस्त्रैः सुतरां सूर्यरश्मिभिः ॥१४॥
देवदानववीराणां ध्वजिन्यौ पाण्डुनन्दन ।
रेजतुर्वीरमालाभिर्यादसामिव सागरौ ॥१५॥

citra-dhvaja-paṭai rājann
ātapatraiḥ sitāmalaiḥ
mahā-dhanair vajra-daṇḍair
vyajanair bārha-cāmaraiḥ

vātoddhūtottaroṣṇīṣair
arcirbhir varma-bhūṣaṇaiḥ
sphuradbhir viśadaiḥ śastraiḥ
sutarāṁ sūrya-raśmibhiḥ

deva-dānava-vīrāṇāṁ
dhvajinyau pāṇḍu-nandana
rejatur vīra-mālābhir
yādasām iva sāgarau

citra-dhvaja-paṭaiḥ—with very nicely decorated flags and canopies; *rājan*—O King; *ātapatraiḥ*—with umbrellas for protection from the sunshine; *sita-amalaiḥ*—most of them very clean and white; *mahā-dhanaiḥ*—by very valuable; *vajra-daṇḍaiḥ*—with rods made of valuable jewels and pearls; *vyajanaiḥ*—with fans; *bārha-cāmaraiḥ*—with other fans made of peacock feathers; *vāta-uddhūta*—flapping with the breeze; *uttara-uṣṇīṣaiḥ*—with upper and lower garments; *arcirbhiḥ*—by the effulgence; *varma-bhūṣaṇaiḥ*—with ornaments and shields; *sphuradbhiḥ*—shining; *viśadaiḥ*—sharp and clean; *śastraiḥ*—with weapons; *sutarām*—excessively; *sūrya-raśmibhiḥ*—with the dazzling illumination of the sunshine; *deva-dānava-vīrāṇām*—of all the heroes of the parties of both the demons and the demigods; *dhvajinyau*—the two parties of soldiers, each one bearing his own flag; *pāṇḍu-nandana*—O descendant of Mahārāja Pāṇḍu; *rejatuḥ*—distinctly recognized; *vīra-mālābhiḥ*—with garlands used by heroes; *yādasām*—of aquatics; *iva*—just like; *sāgarau*—two oceans.

TRANSLATION

O King, O descendant of Mahārāja Pāṇḍu, the soldiers of both the demigods and demons were decorated by canopies, colorful flags, and umbrellas with handles made of valuable jewels and pearls. They were further decorated by fans made of peacock feathers and by other fans also. The soldiers, their upper and lower garments waving in the breeze, naturally looked very beautiful, and in the light of the glittering sunshine their shields, ornaments and sharp, clean weapons appeared dazzling. Thus the ranks of soldiers seemed like two oceans with bands of aquatics.

TEXTS 16–18

वैरोचनो बलिः संख्ये सोऽसुराणां चमूपतिः ।
यानं वैहायसं नाम कामगं मयनिर्मितम् ॥१६॥
सर्वसाङ्ग्रामिकोपेतं सर्वाश्चर्यमयं प्रभो ।
अप्रतर्क्यमनिर्देश्यं दृश्यमानमदर्शनम् ॥१७॥
आस्थितस्तद् विमानाग्र्यं सर्वानीकाधिपैर्वृतः ।
वालव्यजनछत्राग्र्यै रेजे चन्द्र इवोदये ॥१८॥

vairocano baliḥ saṅkhye
so 'surāṇāṁ camū-patiḥ
yānaṁ vaihāyasaṁ nāma
kāma-gaṁ maya-nirmitam

sarva-sāṅgrāmikopetaṁ
sarvāścaryamayaṁ prabho
apratarkyam anirdeśyaṁ
dṛśyamānam adarśanam

āsthitas tad vimānāgryaṁ
sarvānīkādhipair vṛtaḥ
bāla-vyajana-chatrāgryai
reje candra ivodaye

vairocanaḥ—the son of Virocana; *baliḥ*—Mahārāja Bali; *saṅkhye*—in the battle; *saḥ*—he, so celebrated; *asurāṇām*—of the demons; *camū-patiḥ*—commander in chief; *yānam*—airplane; *vaihāyasam*—called Vaihāyasa; *nāma*—by the name; *kāma-gam*—able to fly anywhere he desired; *maya-nirmitam*—made by the demon Maya; *sarva*—all; *sāṅgrāmika-upetam*—equipped with all kinds of weapons required for fighting with all different types of enemies; *sarva-āścarya-mayam*—wonderful in every respect; *prabho*—O King; *apratarkyam*—inexplicable; *anirdeśyam*—indescribable; *dṛśyamānam*—sometimes visible; *adarśanam*—sometimes not visible; *āsthitaḥ*—being seated on such; *tat*—that; *vimāna-agryam*—excellent airplane; *sarva*—all; *anīka-adhipaiḥ*—by the commanders of soldiers; *vṛtaḥ*—surrounded; *bāla-vyajana-chatra-agryaiḥ*—protected by beautifully decorated umbrellas and the best of *cāmaras; reje*—brilliantly situated; *candraḥ*—the moon; *iva*—like; *udaye*—at the time of rising in the evening.

TRANSLATION

For that battle the most celebrated commander in chief, Mahārāja Bali, son of Virocana, was seated on a wonderful airplane named Vaihāyasa. O King, this beautifully decorated airplane had been manufactured by the demon Maya and was equipped with weapons for all types of combat. It was inconceivable and indescribable. Indeed, it was sometimes visible and sometimes not. Seated in this airplane under a beautiful protective umbrella and being fanned by the best of cāmaras, Mahārāja Bali, surrounded by his captains and commanders, appeared just like the moon rising in the evening, illuminating all directions.

TEXTS 19–24

तस्यासन्सर्वतो यानैर्यूथानां पतयोऽसुराः ।
नमुचिः शम्बरो बाणो विप्रचित्तिरयोमुखः ॥१९॥

द्विमूर्धा कालनाभोऽथ प्रहेतिर्हेतिरिल्वलः ।
शकुनिर्भूतसंतापो वज्रदंष्ट्रो विरोचनः ॥२०॥
हयग्रीवः शङ्कुशिराः कपिलो मेघदुन्दुभिः ।
तारकश्चक्रदृक् शुम्भो निशुम्भो जम्भ उत्कलः ॥२१॥
अरिष्टोऽरिष्टनेमिश्च मयश्च त्रिपुराधिपः ।
अन्ये पौलोमकालेया निवातकवचादयः ॥२२॥
अलब्धभागाः सोमस्य केवलं क्लेशभागिनः ।
सर्वं एते रणमुखे बहुशो निर्जितामराः ॥२३॥
सिंहनादान्विमुञ्चन्तः शङ्खान्दध्मुर्महारवान् ।
दृष्ट्वा सपत्नानुत्सिक्तान्बलभित् कुपितो भृशम् ॥२४॥

tasyāsan sarvato yānair
yūthānāṁ patayo 'surāḥ
namuciḥ śambaro bāṇo
vipracittir ayomukhaḥ

dvimūrdhā kālanābho 'tha
prahetir hetir ilvalaḥ
śakunir bhūtasantāpo
vajradaṁṣṭro virocanaḥ

hayagrīvaḥ śaṅkuśirāḥ
kapilo meghadundubhiḥ
tārakaś cakradṛk śumbho
niśumbho jambha utkalaḥ

ariṣṭo 'riṣṭanemiś ca
mayaś ca tripurādhipaḥ
anye pauloma-kāleyā
nivātakavacādayaḥ

alabdha-bhāgāḥ somasya
kevalaṁ kleśa-bhāginaḥ

sarva ete raṇa-mukhe
bahuśo nirjitāmarāḥ

siṁha-nādān vimuñcantaḥ
śaṅkhān dadhmur mahā-ravān
dṛṣṭvā sapatnān utsiktān
balabhit kupito bhṛśam

tasya—of him (Mahārāja Bali); *āsan*—situated; *sarvataḥ*—all around; *yānaiḥ*—by different vehicles; *yūthānām*—of the soldiers; *patayaḥ*—the commanders; *asurāḥ*—demons; *namuciḥ*—Namuci; *śambaraḥ*—Śambara; *bāṇaḥ*—Bāṇa; *vipracittiḥ*—Vipracitti; *ayomukhaḥ*—Ayomukha; *dvimūrdhā*—Dvimūrdhā; *kālanābhaḥ*—Kālanābha; *atha*—also; *prahetiḥ*—Praheti; *hetiḥ*—Heti; *ilvalaḥ*—Ilvala; *śakuniḥ*—Śakuni; *bhūtasantāpaḥ*—Bhūtasantāpa; *vajra-daṁṣṭraḥ*—Vajradaṁṣṭra; *virocanaḥ*—Virocana; *hayagrīvaḥ*—Hayagrīva; *śaṅkuśirāḥ*—Śaṅkuśirā; *kapilaḥ*—Kapila; *megha-dundubhiḥ*—Meghadundubhi; *tārakaḥ*—Tāraka; *cakradṛk*—Cakradṛk; *śumbhaḥ*—Śumbha; *niśumbhaḥ*—Niśumbha; *jambhaḥ*—Jambha; *utkalaḥ*—Utkala; *ariṣṭaḥ*—Ariṣṭa; *ariṣṭanemiḥ*—Ariṣṭanemi; *ca*—and; *mayaḥ ca*—and Maya; *tripurādhipaḥ*—Tripurādhipa; *anye*—others; *pauloma-kāleyāḥ*—the sons of Puloma and the Kāleyas; *nivātakavaca-ādayaḥ*—Nivātakavaca and other demons; *alabdha-bhāgāḥ*—all unable to take a share; *somasya*—of the nectar; *kevalam*—merely; *kleśa-bhāginaḥ*—the demons took a share of the labor; *sarve*—all of them; *ete*—the demons; *raṇa-mukhe*—in the front of the battle; *bahuśaḥ*—by excessive strength; *nirjita-amarāḥ*—being very troublesome to the demigods; *siṁha-nādān*—vibrations like those of lions; *vimuñcantaḥ*—uttering; *śaṅkhān*—conchshells; *dadhmuḥ*—blew; *mahā-ravān*—making a tumultuous sound; *dṛṣṭvā*—after seeing; *sapatnān*—their rivals; *utsiktān*—ferocious; *balabhit*—(Lord Indra) being afraid of the strength; *kupitaḥ*—having become angry; *bhṛśam*—extremely.

TRANSLATION

Surrounding Mahārāja Bali on all sides were the commanders and captains of the demons, sitting on their respective chariots.

Among them were the following demons: Namuci, Śambara, Bāṇa, Vipracitti, Ayomukha, Dvimūrdhā, Kālanābha, Praheti, Heti, Ilvala, Śakuni, Bhūtasantāpa, Vajradaṁṣṭra, Virocana, Hayagrīva, Śaṅkuśirā, Kapila, Meghadundubhi, Tāraka, Cakradṛk, Śumbha, Niśumbha, Jambha, Utkala, Ariṣṭa, Ariṣṭanemi, Tripurādhipa, Maya, the sons of Puloma, the Kāleyas and Nivātakavaca. All of these demons had been deprived of their share of the nectar and had shared merely in the labor of churning the ocean. Now, they fought against the demigods, and to encourage their armies, they made a tumultuous sound like the roaring of lions and blew loudly on conchshells. Balabhit, Lord Indra, upon seeing this situation of his ferocious rivals, became extremely angry.

TEXT 25

ऐरावतं दिक्करिणमारूढः शुशुभे स्वराट् ।
यथा स्रवत्प्रस्रवणमुदयाद्रिमहर्पतिः ॥२५॥

airāvataṁ dik-kariṇam
ārūḍhaḥ śuśubhe sva-rāṭ
yathā sravat-prasravaṇam
udayādrim ahar-patiḥ

airāvatam—Airāvata; *dik-kariṇam*—the great elephant who could go everywhere; *ārūḍhaḥ*—mounted on; *śuśubhe*—became very beautiful to see; *sva-rāṭ*—Indra; *yathā*—just as; *sravat*—flowing; *prasravaṇam*—waves of wine; *udaya-adrim*—on Udayagiri; *ahaḥ-patiḥ*—the sun.

TRANSLATION

Sitting on Airāvata, an elephant who can go anywhere and who holds water and wine in reserve for showering, Lord Indra looked just like the sun rising from Udayagiri, where there are reservoirs of water.

PURPORT

On the top of the mountain called Udayagiri are large lakes from which water continuously pours in waterfalls. Similarly, Indra's carrier,

Airāvata, holds water and wine in reserve and showers it in the direction of Lord Indra. Thus Indra, King of heaven, sitting on the back of Airāvata, appeared like the brilliant sun rising above Udayagiri.

TEXT 26

तस्यासन्सर्वतो देवा नानावाहध्वजायुधाः ।
लोकपालाः सहगणैर्वाय्वग्निवरुणादयः ॥२६॥

tasyāsan sarvato devā
nānā-vāha-dhvajāyudhāḥ
lokapālāḥ saha-gaṇair
vāyv-agni-varuṇādayaḥ

tasya—of Lord Indra; *āsan*—situated; *sarvataḥ*—all around; *devāḥ*—all the demigods; *nānā-vāha*—with varieties of carriers; *dhvaja-āyudhāḥ*—and with flags and weapons; *loka-pālāḥ*—all the chiefs of various higher planetary systems; *saha*—with; *gaṇaiḥ*—their associates; *vāyu*—the demigod controlling air; *agni*—the demigod controlling fire; *varuṇa*—the demigod controlling water; *ādayaḥ*—all of them surrounding Lord Indra.

TRANSLATION

Surrounding Lord Indra, King of heaven, were the demigods, seated on various types of vehicles and decorated with flags and weapons. Present among them were Vāyu, Agni, Varuṇa and other rulers of various planets, along with their associates.

TEXT 27

तेऽन्योन्यमभिसंसृत्य क्षिपन्तो मर्मभिर्मिथः ।
आह्वयन्तो विशन्तोऽग्रे युयुधुर्द्वन्द्वयोधिनः ॥२७॥

te 'nyonyam abhisaṁsṛtya
kṣipanto marmabhir mithaḥ
āhvayanto viśanto 'gre
yuyudhur dvandva-yodhinaḥ

te—all of them (the demigods and the demons); *anyonyam*—one another; *abhisaṁsṛtya*—having come forward face to face; *kṣipantaḥ*—chastising one another; *marmabhiḥ mithaḥ*—with much pain to the cores of the hearts of one another; *āhvayantaḥ*—addressing one another; *viśantaḥ*—having entered the battlefield; *agre*—in front; *yuyudhuḥ*—fought; *dvandva-yodhinaḥ*—two combatants chose each other.

TRANSLATION

The demigods and demons came before each other and reproached one another with words piercing to the heart. Then they drew near and began fighting face to face in pairs.

TEXT 28

युयोध बलिरिन्द्रेण तारकेण गुहोऽस्यत ।
वरुणो हेतिनायुध्यन्मित्रो राजन्प्रहेतिना ॥२८॥

yuyodha balir indreṇa
tārakeṇa guho 'syata
varuṇo hetināyudhyan
mitro rājan prahetinā

yuyodha—fought; *baliḥ*—Mahārāja Bali; *indreṇa*—with King Indra; *tārakeṇa*—with Tāraka; *guhaḥ*—Kārttikeya; *asyata*—engaged in fighting; *varuṇaḥ*—the demigod Varuṇa; *hetinā*—with Heti; *ayudhyat*—fought one another; *mitraḥ*—the demigod Mitra; *rājan*—O King; *prahetinā*—with Praheti.

TRANSLATION

O King, Mahārāja Bali fought with Indra, Kārttikeya with Tāraka, Varuṇa with Heti, and Mitra with Praheti.

TEXT 29

यमस्तु कालनाभेन विश्वकर्मा मयेन वै ।
शम्बरो युयुधे त्वष्ट्रा सवित्रा तु विरोचनः ॥२९॥

yamas tu kālanābhena
viśvakarmā mayena vai
śambaro yuyudhe tvaṣṭrā
savitrā tu virocanaḥ

yamaḥ—Yamarāja; *tu*—indeed; *kālanābhena*—with Kālanābha; *viśvakarmā*—Viśvakarmā; *mayena*—with Maya; *vai*—indeed; *śambaraḥ*—Śambara; *yuyudhe*—fought; *tvaṣṭrā*—with Tvaṣṭā; *savitrā*—with the sun-god; *tu*—indeed; *virocanaḥ*—the demon Virocana.

TRANSLATION

Yamarāja fought with Kālanābha, Viśvakarmā with Maya Dānava, Tvaṣṭā with Sambara, and the sun-god with Virocana.

TEXTS 30–31

अपराजितेन नमुचिरश्विनौ वृषपर्वणा ।
सूर्यो बलिसुतैर्देवो बाणज्येष्ठैः शतेन च ॥३०॥
राहुणा च तथा सोमः पुलोम्ना युयुधेऽनिलः ।
निशुम्भशुम्भयोर्देवी भद्रकाली तरस्विनी ॥३१॥

aparājitena namucir
aśvinau vṛṣaparvaṇā
sūryo bali-sutair devo
bāṇa-jyeṣṭhaiḥ śatena ca

rāhuṇā ca tathā somaḥ
pulomnā yuyudhe 'nilaḥ
niśumbha-śumbhayor devī
bhadrakālī tarasvinī

aparājitena—with the demigod Aparājita; *namuciḥ*—the demon Namuci; *aśvinau*—the Aśvinī brothers; *vṛṣaparvaṇā*—with the demon Vṛṣaparvā; *sūryaḥ*—the sun-god; *bali-sutaiḥ*—with the sons of Bali; *devaḥ*—the god; *bāṇa-jyeṣṭhaiḥ*—the chief of whom is Bāṇa; *śatena*—numbering one hundred; *ca*—and; *rāhuṇā*—by Rāhu; *ca*—also;

tathā—as well as; *somaḥ*—the moon-god; *pulomnā*—Pulomā; *yuyudhe*—fought; *anilaḥ*—the demigod Anila, who controls air; *niśumbha*—the demon Niśumbha; *śumbhayoḥ*—with Śumbha; *devī*—the goddess Durgā; *bhadrakālī*—Bhadra Kālī; *tarasvinī*—extremely powerful.

TRANSLATION

The demigod Aparājita fought with Namuci, and the two Aśvinī-kumāra brothers fought with Vṛṣaparvā. The sun-god fought with the one hundred sons of Mahārāja Bali, headed by Bāṇa, and the moon-god fought with Rāhu. The demigod controlling air fought with Pulomā, and Śumbha and Niśumbha fought the supremely powerful material energy, Durgādevī, who is called Bhadra Kālī.

TEXTS 32–34

वृषाकपिस्तु जम्भेन महिषेण विभावसुः ।
इल्वलः सह वातापिर्ब्रह्मपुत्रैररिन्दम ॥३२॥
कामदेवेन दुर्मर्ष उत्कलो मातृभिः सह ।
बृहस्पतिश्चोशनसा नरकेण शनैश्चरः ॥३३॥
मरुतो निवातकवचैः कालेयैर्वसवोऽमराः ।
विश्वेदेवास्तु पौलोमै रुद्राः क्रोधवशैः सह ॥३४॥

vṛṣākapis tu jambhena
mahiṣeṇa vibhāvasuḥ
ilvalaḥ saha vātāpir
brahma-putrair arindama

kāmadevena durmarṣa
utkalo mātṛbhiḥ saha
bṛhaspatiś cośanasā
narakeṇa śanaiścaraḥ

maruto nivātakavacaiḥ
kāleyair vasavo 'marāḥ

viśvedevās tu paulomai
rudrāḥ krodhavaśaiḥ saha

vṛṣākapiḥ—Lord Śiva; *tu*—indeed; *jambhena*—with Jambha; *mahiṣeṇa*—with Mahiṣāsura; *vibhāvasuḥ*—the fire-god; *ilvalaḥ*—the demon Ilvala; *saha vātāpiḥ*—with his brother, Vātāpi; *brahma-putraiḥ*—with the sons of Brahmā, such as Vasiṣṭha; *arim-dama*—O Mahārāja Parīkṣit, suppressor of enemies; *kāmadevena*—with Kāmadeva; *durmarṣaḥ*—Durmarṣa; *utkalaḥ*—the demon Utkala; *mātṛbhiḥ saha*—with the demigoddesses known as the Mātṛkās; *bṛhaspatiḥ*—the demigod Bṛhaspati; *ca*—and; *uśanasā*—with Śukrācārya; *narakeṇa*—with the demon known as Naraka; *śanaiścaraḥ*—the demigod Śani, or Saturn; *marutaḥ*—the demigods of air; *nivātakavacaiḥ*—with the demon Nivātakavaca; *kāleyaiḥ*—with the Kālakeyas; *vasavaḥ amarāḥ*—the Vasus fought; *viśvedevāḥ*—the Viśvedeva demigods; *tu*—indeed; *paulomaiḥ*—with the Paulomas; *rudrāḥ*—the eleven Rudras; *krodhavaśaiḥ saha*—with the Krodhavaśa demons.

TRANSLATION

O Mahārāja Parīkṣit, suppressor of enemies [Arindama], Lord Śiva fought with Jambha, and Vibhāvasu fought with Mahiṣāsura. Ilvala, along with his brother Vātāpi, fought the sons of Lord Brahmā. Durmarṣa fought with Cupid, the demon Utkala with the Mātṛkā demigoddesses, Bṛhaspati with Śukrācārya, and Śanaiścara [Saturn] with Narakāsura. The Maruts fought Nivātakavaca, the Vasus fought the Kālakeya demons, the Viśvedeva demigods fought the Pauloma demons, and the Rudras fought the Krodhavaśa demons, who were victims of anger.

TEXT 35

त एवमाजावसुराः सुरेन्द्रा
द्वन्द्वेन संहत्य च युध्यमानाः ।
अन्योन्यमासाद्य निजघ्नुरोजसा
जिगीषवस्तीक्ष्णशरासितोमरैः ॥३५॥

ta evam ājāv asurāḥ surendrā
dvandvena saṁhatya ca yudhyamānāḥ
anyonyam āsādya nijaghnur ojasā
jigīṣavas tīkṣṇa-śarāsi-tomaraiḥ

te—all of them; *evam*—in this way; *ājau*—on the battlefield; *asurāḥ*—the demons; *sura-indrāḥ*—and the demigods; *dvandvena*—two by two; *saṁhatya*—mixing together; *ca*—and; *yudhyamānāḥ*—engaged in fighting; *anyonyam*—with one another; *āsādya*—approaching; *nijaghnuḥ*—slashed with weapons and killed; *ojasā*—with great strength; *jigīṣavaḥ*—everyone desiring victory; *tīkṣṇa*—sharp; *śara*—with arrows; *asi*—with swords; *tomaraiḥ*—with lances.

TRANSLATION

All of these demigods and demons assembled on the battlefield with a fighting spirit and attacked one another with great strength. All of them desiring victory, they fought in pairs, hitting one another severely with sharpened arrows, swords and lances.

TEXT 36

भुशुण्डिभिश्चक्रगदर्ष्टिपट्टिशैः
शक्त्युल्मुकैः प्रासपरश्वधैरपि ।
निस्त्रिंशभल्लैः परिघैः समुद्गरैः
सभिन्दिपालैश्च शिरांसि चिच्छिदुः ॥३६॥

bhuśuṇḍibhiś cakra-gadarṣṭi-paṭṭiśaiḥ
śakty-ulmukaiḥ prāsa-paraśvadhair api
nistriṁśa-bhallaiḥ parighaiḥ samudgaraiḥ
sabhindipālaiś ca śirāṁsi cicchiduḥ

bhuśuṇḍibhiḥ—with weapons called *bhuśuṇḍi; cakra*—with discs; *gadā*—with clubs; *ṛṣṭi*—with the weapons called *ṛṣṭi; paṭṭiśaiḥ*—with the weapons called *paṭṭiśa; śakti*—with the *śakti* weapons; *ulmukaiḥ*—with the weapons called *ulmukas; prāsa*—with the *prāsa* weapons; *paraśvadhaiḥ*—with the weapons called *paraśvadha; api*—also;

nistriṁśa—with *nistriṁśas; bhallaiḥ*—with lances; *parighaiḥ*—with the weapons named *parighas; sa-mudgaraiḥ*—with the weapons known as *mudgara; sa-bhindipālaiḥ*—with the *bhindipāla* weapons; *ca*—also; *śirāṁsi*—heads; *cicchiduḥ*—cut off.

TRANSLATION

They severed one another's heads, using weapons like bhuśuṇḍis, cakras, clubs, ṛṣṭis, paṭṭiśas, śaktis, ulmukas, prāsas, paraśvadhas, nistriṁśas, lances, parighas, mudgaras and bhindipālas.

TEXT 37

गजास्तुरङ्गाः सरथाः पदातयः
सारोहवाहा विविधा विखण्डिताः ।
निकृत्तबाहूरुशिरोधराङ्घ्रय-
श्छिन्नध्वजेष्वासतनुत्रभूषणाः ॥३७॥

gajās turaṅgāḥ sarathāḥ padātayaḥ
sāroha-vāhā vividhā vikhaṇḍitāḥ
nikṛtta-bāhūru-śirodharāṅghrayaś
chinna-dhvajeṣvāsa-tanutra-bhūṣaṇāḥ

gajāḥ—elephants; *turaṅgāḥ*—horses; *sa-rathāḥ*—with chariots; *padātayaḥ*—infantry soldiers; *sāroha-vāhāḥ*—carriers with the riders; *vividhāḥ*—varieties; *vikhaṇḍitāḥ*—cut to pieces; *nikṛtta-bāhu*—cut off arms; *ūru*—thighs; *śirodhara*—necks; *aṅghrayaḥ*—legs; *chinna*—cut up; *dhvaja*—flags; *iṣvāsa*—bows; *tanutra*—armor; *bhūṣaṇāḥ*—ornaments.

TRANSLATION

The elephants, horses, chariots, charioteers, infantry soldiers and various kinds of carriers, along with their riders, were slashed to pieces. The arms, thighs, necks and legs of the soldiers were severed, and their flags, bows, armor and ornaments were torn apart.

TEXT 38

तेषां पदाघातरथाङ्गचूर्णिता-
दायोधनादुल्बण उत्थितस्तदा ।
रेणुर्दिशः खं द्युमणिं च छादयन्
न्यवर्ततासृक्स्रुतिभिः परिप्लुतात् ॥३८॥

teṣāṁ padāghāta-rathāṅga-cūrṇitād
āyodhanād ulbaṇa utthitas tadā
reṇur diśaḥ khaṁ dyumaṇiṁ ca chādayan
nyavartatāsṛk-srutibhiḥ pariplutāt

teṣām—of all the people engaged on the battlefield; *padāghāta*—because of beating on the ground by the legs of the demons and demigods; *ratha-aṅga*—and by the wheels of the chariots; *cūrṇitāt*—which was made into pieces of dust; *āyodhanāt*—from the battlefield; *ulbaṇaḥ*—very forceful; *utthitaḥ*—rising; *tadā*—at that time; *reṇuḥ*—the dust particles; *diśaḥ*—all directions; *kham*—outer space; *dyumaṇim*—up to the sun; *ca*—also; *chādayan*—covering all of space up to that; *nyavartata*—dropped floating in the air; *asṛk*—of blood; *srutibhiḥ*—by particles; *pariplutāt*—because of being widely sprinkled.

TRANSLATION

Because of the impact on the ground of the legs of the demons and demigods and the wheels of the chariots, particles of dust flew violently into the sky and made a dust cloud that covered all directions of outer space, as far as the sun. But when the particles of dust were followed by drops of blood being sprinkled all over space, the dust cloud could no longer float in the sky.

PURPORT

The cloud of dust covered the entire horizon, but when drops of blood sprayed up as far as the sun, the dust cloud could no longer float in the sky. A point to be observed here is that although the blood is stated to have reached the sun, it is not said to have reached the moon. Apparently, therefore, as stated elsewhere in *Śrīmad-Bhāgavatam*, the sun, not the moon, is the planet nearest the earth. We have already discussed this point in many places. The sun is first, then the moon, then Mars, Jupiter and so on. The sun is supposed to be 93,000,000 miles above the surface of the earth, and from the *Śrīmad-Bhāgavatam* we understand that the moon is 1,600,000 miles above the sun. Therefore the distance between the earth and the moon would be about 95,000,000 miles. So if a space capsule were traveling at the speed of 18,000 miles per hour, how could it reach the moon in four days? At that speed, going to the moon would take at least seven months. That a space capsule on a moon excursion has reached the moon in four days is therefore impossible.

TEXT 39

शिरोभिरुद्धूतकिरीटकुण्डलैः
संरम्भदृग्भिः परिदष्टदच्छदैः ।
महाभुजैः साभरणैः सहायुधैः
सा प्रास्तृता भूः करभोरुभिर्बभौ ॥३९॥

śirobhir uddhūta-kirīṭa-kuṇḍalaiḥ
saṁrambha-dṛgbhiḥ paridaṣṭa-dacchadaiḥ
mahā-bhujaiḥ sābharaṇaiḥ sahāyudhaiḥ
sā prāstṛtā bhūḥ karabhorubhir babhau

śirobhiḥ—by the heads; *uddhūta*—separated, scattered from; *kirīṭa*—having their helmets; *kuṇḍalaiḥ*—and earrings; *saṁrambha-dṛgbhiḥ*—eyes staring in anger (although the heads were severed from their bodies); *paridaṣṭa*—having been bitten by the teeth; *dacchadaiḥ*—the lips; *mahā-bhujaiḥ*—with big arms; *sa-ābharaṇaiḥ*—decorated with ornaments; *saha-āyudhaiḥ*—and with weapons in their hands, although the hands were severed; *sā*—that battlefield; *prāstṛtā*—scattered; *bhūḥ*—the warfield; *karabha-ūrubhiḥ*—and with thighs and legs resembling the trunks of elephants; *babhau*—it so became.

TRANSLATION

In the course of the battle, the warfield became strewn with the severed heads of heroes, their eyes still staring and their teeth still

pressed against their lips in anger. Helmets and earrings were scattered from these severed heads. Similarly, many arms, decorated with ornaments and clutching various weapons, were strewn here and there, as were many legs and thighs, which resembled the trunks of elephants.

TEXT 40

कबन्धास्तत्र चोत्पेतुः पतितस्वशिरोऽक्षिभिः ।
उद्यतायुधदोर्दण्डैराधावन्तो भटान् मृधे ॥४०॥

kabandhās tatra cotpetuḥ
patita-sva-śiro-'kṣibhiḥ
udyatāyudha-dordaṇḍair
ādhāvanto bhaṭān mṛdhe

kabandhāḥ—trunks (bodies without heads); *tatra*—there (on the battlefield); *ca*—also; *utpetuḥ*—generated; *patita*—fallen; *sva-śiraḥ-akṣibhiḥ*—by the eyes in one's head; *udyata*—raised; *āyudha*—equipped with weapons; *dordaṇḍaiḥ*—the arms of whom; *ādhāvantaḥ*—rushing toward; *bhaṭān*—the soldiers; *mṛdhe*—on the battlefield.

TRANSLATION

Many headless trunks were generated on that battlefield. With weapons in their arms, those ghostly trunks, which could see with the eyes in the fallen heads, attacked the enemy soldiers.

PURPORT

It appears that the heroes who died on the battlefield immediately became ghosts, and although their heads had been severed from their bodies, new trunks were generated, and these new trunks, seeing with the eyes in the severed heads, began to attack the enemy. In other words, many ghosts were generated to join the fight, and thus new trunks appeared on the battlefield.

TEXT 41

बलिर्महेन्द्रं दशभिस्त्रिभिरैरावतं शरैः ।
चतुर्भिश्चतुरो वाहानेकेनारोहमार्च्छयत् ॥४१॥

balir mahendraṁ daśabhis
tribhir airāvataṁ śaraiḥ
caturbhiś caturo vāhān
ekenāroham ārcchayat

baliḥ—Mahārāja Bali; *mahā-indram*—the King of heaven; *daśabhiḥ*—with ten; *tribhiḥ*—with three; *airāvatam*—Airāvata, carrying Indra; *śaraiḥ*—by arrows; *caturbhiḥ*—by four arrows; *caturaḥ*—the four; *vāhān*—mounted soldiers; *ekena*—by one; *āroham*—the driver of the elephants; *ārcchayat*—attacked.

TRANSLATION

Mahārāja Bali then attacked Indra with ten arrows and attacked Airāvata, Indra's carrier elephant, with three arrows. With four arrows he attacked the four horsemen guarding Airāvata's legs, and with one arrow he attacked the driver of the elephant.

PURPORT

The word *vāhān* refers to the soldiers on horseback who protected the legs of the carrier elephants. According to the system of military arrangement, the legs of the elephant bearing the commander were also protected.

TEXT 42

स तानापततः शक्रस्तावद्भिः शीघ्रविक्रमः ।
चिच्छेद निशितैर्भल्लैरसम्प्राप्तान्हसन्निव ॥४२॥

sa tān āpatataḥ śakras
tāvadbhiḥ śīghra-vikramaḥ
ciccheda niśitair bhallair
asamprāptān hasann iva

saḥ—he (Indra); *tān*—arrows; *āpatataḥ*—while moving toward him and falling down; *śakraḥ*—Indra; *tāvadbhiḥ*—immediately; *śīghra-vikramaḥ*—was practiced to oppress very soon; *ciccheda*—cut to pieces; *niśitaiḥ*—very sharp; *bhallaiḥ*—with another type of arrow;

asamprāptān—the enemy's arrows not being received; *hasan iva*—as if smiling.

TRANSLATION

Before Bali Mahārāja's arrows could reach him, Indra, King of heaven, who is expert in dealing with arrows, smiled and counteracted the arrows with arrows of another type, known as bhalla, which were extremely sharp.

TEXT 43

तस्य कर्मोत्तमं वीक्ष्य दुर्मर्षः शक्तिमाददे ।
तां ज्वलन्तीं महोल्काभां हस्तस्थामच्छिनद्धरिः ॥४३॥

tasya karmottamaṁ vīkṣya
durmarṣaḥ śaktim ādade
tāṁ jvalantīṁ maholkābhāṁ
hasta-sthām acchinad dhariḥ

tasya—of King Indra; *karma-uttamam*—the very expert service in military art; *vīkṣya*—after observing; *durmarṣaḥ*—being in a very angry mood; *śaktim*—the *śakti* weapon; *ādade*—took up; *tām*—that weapon; *jvalantīm*—blazing fire; *mahā-ulkā-ābhām*—appearing like a great firebrand; *hasta-sthām*—while still in the hand of Bali; *acchinat*—cut to pieces; *hariḥ*—Indra.

TRANSLATION

When Bali Mahārāja saw the expert military activities of Indra, he could not restrain his anger. Thus he took up another weapon, known as śakti, which blazed like a great firebrand. But Indra cut that weapon to pieces while it was still in Bali's hand.

TEXT 44

ततः शूलं ततः प्रासं ततस्तोमरमृष्टयः ।
यद् यच्छस्त्रं समादद्यात्सर्वं तदच्छिनद् विभुः ॥४४॥

tataḥ śūlaṁ tataḥ prāsaṁ
tatas tomaram ṛṣṭayaḥ
yad yac chastraṁ samādadyāt
sarvaṁ tad acchinad vibhuḥ

tataḥ—thereafter; *śūlam*—lance; *tataḥ*—thereafter; *prāsam*—the *prāsa* weapon; *tataḥ*—thereafter; *tomaram*—the *tomara* weapon; *ṛṣṭayaḥ*—the *ṛṣṭi* weapons; *yat yat*—whatever and whichever; *śastram*—weapon; *samādadyāt*—Bali Mahārāja tried to use; *sarvam*—all of them; *tat*—those same weapons; *acchinat*—cut to pieces; *vibhuḥ*—the great Indra.

TRANSLATION

Thereafter, one by one, Bali Mahārāja used a lance, prāsa, tomara, ṛṣṭis and other weapons, but whatever weapons he took up, Indra immediately cut them to pieces.

TEXT 45

ससर्जाथासुरीं मायामन्तर्धानगतोऽसुरः ।
ततः प्रादुरभूच्छैलः सुरानीकोपरि प्रभो ॥४५॥

sasarjāthāsurīṁ māyām
antardhāna-gato 'suraḥ
tataḥ prādurabhūc chailaḥ
surānīkopari prabho

sasarja—released; *atha*—now; *āsurīm*—demoniac; *māyām*—illusion; *antardhāna*—out of vision; *gataḥ*—having gone; *asuraḥ*—Bali Mahārāja; *tataḥ*—thereafter; *prādurabhūt*—there appeared; *śailaḥ*—a big mountain; *sura-anīka-upari*—above the heads of the soldiers of the demigods; *prabho*—O my lord.

TRANSLATION

My dear King, Bali Mahārāja then disappeared and resorted to demoniac illusions. A giant mountain, generated from illusion, then appeared above the heads of the demigod soldiers.

TEXT 46

ततो निपेतुस्तरवो दह्यमाना दवाग्निना ।
शिलाः सटङ्कशिखराश्चूर्णयन्त्यो द्विषद्बलम् ॥४६॥

tato nipetus taravo
dahyamānā davāgninā
śilāḥ saṭaṅka-śikharāś
cūrṇayantyo dviṣad-balam

tataḥ—from that great mountain; *nipetuḥ*—began to fall; *taravaḥ*—large trees; *dahyamānāḥ*—blazing in fire; *dava-agninā*—by the forest fire; *śilāḥ*—and stones; *sa-ṭaṅka-śikharāḥ*—having edges with points as sharp as stone picks; *cūrṇayantyaḥ*—smashing; *dviṣat-balam*—the strength of the enemies.

TRANSLATION

From that mountain fell trees blazing in a forest fire. Chips of stone, with sharp edges like picks, also fell and smashed the heads of the demigod soldiers.

TEXT 47

महोरगाः समुत्पेतुर्दन्दशूकाः सवृश्चिकाः ।
सिंहव्याघ्रवराहाश्च मर्दयन्तो महागजाः ॥४७॥

mahoragāḥ samutpetur
dandaśūkāḥ savṛścikāḥ
siṁha-vyāghra-varāhāś ca
mardayanto mahā-gajāḥ

mahā-uragāḥ—big serpents; *samutpetuḥ*—fell upon them; *dandaśūkāḥ*—other poisonous animals and insects; *sa-vṛścikāḥ*—with scorpions; *siṁha*—lions; *vyāghra*—tigers; *varāhāḥ ca*—and forest boars; *mardayantaḥ*—smashing; *mahā-gajāḥ*—great elephants.

TRANSLATION

Scorpions, large snakes and many other poisonous animals, as well as lions, tigers, boars and great elephants, all began falling upon the demigod soldiers, crushing everything.

TEXT 48

यातुधान्यश्च शतशः शूलहस्ता विवाससः ।
छिन्धि भिन्धीति वादिन्यस्तथा रक्षोगणाः प्रभो ॥ ४८ ॥

yātudhānyaś ca śataśaḥ
śūla-hastā vivāsasaḥ
chindhi bhindhīti vādinyas
tathā rakṣo-gaṇāḥ prabho

yātudhānyaḥ—carnivorous female demons; *ca*—and; *śataśaḥ*—hundreds upon hundreds; *śūla-hastāḥ*—every one of them with a trident in hand; *vivāsasaḥ*—completely naked; *chindhi*—cut to pieces; *bhindhi*—pierce; *iti*—thus; *vādinyaḥ*—talking; *tathā*—in that way; *rakṣaḥ-gaṇāḥ*—a band of Rākṣasas (a type of demon); *prabho*—O my King.

TRANSLATION

O my King, many hundreds of male and female carnivorous demons, completely naked and carrying tridents in their hands, then appeared, crying the slogans "Cut them to pieces! Pierce them!"

TEXT 49

ततो महाघना व्योम्नि गम्भीरपरुषस्वनाः ।
अङ्गारान्मुमुचुर्वातैराहताः स्तनयित्नवः ॥४९॥

tato mahā-ghanā vyomni
gambhīra-paruṣa-svanāḥ
aṅgārān mumucur vātair
āhatāḥ stanayitnavaḥ

tataḥ—thereafter; *mahā-ghanāḥ*—big clouds; *vyomni*—in the sky; *gambhīra-paruṣa-svanāḥ*—making very deep rumbling sounds; *aṅgārān*—embers; *mumucuḥ*—released; *vātaiḥ*—by the strong winds; *āhatāḥ*—harassed; *stanayitnavaḥ*—with the sound of thunder.

TRANSLATION

Fierce clouds, harassed by strong winds, then appeared in the sky. Rumbling very gravely with the sound of thunder, they began to shower live coals.

TEXT 50

सृष्टो दैत्येन सुमहान्वह्निः श्वसनसारथिः ।
सांवर्तक इवात्युग्रो विबुधध्वजिनीमधाक् ॥५०॥

sṛṣṭo daityena sumahān
vahniḥ śvasana-sārathiḥ
sāṁvartaka ivātyugro
vibudha-dhvajinīm adhāk

sṛṣṭaḥ—created; *daityena*—by the demon (Bali Mahārāja); *su-mahān*—very great, devastating; *vahniḥ*—a fire; *śvasana-sārathiḥ*—being carried by the blasting wind; *sāṁvartakaḥ*—the fire named Sāṁvartaka, which appears during the time of dissolution; *iva*—just like; *ati*—very much; *ugraḥ*—terrible; *vibudha*—of the demigods; *dhvajinīm*—the soldiers; *adhāk*—burned to ashes.

TRANSLATION

A great devastating fire created by Bali Mahārāja began burning all the soldiers of the demigods. This fire, accompanied by blasting winds, seemed as terrible as the Sāṁvartaka fire, which appears at the time of dissolution.

TEXT 51

ततः समुद्र उद्वेलः सर्वतः प्रत्यदृश्यत ।
प्रचण्डवातैरुद्धूततरङ्गावर्तभीषणः ॥५१॥

tataḥ samudra udvelaḥ
sarvataḥ pratyadṛśyata
pracaṇḍa-vātair uddhūta-
taraṅgāvarta-bhīṣaṇaḥ

tataḥ—thereafter; *samudraḥ*—the sea; *udvelaḥ*—being agitated; *sarvataḥ*—everywhere; *pratyadṛśyata*—appeared before everyone's vision; *pracaṇḍa*—fierce; *vātaiḥ*—by the winds; *uddhūta*—agitated; *taraṅga*—of the waves; *āvarta*—whirling water; *bhīṣaṇaḥ*—ferocious.

TRANSLATION

Thereafter, whirlpools and sea waves, agitated by fierce blasts of wind, appeared everywhere, before everyone's vision, in a furious flood.

TEXT 52

एवं दैत्यैर्महामायैरलक्ष्यगतिभीरणे ।
सृज्यमानासु मायासु विषेदुः सुरसैनिकाः ॥५२॥

evaṁ daityair mahā-māyair
alakṣya-gatibhī raṇe
sṛjyamānāsu māyāsu
viṣeduḥ sura-sainikāḥ

evam—thus; *daityaiḥ*—by the demons; *mahā-māyaiḥ*—who were expert in creating illusions; *alakṣya-gatibhiḥ*—but invisible; *raṇe*—in the fight; *sṛjyamānāsu māyāsu*—because of the creation of such an illusory atmosphere; *viṣeduḥ*—became morose; *sura-sainikāḥ*—the soldiers of the demigods.

TRANSLATION

While this magical atmosphere in the fight was being created by the invisible demons, who were expert in such illusions, the soldiers of the demigods became morose.

TEXT 53

न तत्प्रतिविधिं यत्र विदुरिन्द्रादयो नृप ।
ध्यातः प्रादुरभूत् तत्र भगवान्विश्वभावनः ॥५३॥

na tat-pratividhiṁ yatra
vidur indrādayo nṛpa
dhyātaḥ prādurabhūt tatra
bhagavān viśva-bhāvanaḥ

na—not; *tat-pratividhim*—the counteraction of such an illusory atmosphere; *yatra*—wherein; *viduḥ*—could understand; *indra-ādayaḥ*—the demigods, headed by Indra; *nṛpa*—O King; *dhyātaḥ*—being meditated upon; *prādurabhūt*—appeared there; *tatra*—in that place; *bhagavān*—the Supreme Personality of Godhead; *viśva-bhāvanaḥ*—the creator of the universe.

TRANSLATION

O King, when the demigods could find no way to counteract the activities of the demons, they wholeheartedly meditated upon the Supreme Personality of Godhead, the creator of the universe, who then immediately appeared.

TEXT 54

ततः सुपर्णांसकृताङ्घ्रिपल्लवः
पिशङ्गवासा नवकञ्जलोचनः ।
अदृश्यताष्टायुधबाहुरुल्लस-
च्छ्रीकौस्तुभानर्घ्यकिरीटकुण्डलः ॥५४॥

tataḥ suparṇāṁsa-kṛtāṅghri-pallavaḥ
piśaṅga-vāsā nava-kañja-locanaḥ
adṛśyatāṣṭāyudha-bāhur ullasac-
chrī-kaustubhānarghya-kirīṭa-kuṇḍalaḥ

tataḥ—thereafter; *suparṇa-aṁsa-kṛta-aṅghri-pallavaḥ*—the Supreme Personality of Godhead, whose lotus feet spread over the two shoulders of Garuḍa; *piśaṅga-vāsāḥ*—whose dress is yellow; *nava-kañja-locanaḥ*—and whose eyes are just like the petals of a newly blossomed lotus; *adṛśyata*—became visible (in the presence of the demigods); *aṣṭa-āyudha*—equipped with eight kinds of weapons; *bāhuḥ*—arms; *ullasat*—brilliantly exhibiting; *śrī*—the goddess of fortune; *kaustubha*—the Kaustubha gem; *anarghya*—of incalculable value; *kirīṭa*—helmet; *kuṇḍalaḥ*—having earrings.

TRANSLATION

The Supreme Personality of Godhead, whose eyes resemble the petals of a newly blossomed lotus, sat on the back of Garuḍa, spreading His lotus feet over Garuḍa's shoulders. Dressed in yellow, decorated by the Kaustubha gem and the goddess of fortune, and wearing an invaluable helmet and earrings, the Supreme Lord, holding various weapons in His eight hands, became visible to the demigods.

TEXT 55

तस्मिन्प्रविष्टेऽसुरकूटकर्मजा
माया विनेशुर्महिना महीयसः ।
स्वप्नो यथा हि प्रतिबोध आगते
हरिस्मृतिः सर्वविपद्विमोक्षणम् ॥५५॥

tasmin praviṣṭe 'sura-kūṭa-karmajā
māyā vineśur mahinā mahīyasaḥ
svapno yathā hi pratibodha āgate
hari-smṛtiḥ sarva-vipad-vimokṣaṇam

tasmin praviṣṭe—upon the entrance of the Supreme Personality of Godhead; *asura*—of the demons; *kūṭa-karma-jā*—because of the illusory, magical activities; *māyā*—the false manifestations; *vineśuḥ*—were immediately curbed; *mahinā*—by the superior power; *mahīyasaḥ*—of the Supreme Personality of Godhead, who is greater than the greatest; *svapnaḥ*—dreams; *yathā*—as; *hi*—indeed; *pratibodhe*—when awakening; *āgate*—has arrived; *hari-smṛtiḥ*—remembrance of the Supreme Personality of Godhead; *sarva-vipat*—of all kinds of dangerous situations; *vimokṣaṇam*—immediately vanquishes.

TRANSLATION

As the dangers of a dream cease when the dreamer awakens, the illusions created by the jugglery of the demons were vanquished by the transcendental prowess of the Supreme Personality of Godhead as soon as He entered the battlefield. Indeed, simply by remembrance of the Supreme Personality of Godhead, one becomes free from all dangers.

TEXT 56

दृष्ट्वा मृधे गरुडवाहमिभारिवाह
आविध्य शूलमहिनोदथ कालनेमिः ।
तल्लीलया गरुडमूर्ध्नि पतद् गृहीत्वा
तेनाहनन्नृप सवाहमरिं त्र्यधीशः ॥५६॥

dṛṣṭvā mṛdhe garuḍa-vāham ibhāri-vāha
āvidhya śūlam ahinod atha kālanemiḥ
tal līlayā garuḍa-mūrdhni patad gṛhītvā
tenāhanan nṛpa savāham ariṁ tryadhīśaḥ

dṛṣṭvā—seeing; *mṛdhe*—on the battlefield; *garuḍa-vāham*—the Supreme Personality of Godhead, carried by Garuḍa; *ibhāri-vāhaḥ*—the demon, who was carried by a big lion; *āvidhya*—whirling around; *śūlam*—trident; *ahinot*—discharged at him; *atha*—thus; *kālanemiḥ*—the demon Kālanemi; *tat*—such an attack by the demon against the Supreme Lord; *līlayā*—very easily; *garuḍa-mūrdhni*—on the head of His carrier, Garuḍa; *patat*—while falling down; *gṛhītvā*—after taking it immediately, without difficulty; *tena*—and by the same weapon; *ahanat*—killed; *nṛpa*—O King; *sa-vāham*—with his carrier; *arim*—the enemy; *tri-adhīśaḥ*—the Supreme Personality of Godhead, the proprietor of the three worlds.

TRANSLATION

O King, when the demon Kālanemi, who was carried by a lion, saw that the Supreme Personality of Godhead, carried by Garuḍa,

was on the battlefield, the demon immediately took his trident, whirled it and discharged it at Garuḍa's head. The Supreme Personality of Godhead, Hari, the master of the three worlds, immediately caught the trident, and with the very same weapon he killed the enemy Kālanemi, along with his carrier, the lion.

PURPORT

In this regard, Śrīla Madhvācārya says:

kālanemy-ādayaḥ sarve
kariṇā nihatā api
śukreṇojjīvitāḥ santaḥ
punas tenaiva pātitāḥ

"Kālanemi and all the other demons were killed by the Supreme Personality of Godhead, Hari, and when Śukrācārya, their spiritual master, brought them back to life, they were again killed by the Supreme Personality of Godhead."

TEXT 57

माली सुमाल्यतिबलौ युधि पेततुर्य-
चक्रेण कृत्तशिरसावथ माल्यवांस्तम् ।
आहत्य तिग्मगदयाहनदण्डजेन्द्रं
तावच्छिरोऽच्छिनदरेर्नदतोऽरिणाद्यः ॥ ५७ ॥

mālī sumāly atibalau yudhi petatur yac-
cakreṇa kṛtta-śirasāv atha mālyavāṁs tam
āhatya tigma-gadayāhanad aṇḍajendraṁ
tāvac chiro 'cchinad arer nadato 'riṇādyaḥ

mālī sumālī—two demons named Mālī and Sumālī; *ati-balau*—very powerful; *yudhi*—on the battlefield; *petatuḥ*—fell down; *yat-cakreṇa*—by whose disc; *kṛtta-śirasau*—their heads having been cut off; *atha*—thereupon; *mālyavān*—Mālyavān; *tam*—the Supreme Personality of Godhead; *āhatya*—attacking; *tigma-gadayā*—with a very sharp club; *ahanat*—attempted to attack, kill; *aṇḍa-ja-indram*—Garuḍa, the king of all the birds, who are born from eggs; *tāvat*—at that time; *śiraḥ*—the head; *acchinat*—cut off; *areḥ*—of the enemy; *nadataḥ*—roaring like a lion; *ariṇā*—by the disc; *ādyaḥ*—the original Personality of Godhead.

TRANSLATION

Thereafter, two very powerful demons named Mālī and Sumālī were killed by the Supreme Lord, who severed their heads with His disc. Then Mālyavān, another demon, attacked the Lord. With his sharp club, the demon, who was roaring like a lion, attacked Garuḍa, the lord of the birds, who are born from eggs. But the Supreme Personality of Godhead, the original person, used His disc to cut off the head of that enemy also.

Thus end the Bhaktivedanta purports of the Eighth Canto, Tenth Chapter, of the Śrīmad-Bhāgavatam, *entitled "The Battle Between the Demigods and the Demons."*

CHAPTER ELEVEN

King Indra Annihilates the Demons

As described in this chapter, the great saint Nārada Muni, being very compassionate to the demons who had been killed by the demigods, forbade the demigods to continue killing. Then Śukrācārya, by his mystic power, renewed the lives of all the demons.

Having been graced by the Supreme Personality of Godhead, the demigods began fighting the demons again, with renewed energy. King Indra released his thunderbolt against Bali, and when Bali fell, his friend Jambhāsura attacked Indra, who then cut off Jambhāsura's head with his thunderbolt. When Nārada Muni learned that Jambhāsura had been killed, he informed Jambhāsura's relatives Namuci, Bala and Pāka, who then went to the battlefield and attacked the demigods. Indra, King of heaven, severed the heads of Bala and Pāka and released the weapon known as *kuliśa*, the thunderbolt, against Namuci's shoulder. The thunderbolt, however, returned unsuccessful, and thus Indra became morose. At that time, an unseen voice came from the sky. The voice declared, "A dry or wet weapon cannot kill Namuci." Hearing this voice, Indra began to think of how Namuci could be killed. He then thought of foam, which is neither moist nor dry. Using a weapon of foam, he was able to kill Namuci. Thus Indra and the other demigods killed many demons. Then, at the request of Lord Brahmā, Nārada went to the demigods and forbade them to kill the demons any longer. All the demigods then returned to their abodes. Following the instructions of Nārada, whatever demons remained alive on the battlefield took Bali Mahārāja to Asta Mountain. There, by the touch of Śukrācārya's hand, Bali Mahārāja regained his senses and consciousness, and those demons whose heads and bodies had not been completely lost were brought back to life by the mystic power of Śukrācārya.

TEXT 1

श्रीशुक उवाच

अथो सुराः प्रत्युपलब्धचेतसः
परस्य पुंसः परयानुकम्पया ।

जघ्नुर्भृशं शक्रसमीरणादय-
स्तांस्तान्रणे यैरभिसंहताः पुरा ॥ १ ॥

śrī-śuka uvāca
atho surāḥ pratyupalabdha-cetasaḥ
parasya puṁsaḥ parayānukampayā
jaghnur bhṛśaṁ śakra-samīraṇādayas
tāṁs tān raṇe yair abhisaṁhatāḥ purā

śrī-śukaḥ uvāca—Śrī Śukadeva Gosvāmī said; *atho*—thereafter; *surāḥ*—all the demigods; *pratyupalabdha-cetasaḥ*—being enlivened again by revival of their consciousness; *parasya*—of the Supreme; *puṁsaḥ*—of the Personality of Godhead; *parayā*—supreme; *anukampayā*—by the mercy; *jaghnuḥ*—began to beat; *bhṛśam*—again and again; *śakra*—Indra; *samīraṇa*—Vāyu; *ādayaḥ*—and others; *tān tān*—to those demons; *raṇe*—in the fight; *yaiḥ*—by whom; *abhisaṁhatāḥ*—they were beaten; *purā*—before.

TRANSLATION

Śukadeva Gosvāmī said: Thereafter, by the supreme grace of the Supreme Personality of Godhead, Śrī Hari, all the demigods, headed by Indra and Vāyu, were brought back to life. Being enlivened, the demigods began severely beating the very same demons who had defeated them before.

TEXT 2

वैरोचनाय संरब्धो भगवान्पाकशासनः ।
उदयच्छद् यदा वज्रं प्रजा हा हेति चुक्रुशुः ॥ २ ॥

vairocanāya saṁrabdho
bhagavān pāka-śāsanaḥ
udayacchad yadā vajraṁ
prajā hā heti cukruśuḥ

vairocanāya—unto Bali Mahārāja (just to kill him); *saṁrabdhaḥ*—being very angry; *bhagavān*—the most powerful; *pāka-śāsanaḥ*—

Indra; *udayacchat*—took in his hand; *yadā*—at which time; *vajram*—the thunderbolt; *prajāḥ*—all the demons; *hā hā*—alas, alas; *iti*—thus; *cukruśuḥ*—began to resound.

TRANSLATION

When the most powerful Indra became angry and took his thunderbolt in hand to kill Mahārāja Bali, the demons began lamenting, "Alas, alas!"

TEXT 3

वज्रपाणिस्तमाहेदं तिरस्कृत्य पुरःस्थितम् ।
मनस्विनं सुसम्पन्नं विचरन्तं महामृधे ॥ ३ ॥

vajra-pāṇis tam āhedaṁ
tiraskṛtya puraḥ-sthitam
manasvinaṁ susampannaṁ
vicarantaṁ mahā-mṛdhe

vajra-pāṇiḥ—Indra, who always carries in his hand the thunderbolt; *tam*—unto Bali Mahārāja; *āha*—addressed; *idam*—in this way; *tiraskṛtya*—chastising him; *puraḥ-sthitam*—standing before him; *manasvinam*—very sober and tolerant; *su-sampannam*—well equipped with paraphernalia for fighting; *vicarantam*—moving; *mahā-mṛdhe*—on the great battlefield.

TRANSLATION

Sober and tolerant and well equipped with paraphernalia for fighting, Bali Mahārāja moved before Indra on the great battlefield. King Indra, who always carries the thunderbolt in his hand, rebuked Bali Mahārāja as follows.

TEXT 4

नटवन्मूढ मायाभिर्मायेशान् नो जिगीषसि ।
जित्वा बालान् निबद्धाक्षान् नटो हरति तद्धनम् ॥ ४ ॥

naṭavan mūḍha māyābhir
māyeśān no jigīṣasi
jitvā bālān nibaddhākṣān
naṭo harati tad-dhanam

naṭa-vat—like a cheater or rogue; *mūḍha*—you rascal; *māyābhiḥ*—by exhibiting illusions; *māyā-īśān*—unto the demigods, who can control all such illusory manifestations; *naḥ*—unto us; *jigīṣasi*—you are trying to become victorious; *jitvā*—conquering; *bālān*—small children; *nibaddha-akṣān*—by binding the eyes; *naṭaḥ*—a cheater; *harati*—takes away; *tat-dhanam*—the property in the possession of a child.

TRANSLATION

Indra said: O rascal, as a cheater sometimes binds the eyes of a child and takes away his possessions, you are trying to defeat us by displaying some mystic power, although you know that we are the masters of all such mystic powers.

TEXT 5

आरुरुक्षन्ति मायाभिरुत्सिसृप्सन्ति ये दिवम् ।
तान्दस्यून्विधुनोम्यज्ञान्पूर्वस्माच्च पदादधः ॥ ५ ॥

ārurukṣanti māyābhir
utsisṛpsanti ye divam
tān dasyūn vidhunomy ajñān
pūrvasmāc ca padād adhaḥ

ārurukṣanti—persons who desire to come to the upper planetary systems; *māyābhiḥ*—by so-called mystic power or material advancement of science; *utsisṛpsanti*—or want to be liberated by such false attempts; *ye*—such persons who; *divam*—the higher planetary system known as Svargaloka; *tān*—such rogues and ruffians; *dasyūn*—such thieves; *vidhunomi*—I force to go down; *ajñān*—rascals; *pūrvasmāt*—previous; *ca*—also; *padāt*—from the position; *adhaḥ*—downward.

TRANSLATION

Those fools and rascals who want to ascend to the upper planetary system by mystic power or mechanical means, or who endeavor to cross even the upper planets and achieve the spiritual world or liberation, I cause to be sent to the lowest region of the universe.

PURPORT

There are undoubtedly different planetary systems for different persons. As stated in *Bhagavad-gītā* (14.18), *ūrdhvaṁ gacchanti sattva-sthāḥ:* persons in the mode of goodness can go to the upper planets. Those in the modes of darkness and passion, however, are not allowed to enter the higher planets. The word *divam* refers to the higher planetary system known as Svargaloka. Indra, King of the higher planetary system, has the power to push down any conditioned soul attempting to go from the lower to the higher planets without proper qualifications. The modern attempt to go to the moon is also an attempt by inferior men to go to Svargaloka by artificial, mechanical means. This attempt cannot be successful. From this statement of Indra it appears that anyone attempting to go to the higher planetary systems by mechanical means, which are here called *māyā*, is condemned to go the the hellish planets in the lower portion of the universe. To go to the higher planetary system, one needs sufficient good qualities. A sinful person situated in the mode of ignorance and addicted to drinking, meat-eating and illicit sex will never enter the higher planets by mechanical means.

TEXT 6

सोऽहं दुर्मायिनस्तेऽद्य वज्रेण शतपर्वणा ।
शिरो हरिष्ये मन्दात्मन्घटस्व ज्ञातिभिः सह ॥ ६ ॥

so 'haṁ durmāyinas te 'dya
vajreṇa śata-parvaṇā
śiro hariṣye mandātman
ghaṭasva jñātibhiḥ saha

saḥ—I am the same powerful person; *aham*—I; *durmāyinaḥ*—of you, who can perform so much jugglery with illusions; *te*—of you;

adya—today; *vajreṇa*—by the thunderbolt; *śata-parvaṇā*—which has hundreds of sharp edges; *śiraḥ*—the head; *hariṣye*—I shall separate; *manda-ātman*—O you with a poor fund of knowledge; *ghaṭasva*—just try to exist on this battlefield; *jñātibhiḥ saha*—with your relatives and assistants.

TRANSLATION

Today, with my thunderbolt, which has hundreds of sharp edges, I, the same powerful person, shall sever your head from your body. Although you can produce so much jugglery through illusion, you are endowed with a poor fund of knowledge. Now, try to exist on this battlefield with your relatives and friends.

TEXT 7

श्रीबलिरुवाच

सङ्ग्रामे वर्तमानानां कालचोदितकर्मणाम् ।
कीर्तिर्जयोऽजयो मृत्युः सर्वेषां स्युरनुक्रमात् ॥ ७ ॥

śrī-balir uvāca
saṅgrāme vartamānānāṁ
kāla-codita-karmaṇām
kīrtir jayo 'jayo mṛtyuḥ
sarveṣāṁ syur anukramāt

śrī-baliḥ uvāca—Bali Mahārāja said; *saṅgrāme*—in the battlefield; *vartamānānām*—of all persons present here; *kāla-codita*—influenced by the course of time; *karmaṇām*—for persons engaged in fighting or any other activities; *kīrtiḥ*—reputation; *jayaḥ*—victory; *ajayaḥ*—defeat; *mṛtyuḥ*—death; *sarveṣām*—of all of them; *syuḥ*—must be done; *anukramāt*—one after another.

TRANSLATION

Bali Mahārāja replied: All those present on this battlefield are certainly under the influence of eternal time, and according to their prescribed activities, they are destined to receive fame, victory, defeat and death, one after another.

PURPORT

If one is victorious on the battlefield, he becomes famous; and if one is not victorious but is defeated, he may die. Both victory and defeat are possible, whether on such a battlefield as this or on the battlefield of the struggle for existence. Everything takes place according to the laws of nature (*prakṛteḥ kriyamāṇāni guṇaiḥ karmāṇi sarvaśaḥ*). Since everyone, without exception, is subject to the modes of material nature, whether one is victorious or defeated he is not independent, but is under the control of material nature. Bali Mahārāja, therefore, was very sensible. He knew that the fighting was arranged by eternal time and that under time's influence one must accept the results of one's own activities. Therefore even though Indra threatened that he would now kill Bali Mahārāja by releasing the thunderbolt, Bali Mahārāja was not at all afraid. This is the spirit of a *kṣatriya: yuddhe cāpy apalāyanam* (Bg. 18.43). A *kṣatriya* must be tolerant in all circumstances, especially on the battlefield. Thus Bali Mahārāja asserted that he was not at all afraid of death, although he was threatened by such a great personality as the King of heaven.

TEXT 8

तदिदं कालरशनं जगत् पश्यन्ति सूरयः ।
न हृष्यन्ति न शोचन्ति तत्र यूयमपण्डिताः ॥ ८ ॥

tad idaṁ kāla-raśanaṁ
jagat paśyanti sūrayaḥ
na hṛṣyanti na śocanti
tatra yūyam apaṇḍitāḥ

tat—therefore; *idam*—this whole material world; *kāla-raśanam*—is moving because of time eternal; *jagat*—moving forward (this whole universe); *paśyanti*—observe; *sūrayaḥ*—those who are intelligent by admission of the truth; *na*—not; *hṛṣyanti*—become jubilant; *na*—nor; *śocanti*—lament; *tatra*—in such; *yūyam*—all of you demigods; *apaṇḍitāḥ*—not very learned (having forgotten that you are working under eternal time).

TRANSLATION

Seeing the movements of time, those who are cognizant of the real truth neither rejoice nor lament for different circumstances. Therefore, because you are jubilant due to your victory, you should be considered not very learned.

PURPORT

Bali Mahārāja knew that Indra, King of heaven, was extremely powerful, certainly more powerful than he himself. Nonetheless, Bali Mahārāja challenged Indra by saying that Indra was not a very learned person. In *Bhagavad-gītā* (2.11) Kṛṣṇa rebuked Arjuna by saying:

aśocyān anvaśocas tvaṁ
prajñā-vādāṁś ca bhāṣase
gatāsūn agatāsūṁś ca
nānuśocanti paṇḍitāḥ

"While speaking learned words, you are mourning for what is not worthy of grief. Those who are wise lament neither for the living nor the dead." Thus as Kṛṣṇa challenged Arjuna by saying that he was not a *paṇḍita*, or a learned person, Bali Mahārāja also challenged King Indra and his associates. In this material world, everything happens under the influence of time. Consequently, for a learned person who sees how things are taking place, there is no question of being sorry or happy because of the waves of material nature. After all, since we are being carried away by these waves, what is the meaning of being jubilant or morose? One who is fully conversant with the laws of nature is never jubilant or morose because of nature's activities. In *Bhagavad-gītā* (2.14), Kṛṣṇa advises that one be tolerant: *tāṁs titikṣasva bhārata.* Following this advice of Kṛṣṇa's, one should not be morose or unhappy because of circumstantial changes. This is the symptom of a devotee. A devotee carries out his duty in Kṛṣṇa consciousness and is never unhappy in awkward circumstances. He has full faith that in such circumstances, Kṛṣṇa protects His devotee. Therefore a devotee never deviates from his prescribed duty of devotional service. The material qualities of jubilation and moroseness are present even in the demigods, who are very highly situated in the upper planetary system. Therefore, when one is undisturbed by the so-called favorable and unfavorable circumstances of this material world, he should be understood to be *brahma-bhūta*, or self-realized. As stated in *Bhagavad-gītā* (18.54), *brahma-bhūtaḥ prasannātmā na śocati na kāṅkṣati:* "One who is transcendentally situated at once realizes the Supreme Brahman and becomes fully joyful." When one is undisturbed by material circumstances, he should be understood to be on the transcendental stage, above the reactions of the three modes of material nature.

TEXT 9

न वयं मन्यमानानामात्मानं तत्र साधनम् ।
गिरो वः साधुशोच्यानां गृह्णीमो मर्मताडनाः ॥ ९ ॥

na vayaṁ manyamānānām
ātmānaṁ tatra sādhanam
giro vaḥ sādhu-śocyānāṁ
gṛhṇīmo marma-tāḍanāḥ

na—not; *vayam*—we; *manyamānānām*—who are considering; *ātmānam*—the self; *tatra*—in victory or defeat; *sādhanam*—the cause; *giraḥ*—the words; *vaḥ*—of you; *sādhu-śocyānām*—who are to be pitied by the saintly persons; *gṛhṇīmaḥ*—accept; *marma-tāḍanāḥ*—which afflict the heart.

TRANSLATION

You demigods think that your own selves are the cause of your attaining fame and victory. Because of your ignorance, saintly persons feel sorry for you. Therefore, although your words afflict the heart, we do not accept them.

TEXT 10

श्रीशुक उवाच

इत्याक्षिप्य विभुं वीरो नाराचैर्वीरमर्दनः ।
आकर्णपूर्णैरहनदाक्षेपैराहतं पुनः ॥१०॥

śrī-śuka uvāca
ity ākṣipya vibhuṁ vīro
nārācair vīra-mardanaḥ
ākarṇa-pūrṇair ahanad
ākṣepair āha taṁ punaḥ

śrī-śukaḥ uvāca—Śrī Śukadeva Gosvāmī said; *iti*—thus; *ākṣipya*—chastising; *vibhum*—unto King Indra; *vīraḥ*—the valiant Bali Mahārāja; *nārācaiḥ*—by the arrows named *nārācas; vīra-mardanaḥ*—Bali Mahārāja, who could subdue even great heros; *ākarṇa-pūrṇaiḥ*—drawn up to his ear; *ahanat*—attacked; *ākṣepaiḥ*—by words of chastisement; *āha*—said; *tam*—unto him; *punaḥ*—again.

TRANSLATION

Śukadeva Gosvāmī said: After thus rebuking Indra, King of heaven, with sharp words, Bali Mahārāja, who could subdue any other hero, drew back to his ear the arrows known as nārācas and attacked Indra with these arrows. Then he again chastised Indra with strong words.

TEXT 11

एवं निराकृतो देवो वैरिणा तथ्यवादिना ।
नामृष्यत् तदधिक्षेपं तोत्राहत इव द्विपः ॥११॥

evaṁ nirākṛto devo
vairiṇā tathya-vādinā
nāmṛṣyat tad-adhikṣepaṁ
totrāhata iva dvipaḥ

evam—thus; *nirākṛtaḥ*—being defeated; *devaḥ*—King Indra; *vairiṇā*—by his enemy; *tathya-vādinā*—who was competent to speak the truth; *na*—not; *amṛṣyat*—lamented; *tat*—of him (Bali); *adhikṣepam*—the chastisement; *totra*—by the scepter or rod; *āhataḥ*—being beaten; *iva*—just like; *dvipaḥ*—an elephant.

TRANSLATION

Since Mahārāja Bali's rebukes were truthful, King Indra did not at all become sorry, just as an elephant beaten by its driver's rod does not become agitated.

TEXT 12

प्राहरत् कुलिशं तस्मा अमोघं परमर्दनः ।
सयानो न्यपतद् भूमौ छिन्नपक्ष इवाचलः ॥१२॥

prāharat kuliśaṁ tasmā
amoghaṁ para-mardanaḥ
sayāno nyapatad bhūmau
chinna-pakṣa ivacalaḥ

prāharat—inflicted; *kuliśam*—thunderbolt scepter; *tasmai*—unto him (Bali Mahārāja); *amogham*—infallibie; *para-mardanaḥ*—Indra, who is expert in defeating the enemy; *sa-yānaḥ*—with his airplane; *nyapatat*—fell down; *bhūmau*—on the ground; *chinna-pakṣaḥ*—whose wings have been taken away; *iva*—like; *acalaḥ*—a mountain.

TRANSLATION

When Indra, the defeater of enemies, released his infallible thunderbolt scepter at Bali Mahārāja with a desire to kill him, Bali Mahārāja indeed fell to the ground with his airplane, like a mountain with its wings cut off.

PURPORT

In many descriptions in Vedic literature it is found that mountains also fly in the sky with wings. When such mountains are dead, they fall to the ground, where they stay as very large dead bodies.

TEXT 13

सखायं पतितं दृष्ट्वा जम्भो बलिसखः सुहृत् ।
अभ्ययात् सौहृदं सख्युर्हतस्यापि समाचरन् ॥१३॥

sakhāyaṁ patitaṁ dṛṣṭvā
jambho bali-sakhaḥ suhṛt
abhyayāt sauhṛdaṁ sakhyur
hatasyāpi samācaran

sakhāyam—his intimate friend; *patitam*—having fallen; *dṛṣṭvā*—after seeing; *jambhaḥ*—the demon Jambha; *bali-sakhaḥ*—a very intimate friend of Bali Mahārāja; *suhṛt*—and constant well-wisher; *abhyayāt*—appeared on the scene; *sauhṛdam*—very compassionate friendship; *sakhyuḥ*—of his friend; *hatasya*—who was injured and fallen; *api*—although; *samācaran*—just to perform friendly duties.

TRANSLATION

When the demon Jambhāsura saw that his friend Bali had fallen, he appeared before Indra, the enemy, just to serve Bali Mahārāja with friendly behavior.

TEXT 14

स सिंहवाह आसाद्य गदामुद्यम्य रंहसा ।
जत्रावताडयच्छक्रं गजं च सुमहाबलः ॥१४॥

sa siṁha-vāha āsādya
gadām udyamya raṁhasā
jatrāv atāḍayac chakraṁ
gajaṁ ca sumahā-balaḥ

saḥ—Jambhāsura; *siṁha-vāhaḥ*—being carried by a lion; *āsādya*—coming before King Indra; *gadām*—his club; *udyamya*—taking up; *raṁhasā*—with great force; *jatrau*—on the base of the neck; *atāḍayat*—hit; *śakram*—Indra; *gajam ca*—as well as his elephant; *su-mahā-balaḥ*—the greatly powerful Jambhāsura.

TRANSLATION

The greatly powerful Jambhāsura, carried by a lion, approached Indra and forcefully struck him on the shoulder with his club. He also struck Indra's elephant.

TEXT 15

गदाप्रहारव्यथितो भृशं विह्वलितो गजः ।
जानुभ्यां धरणीं स्पृष्ट्वा कश्मलं परमं ययौ ॥१५॥

gadā-prahāra-vyathito
bhṛśaṁ vihvalito gajaḥ
jānubhyāṁ dharaṇīṁ spṛṣṭvā
kaśmalaṁ paramaṁ yayau

gadā-prahāra-vyathitaḥ—being aggrieved because of the blow from Jambhāsura's club; *bhṛśam*—very much; *vihvalitaḥ*—upset; *gajaḥ*—the elephant; *jānubhyām*—with its two knees; *dharaṇīm*—the earth; *spṛṣṭvā*—touching; *kaśmalam*—unconsciousness; *paramam*—ultimate; *yayau*—entered.

TRANSLATION

Being beaten by Jambhāsura's club, Indra's elephant was confused and aggrieved. Thus it touched its knees to the ground and fell unconscious.

TEXT 16

ततो रथो मातलिना हरिभिर्दशशतैर्वृतः ।
आनीतो द्विपमुत्सृज्य रथमारुरुहे विभुः ॥१६॥

tato ratho mātalinā
haribhir daśa-śatair vṛtaḥ
ānīto dvipam utsṛjya
ratham āruruhe vibhuḥ

tataḥ—thereafter; *rathaḥ*—chariot; *mātalinā*—by his chariot driver named Mātali; *haribhiḥ*—with horses; *daśa-śataiḥ*—by ten times one hundred (one thousand); *vṛtaḥ*—yoked; *ānītaḥ*—being brought in; *dvipam*—the elephant; *utsṛjya*—keeping aside; *ratham*—the chariot; *āruruhe*—got up; *vibhuḥ*—the great Indra.

TRANSLATION

Thereafter, Mātali, Indra's chariot driver, brought Indra's chariot, which was drawn by one thousand horses. Indra then left his elephant and got onto the chariot.

TEXT 17

तस्य तत् पूजयन् कर्म यन्तुर्दानवसत्तमः ।
शूलेन ज्वलता तं तु स्मयमानोऽहनन्मृधे ॥१७॥

tasya tat pūjayan karma
yantur dānava-sattamaḥ
śūlena jvalatā taṁ tu
smayamāno 'hanan mṛdhe

tasya—of Mātali; *tat*—that service (bringing the chariot before Indra); *pūjayan*—appreciating; *karma*—such service to the master; *yantuḥ*—of the chariot driver; *dānava-sat-tamaḥ*—the best of the demons, namely Jambhāsura; *śūlena*—by his trident; *jvalatā*—which was blazing fire; *tam*—Mātali; *tu*—indeed; *smayamānaḥ*—smiling; *ahanat*—struck; *mṛdhe*—in the battle.

TRANSLATION

Appreciating Mātali's service, Jambhāsura, the best of the demons, smiled. Nonetheless, he struck Mātali in the battle with a trident of blazing fire.

TEXT 18

सेहे रुजं सुदुर्मर्षां सत्त्वमालम्ब्य मातलिः ।
इन्द्रो जम्भस्य संक्रुद्धो वज्रेणापाहरच्छिरः ॥१८॥

sehe rujaṁ sudurmarṣāṁ
sattvam ālambya mātaliḥ
indro jambhasya saṅkruddho
vajreṇāpāharac chiraḥ

sehe—tolerated; *rujam*—the pain; *su-durmarṣām*—intolerable; *sattvam*—patience; *ālambya*—taking shelter of; *mātaliḥ*—the charioteer Mātali; *indraḥ*—King Indra; *jambhasya*—of the great demon Jambha; *saṅkruddhaḥ*—being very angry at him; *vajreṇa*—with his thunderbolt; *apāharat*—separated; *śiraḥ*—the head.

TRANSLATION

Although the pain was extremely severe, Mātali tolerated it with great patience. Indra, however, became extremely angry at Jambhāsura. He struck Jambhāsura with his thunderbolt and thus severed his head from his body.

TEXT 19

जम्भं श्रुत्वा हतं तस्य ज्ञातयो नारदादृषेः ।
नमुचिश्च बलः पाकस्तत्रापेतुस्त्वरान्विताः ॥१९॥

jambhaṁ śrutvā hataṁ tasya
jñātayo nāradād ṛṣeḥ
namuciś ca balaḥ pākas
tatrāpetus tvarānvitāḥ

jambham—Jambhāsura; *śrutvā*—after hearing; *hatam*—had been killed; *tasya*—his; *jñātayaḥ*—friends and relatives; *nāradāt*—from the source Nārada; *ṛṣeḥ*—from the great saint; *namuciḥ*—the demon Namuci; *ca*—also; *balaḥ*—the demon Bala; *pākaḥ*—the demon Pāka; *tatra*—there; *āpetuḥ*—immediately arrived; *tvarā-anvitāḥ*—with great haste.

TRANSLATION

When Nārada Ṛṣi informed Jambhāsura's friends and relatives that Jambhāsura had been killed, the three demons named Namuci, Bala and Pāka arrived on the battlefield in great haste.

TEXT 20

वचोभिः परुषैरिन्द्रमर्दयन्तोऽस्य मर्मसु ।
शरैरवाकिरन् मेघा धाराभिरिव पर्वतम् ॥२०॥

vacobhiḥ paruṣair indram
ardayanto 'sya marmasu
śarair avākiran meghā
dhārābhir iva parvatam

vacobhiḥ—with harsh words; *paruṣaiḥ*—very rough and cruel; *indram*—King Indra; *ardayantaḥ*—chastising, piercing; *asya*—of Indra; *marmasu*—in the heart, etc.; *śaraiḥ*—with arrows; *avākiran*—covered all around; *meghāḥ*—clouds; *dhārābhiḥ*—with showers of rain; *iva*—just as; *parvatam*—a mountain.

TRANSLATION

Rebuking Indra with harsh, cruel words that were piercing to the heart, these demons showered him with arrows, just as torrents of rain wash a great mountain.

TEXT 21

हरीन्दशशतान्याजौ हर्यश्वस्य बलः शरैः ।
तावद्भिरर्दयामास युगपल्लघुहस्तवान् ॥२१॥

harīn daśa-śatāny ājau
haryaśvasya balaḥ śaraiḥ
tāvadbhir ardayām āsa
yugapal laghu-hastavān

harīn—horses; *daśa-śatāni*—ten times one hundred (one thousand); *ājau*—on the battlefield; *haryaśvasya*—of King Indra; *balaḥ*—the demon Bala; *śaraiḥ*—with arrows; *tāvadbhiḥ*—with so many; *ardayām āsa*—put into tribulation; *yugapat*—simultaneously; *laghu-hastavān*—with quick handling.

TRANSLATION

Quickly handling the situation on the battlefield, the demon Bala put all of Indra's one thousand horses into tribulation by simultaneously piercing them all with an equal number of arrows.

TEXT 22

शताभ्यां मातलिं पाको रथं सावयवं पृथक् ।
सकृत्सन्धानमोक्षेण तदद्भुतमभूद् रणे ॥२२॥

śatābhyāṁ mātaliṁ pāko
rathaṁ sāvayavaṁ pṛthak
sakṛt sandhāna-mokṣeṇa
tad adbhutam abhūd raṇe

śatābhyām—with two hundred arrows; *mātalim*—unto the chariot driver Mātali; *pākaḥ*—the demon named Pāka; *ratham*—the chariot; *sa-avayavam*—with all paraphernalia; *pṛthak*—separately; *sakṛt*—once, at one time; *sandhāna*—by yoking the arrows to the bow; *mokṣeṇa*—and releasing; *tat*—such an action; *adbhutam*—wonderful; *abhūt*—so became; *raṇe*—on the battlefield.

TRANSLATION

Pāka, another demon, attacked both the chariot, with all its paraphernalia, and the chariot driver, Mātali, by fitting two hundred arrows to his bow and releasing them all simultaneously. This was indeed a wonderful act on the battlefield.

TEXT 23

नमुचिः पञ्चदशभिः स्वर्णपुङ्खैर्महेषुभिः ।
आहत्य व्यनदत्संख्ये सतोय इव तोयदः ॥२३॥

namuciḥ pañca-daśabhiḥ
svarṇa-puṅkhair maheṣubhiḥ
āhatya vyanadat saṅkhye
satoya iva toyadaḥ

namuciḥ—the demon named Namuci; *pañca-daśabhiḥ*—with fifteen; *svarṇa-puṅkhaiḥ*—with golden feathers attached; *mahā-iṣubhiḥ*—very powerful arrows; *āhatya*—piercing; *vyanadat*—resounded; *saṅkhye*—

on the battlefield; *sa-toyaḥ*—bearing water; *iva*—like; *toya-daḥ*—a cloud that delivers rain.

TRANSLATION

Then Namuci, another demon, attacked Indra and injured him with fifteen very powerful golden-feathered arrows, which roared like a cloud full of water.

TEXT 24

सर्वतः शरकूटेन शक्रं सरथसारथिम् ।
छादयामासुरसुराः प्रावृट्सूर्यमिवाम्बुदाः ॥२४॥

sarvataḥ śara-kūṭena
śakraṁ saratha-sārathim
chādayām āsur asurāḥ
prāvṛṭ-sūryam ivāmbudāḥ

sarvataḥ—all around; *śara-kūṭena*—by a dense shower of arrows; *śakram*—Indra; *sa-ratha*—with his chariot; *sārathim*—and with his chariot driver; *chādayām āsuḥ*—covered; *asurāḥ*—all the demons; *prāvṛṭ*—in the rainy season; *sūryam*—the sun; *iva*—like; *ambu-dāḥ*—clouds.

TRANSLATION

Other demons covered Indra, along with his chariot and chariot driver, with incessant showers of arrows, just as clouds cover the sun in the rainy season.

TEXT 25

अलक्षयन्तस्तमतीव विह्वला
विचुक्रुशुर्देवगणाः सहानुगाः ।
अनायकाः शत्रुबलेन निर्जिता
वणिक्पथा भिन्ननवो यथार्णवे ॥२५॥

alakṣayantas tam atīva vihvalā
vicukruśur deva-gaṇāḥ sahānugāḥ
anāyakāḥ śatru-balena nirjitā
vaṇik-pathā bhinna-navo yathārṇave

alakṣayantaḥ—being unable to see; *tam*—King Indra; *atīva*—fiercely; *vihvalāḥ*—bewildered; *vicukruśuḥ*—began to lament; *deva-gaṇāḥ*—all the demigods; *saha-anugāḥ*—with their followers; *anāyakāḥ*—without any captain or leader; *śatru-balena*—by the superior power of their enemies; *nirjitāḥ*—oppressed severely; *vaṇik-pathaḥ*—traders; *bhinna-navaḥ*—whose ship is wrecked; *yathā arṇave*—as in the middle of the ocean.

TRANSLATION

The demigods, being severely oppressed by their enemies and being unable to see Indra on the battlefield, were very anxious. Having no captain or leader, they began lamenting like traders in a wrecked vessel in the midst of the ocean.

PURPORT

From this statement it appears that in the upper planetary system there is shipping and that traders there engage in navigation as their occupational duty. Sometimes, as on this planet, these traders are shipwrecked in the middle of the ocean. It appears that even in the upper planetary system, such calamities occasionally take place. The upper planetary system in the creation of the Lord is certainly not vacant or devoid of living entities. From *Śrīmad-Bhāgavatam* we understand that every planet is full of living entities, just as earth is. There is no reason to accept that on other planetary systems there are no living beings.

TEXT 26

ततस्तुराषाडिषुबद्धपञ्जराद्
विनिर्गतः साश्वरथध्वजाग्रणीः ।
बभौ दिशः खं पृथिवीं च रोचयन्
स्वतेजसा सूर्य इव क्षपात्यये ॥२६॥

tatas turāṣāḍ iṣu-baddha-pañjarād
vinirgataḥ sāśva-ratha-dhvajāgraṇīḥ
babhau diśaḥ khaṁ pṛthivīṁ ca rocayan
sva-tejasā sūrya iva kṣapātyaye

tataḥ—thereafter; *turāṣāṭ*—another name of Indra; *iṣu-baddha-pañjarāt*—from the cage of the network of arrows; *vinirgataḥ*—being released; *sa*—with; *aśva*—horses; *ratha*—chariot; *dhvaja*—flag; *agraṇīḥ*—and chariot driver; *babhau*—became; *diśaḥ*—all directions; *kham*—the sky; *pṛthivīm*—the earth; *ca*—and; *rocayan*—pleasing everywhere; *sva-tejasā*—by his personal effulgence; *sūryaḥ*—the sun; *iva*—like; *kṣapā-atyaye*—at the end of night.

TRANSLATION

Thereafter, Indra released himself from the cage of the network of arrows. Appearing with his chariot, flag, horses and chariot driver and thus pleasing the sky, the earth and all directions, he shone effulgently like the sun at the end of night. Indra was bright and beautiful in the vision of everyone.

TEXT 27

निरीक्ष्य पृतनां देवः परैरभ्यर्दितां रणे ।
उदयच्छद् रिपुं हन्तुं वज्रं वज्रधरो रुषा ॥२७॥

nirīkṣya pṛtanāṁ devaḥ
parair abhyarditāṁ raṇe
udayacchad ripuṁ hantuṁ
vajraṁ vajra-dharo ruṣā

nirīkṣya—after observing; *pṛtanām*—his own soldiers; *devaḥ*—the demigod Indra; *paraiḥ*—by the enemies; *abhyarditām*—put into great difficulties or oppressed; *raṇe*—in the battlefield; *udayacchat*—took up; *ripum*—the enemies; *hantum*—to kill; *vajram*—the thunderbolt; *vajra-dharaḥ*—the carrier of the thunderbolt; *ruṣā*—in great anger.

TRANSLATION

When Indra, who is known as Vajra-dhara, the carrier of the thunderbolt, saw his own soldiers so oppressed by the enemies on the battlefield, he became very angry. Thus he took up his thunderbolt to kill the enemies.

TEXT 28

स तेनैवाष्टधारेण शिरसी बलपाकयोः ।
ज्ञातीनां पश्यतां राजञ्जहार जनयन्भयम् ॥२८॥

sa tenaivāṣṭa-dhāreṇa
śirasī bala-pākayoḥ
jñātīnāṁ paśyatāṁ rājan
jahāra janayan bhayam

saḥ—he (Indra); *tena*—by that; *eva*—indeed; *aṣṭa-dhāreṇa*—by the thunderbolt; *śirasī*—the two heads; *bala-pākayoḥ*—of the two demons known as Bala and Pāka; *jñātīnām paśyatām*—while their relatives and soldiers were watching; *rājan*—O King; *jahāra*—(Indra) cut off; *janayan*—creating; *bhayam*—fear (among them).

TRANSLATION

O King Parīkṣit, King Indra used his thunderbolt to cut off the heads of both Bala and Pāka in the presence of all their relatives and followers. In this way he created a very fearful atmosphere on the battlefield.

TEXT 29

नमुचिस्तद्वधं दृष्ट्वा शोकामर्षरुषान्वितः ।
जिघांसुरिन्द्रं नृपते चकार परमोद्यमम् ॥२९॥

namucis tad-vadhaṁ dṛṣṭvā
śokāmarṣa-ruṣānvitaḥ
jighāṁsur indraṁ nṛpate
cakāra paramodyamam

namuciḥ—the demon Namuci; *tat*—of those two demons; *vadham*—the massacre; *dṛṣṭvā*—after seeing; *śoka-amarṣa*—lamentation and grief; *ruṣā-anvitaḥ*—being very angry at this; *jighāṁsuḥ*—wanted to kill; *indram*—King Indra; *nṛ-pate*—O Mahārāja Parīkṣit; *cakāra*—made; *parama*—a great; *udyamam*—endeavor.

TRANSLATION

O King, when Namuci, another demon, saw the killing of both Bala and Pāka, he was full of grief and lamentation. Thus he angrily made a great attempt to kill Indra.

TEXT 30

अश्मसारमयं शूलं घण्टावद्धेमभूषणम् ।
प्रगृह्याभ्यद्रवत् क्रुद्धो हतोऽसीति वितर्जयन् ।
प्राहिणोद् देवराजाय निनदन् मृगराडिव ॥३०॥

aśmasāramayaṁ śūlaṁ
ghaṇṭāvad dhema-bhūṣaṇam
pragṛhyābhyadravat kruddho
hato 'sīti vitarjayan
prāhiṇod deva-rājāya
ninadan mṛga-rāḍ iva

aśmasāra-mayam—made of steel; *śūlam*—a spear; *ghaṇṭā-vat*—bound with bells; *hema-bhūṣaṇam*—decorated with ornaments of gold; *pragṛhya*—taking in his hand; *abhyadravat*—forcefully went; *kruddhaḥ*—in an angry mood; *hataḥ asi iti*—now you are killed; *vitarjayan*—roaring like that; *prāhiṇot*—struck; *deva-rājāya*—unto King Indra; *ninadan*—resounding; *mṛga-rāṭ*—a lion; *iva*—like.

TRANSLATION

Being angry and roaring like a lion, the demon Namuci took up a steel spear, which was bound with bells and decorated with ornaments of gold. He loudly cried, "Now you are killed!" Thus coming before Indra to kill him, Namuci released his weapon.

TEXT 31

तदापतद् गगनतले महाजवं
विचिच्छिदे हरिरिषुभिः सहस्रधा ।
तमाहनन्नृप कुलिशेन कन्धरे
रुषान्वितस्त्रिदशपतिः शिरो हरन् ॥३१॥

tadāpatad gagana-tale mahā-javaṁ
vicicchide harir iṣubhiḥ sahasradhā
tam āhanan nṛpa kuliśena kandhare
ruṣānvitas tridaśa-patiḥ śiro haran

tadā—at that time; *apatat*—falling like a meteor; *gagana-tale*—beneath the sky or on the ground; *mahā-javam*—extremely powerful; *vicicchide*—cut to pieces; *hariḥ*—Indra; *iṣubhiḥ*—by his arrows; *sahasradhā*—into thousands of pieces; *tam*—that Namuci; *āhanat*—struck; *nṛpa*—O King; *kuliśena*—with his thunderbolt; *kandhare*—on the shoulder; *ruṣā-anvitaḥ*—being very angry; *tridaśa-patiḥ*—Indra, the King of the demigods; *śiraḥ*—the head; *haran*—to separate.

TRANSLATION

O King, when Indra, King of heaven, saw this very powerful spear falling toward the ground like a blazing meteor, he immediately cut it to pieces with his arrows. Then, being very angry, he struck Namuci's shoulder with his thunderbolt to cut off Namuci's head.

TEXT 32

न तस्य हि त्वचमपि वज्र ऊर्जितो
बिभेद यः सुरपतिनौजसेरितः ।
तदद्भुतं परमतिवीर्यवृत्रभित्
तिरस्कृतो नमुचिशिरोधरत्वचा ॥३२॥

na tasya hi tvacam api vajra ūrjito
bibheda yaḥ sura-patinaujaseritaḥ

tad adbhutaṁ param ativīrya-vṛtra-bhit
tiraskṛto namuci-śirodhara-tvacā

na—not; *tasya*—of him (Namuci); *hi*—indeed; *tvacam api*—even the skin; *vajraḥ*—the thunderbolt; *ūrjitaḥ*—very powerful; *bibheda*—could pierce; *yaḥ*—the weapon which; *sura-patinā*—by the king of the demigods; *ojasā*—very forcefully; *īritaḥ*—had been released; *tat*—therefore; *adbhutam param*—it was extraordinarily wonderful; *ati-vīrya-vṛtra-bhit*—so powerful that it could pierce the body of the very powerful Vṛtrāsura; *tiraskṛtaḥ*—(now in the future) which had been repelled; *namuci-śirodhara-tvacā*—by the skin of Namuci's neck.

TRANSLATION

Although King Indra hurled his thunderbolt at Namuci with great force, it could not even pierce his skin. It is very wonderful that the famed thunderbolt that had pierced the body of Vṛtrāsura could not even slightly injure the skin of Namuci's neck.

TEXT 33

तस्मादिन्द्रोऽबिभेच्छत्रोर्वज्रः प्रतिहतो यतः ।
किमिदं दैवयोगेन भूतं लोकविमोहनम् ॥३३॥

tasmād indro 'bibhec chatror
vajraḥ pratihato yataḥ
kim idaṁ daiva-yogena
bhūtaṁ loka-vimohanam

tasmāt—therefore; *indraḥ*—the King of heaven; *abibhet*—became very fearful; *śatroḥ*—from the enemy (Namuci); *vajraḥ*—the thunderbolt; *pratihataḥ*—was unable to hit and returned; *yataḥ*—because; *kim idam*—what is this; *daiva-yogena*—by some superior force; *bhūtam*—it has happened; *loka-vimohanam*—so wonderful to the people in general.

TRANSLATION

When Indra saw the thunderbolt return from the enemy, he was very much afraid. He began to wonder whether this had happened because of some miraculous superior power.

PURPORT

Indra's thunderbolt is invincible, and therefore when Indra saw that it had returned without doing any injury to Namuci, he was certainly very much afraid.

TEXT 34

येन मे पूर्वमद्रीणां पक्षच्छेदः प्रजात्यये ।
कृतो निविशतां भारैः पतत्त्रैः पततां भुवि ॥३४॥

yena me pūrvam adrīṇāṁ
pakṣa-cchedaḥ prajātyaye
kṛto niviśatāṁ bhāraiḥ
patattraiḥ patatāṁ bhuvi

yena—by the same thunderbolt; *me*—by me; *pūrvam*—formerly; *adrīṇām*—of the mountains; *pakṣa-cchedaḥ*—the cutting of the wings; *prajā-atyaye*—when there was killing of the people in general; *kṛtaḥ*—was done; *niviśatām*—of those mountains which entered; *bhāraiḥ*—by the great weight; *patattraiḥ*—by wings; *patatām*—falling; *bhuvi*—on the ground.

TRANSLATION

Indra thought: Formerly, when many mountains flying in the sky with wings would fall to the ground and kill people, I cut their wings with this same thunderbolt.

TEXT 35

तपःसारमयं त्वाष्ट्रं वृत्रो येन विपाटितः ।
अन्ये चापि बलोपेताः सर्वास्त्रैरक्षतत्वचः ॥३५॥

tapaḥ-sāramayaṁ tvāṣṭraṁ
vṛtro yena vipāṭitaḥ
anye cāpi balopetāḥ
sarvāstrair akṣata-tvacaḥ

tapaḥ—austerities; *sāra-mayam*—greatly powerful; *tvāṣṭram*—performed by Tvaṣṭā; *vṛtraḥ*—Vṛtrāsura; *yena*—by which; *vipāṭitaḥ*—was killed; *anye*—others; *ca*—also; *api*—indeed; *bala-upetāḥ*—very powerful persons; *sarva*—all kinds; *astraiḥ*—by weapons; *akṣata*—without being injured; *tvacaḥ*—their skin.

TRANSLATION

Vṛtrāsura was the essence of the austerities undergone by Tvaṣṭā, yet the thunderbolt killed him. Indeed, not only he but also many other stalwart heroes, whose very skin could not be injured even by all kinds of weapons, were killed by the same thunderbolt.

TEXT 36

सोऽयं प्रतिहतो वज्रो मया मुक्तोऽसुरेऽल्पके ।
नाहं तदाददे दण्डं ब्रह्मतेजोऽप्यकारणम् ॥३६॥

so 'yaṁ pratihato vajro
mayā mukto 'sure 'lpake
nāhaṁ tad ādade daṇḍaṁ
brahma-tejo 'py akāraṇam

saḥ ayam—therefore, this thunderbolt; *pratihataḥ*—repelled; *vajraḥ*—thunderbolt; *mayā*—by me; *muktaḥ*—released; *asure*—unto that demon; *alpake*—less important; *na*—not; *aham*—I; *tat*—that; *ādade*—hold; *daṇḍam*—it is now just like a rod; *brahma-tejaḥ*—as powerful as a *brahmāstra; api*—although; *akāraṇam*—now it is useless.

TRANSLATION

But now, although the same thunderbolt has been released against a less important demon, it has been ineffectual. Therefore, although it was as good as a brahmāstra, it has now become useless like an ordinary rod. I shall therefore hold it no longer.

TEXT 37

इति शक्रं विषीदन्तमाह वागशरीरिणी ।
नायं शुष्कैरथो नार्द्रैर्वधमर्हति दानवः ॥३७॥

iti śakraṁ viṣīdantam
āha vāg aśarīriṇī
nāyaṁ śuṣkair atho nārdrair
vadham arhati dānavaḥ

iti—in this way; *śakram*—unto Indra; *viṣīdantam*—lamenting; *āha*—spoke; *vāk*—a voice; *aśarīriṇī*—without any body, or from the sky; *na*—not; *ayam*—this; *śuṣkaiḥ*—by anything dry; *atho*—also; *na*—nor; *ārdraiḥ*—by anything moist; *vadham*—annihilation; *arhati*—is befitting; *dānavaḥ*—this demon (Namuci).

TRANSLATION

Śukadeva Gosvāmī continued: While the morose Indra was lamenting in this way, an ominous, unembodied voice said from the sky, "This demon Namuci is not to be annihilated by anything dry or moist."

TEXT 38

मयास्मै यद् वरो दत्तो मृत्युर्नैवार्द्रशुष्कयोः ।
अतोऽन्यश्चिन्तनीयस्ते उपायो मघवन् रिपोः ॥३८॥

mayāsmai yad varo datto
mṛtyur naivārdra-śuṣkayoḥ
ato 'nyaś cintanīyas te
upāyo maghavan ripoḥ

mayā—by me; *asmai*—unto him; *yat*—because; *varaḥ*—a benediction; *dattaḥ*—has been granted; *mṛtyuḥ*—death; *na*—not; *eva*—indeed; *ārdra*—by either a moist; *śuṣkayoḥ*—or by a dry medium; *ataḥ*—therefore; *anyaḥ*—something else, another; *cintanīyaḥ*—has to be thought of; *te*—by you; *upāyaḥ*—means; *maghavan*—O Indra; *ripoḥ*—of your enemy.

TRANSLATION

The voice also said, "O Indra, because I have given this demon the benediction that he will never be killed by any weapon that is dry or moist, you have to think of another way to kill him."

TEXT 39

तां दैवीं गिरमाकर्ण्य मघवान्सुसमाहितः ।
ध्यायन् फेनमथापश्यदुपायमुभयात्मकम् ॥३९॥

tāṁ daivīṁ giram ākarṇya
maghavān susamāhitaḥ
dhyāyan phenam athāpaśyad
upāyam ubhayātmakam

tām—that; *daivīm*—ominous; *giram*—voice; *ākarṇya*—after hearing; *maghavān*—Lord Indra; *su-samāhitaḥ*—becoming very careful; *dhyāyan*—meditating; *phenam*—appearance of foam; *atha*—thereafter; *apaśyat*—he saw; *upāyam*—the means; *ubhaya-ātmakam*—simultaneously dry and moist.

TRANSLATION

After hearing the ominous voice, Indra, with great attention, began to meditate on how to kill the demon. He then saw that foam would be the means, for it is neither moist nor dry.

TEXT 40

न शुष्केण न चार्द्रेण जहार नमुचेः शिरः ।
तं तुष्टुवुर्मुनिगणा माल्यैश्चावाकिरन्विभुम् ॥४०॥

na śuṣkeṇa na cārdreṇa
jahāra namuceḥ śiraḥ
taṁ tuṣṭuvur muni-gaṇā
mālyaiś cāvākiran vibhum

na—neither; *śuṣkeṇa*—by dry means; *na*—nor; *ca*—also; *ārdreṇa*—by a moist weapon; *jahāra*—he separated; *namuceḥ*—of Namuci; *śiraḥ*—the head; *tam*—him (Indra); *tuṣṭuvuḥ*—satisfied; *muni-gaṇāḥ*—all the sages; *mālyaiḥ*—with flower garlands; *ca*—also; *avākiran*—covered; *vibhum*—that great personality.

TRANSLATION

Thus Indra, King of heaven, severed Namuci's head with a weapon of foam, which was neither dry nor moist. Then all the sages satisfied Indra, the exalted personality, by showering flowers and garlands upon him, almost covering him.

PURPORT

In this regard, the *śruti-mantras* say, *apāṁ phenena namuceḥ śira indro 'dārayat:* Indra killed Namuci with watery foam, which is neither moist nor dry.

TEXT 41

गन्धर्वमुख्यौ जगतुर्विश्वावसुपरावसू ।
देवदुन्दुभयो नेदुर्नर्तक्यो ननृतुर्मुदा ॥४१॥

gandharva-mukhyau jagatur
viśvāvasu-parāvasū
deva-dundubhayo nedur
nartakyo nanṛtur mudā

gandharva-mukhyau—the two chiefs of the Gandharvas; *jagatuḥ*—began to sing nice songs; *viśvāvasu*—named Viśvāvasu; *parāvasū*—named Parāvasu; *deva-dundubhayaḥ*—the kettledrums beaten by the demigods; *neduḥ*—made their sound; *nartakyaḥ*—the dancers known as Apsarās; *nanṛtuḥ*—began to dance; *mudā*—in great happiness.

TRANSLATION

Viśvāvasu and Parāvasu, the two chiefs of the Gandharvas, sang in great happiness. The kettledrums of the demigods sounded, and the Apsarās danced in jubilation.

TEXT 42

अन्येऽप्येवं प्रतिद्वन्द्वान्वाय्वग्निवरुणादयः ।
सूदयामासुरसुरान् मृगान्केसरिणो यथा ॥४२॥

anye 'py evaṁ pratidvandvān
vāyv-agni-varuṇādayaḥ
sūdayām āsur asurān
mṛgān kesariṇo yathā

anye—others; *api*—also; *evam*—in this way; *pratidvandvān*—the opposing party of belligerants; *vāyu*—the demigod known as Vāyu; *agni*—the demigod known as Agni; *varuṇa-ādayaḥ*—the demigod known as Varuṇa and others; *sūdayām āsuḥ*—began to kill vigorously; *asurān*—all the demons; *mṛgān*—deer; *kesariṇaḥ*—lions; *yathā*—just as.

TRANSLATION

Vāyu, Agni, Varuṇa and other demigods began killing the demons who opposed them, just as lions kill deer in a forest.

TEXT 43

ब्रह्मणा प्रेषितो देवान्देवर्षिर्नारदो नृप ।
वारयामास विबुधान्दृष्ट्वा दानवसंक्षयम् ॥४३॥

brahmaṇā preṣito devān
devarṣir nārado nṛpa
vārayām āsa vibudhān
dṛṣṭvā dānava-saṅkṣayam

brahmaṇā—by Lord Brahmā; *preṣitaḥ*—sent; *devān*—unto the demigods; *deva-ṛṣiḥ*—the great sage of the heavenly planets; *nāradaḥ*—Nārada Muni; *nṛpa*—O King; *vārayām āsa*—forbade; *vibudhān*—all the demigods; *dṛṣṭvā*—after seeing; *dānava-saṅkṣayam*—the total annihilation of the demons.

TRANSLATION

O King, when Lord Brahmā saw the imminent total annihilation of the demons, he sent a message with Nārada, who went before the demigods to make them stop fighting.

TEXT 44

श्रीनारद उवाच
भवद्भिरमृतं प्राप्तं नारायणभुजाश्रयैः ।
श्रिया समेधिताः सर्व उपारमत विग्रहात् ॥४४॥

śrī-nārada uvāca
bhavadbhir amṛtaṁ prāptaṁ
nārāyaṇa-bhujāśrayaiḥ
śriyā samedhitāḥ sarva
upāramata vigrahāt

śrī-nāradaḥ uvāca—Nārada Muni prayed to the demigods; *bhavadbhiḥ*—by all of you; *amṛtam*—nectar; *prāptam*—has been obtained; *nārāyaṇa*—of the Supreme Personality of Godhead; *bhuja-āśrayaiḥ*—being protected by the arms; *śriyā*—by all fortune; *samedhitāḥ*—have flourished; *sarve*—all of you; *upāramata*—now cease; *vigrahāt*—from this fighting.

TRANSLATION

The great sage Nārada said: All of you demigods are protected by the arms of Nārāyaṇa, the Supreme Personality of Godhead, and by His grace you have gotten the nectar. By the grace of the goddess of fortune, you are glorious in every way. Therefore, please stop this fighting.

TEXT 45

श्रीशुक उवाच
संयम्य मन्युसंरम्भं मानयन्तो मुनेर्वचः ।
उपगीयमानानुचरैर्ययुः सर्वे त्रिविष्टपम् ॥४५॥

śrī-śuka uvāca
saṁyamya manyu-saṁrambhaṁ
mānayanto muner vacaḥ
upagīyamānānucarair
yayuḥ sarve triviṣṭapam

śrī-śukaḥ uvāca—Śrī Śukadeva Gosvāmī said; *saṁyamya*—controlling; *manyu*—of anger; *saṁrambham*—the aggravation; *mānayantaḥ*—accepting; *muneḥ vacaḥ*—the words of Nārada Muni; *upagīyamāna*—being praised; *anucaraiḥ*—by their followers; *yayuḥ*—returned; *sarve*—all of the demigods; *triviṣṭapam*—to the heavenly planets.

TRANSLATION

Śrī Śukadeva Gosvāmī said: Accepting the words of Nārada, the demigods gave up their anger and stopped fighting. Being praised by their followers, they returned to their heavenly planets.

TEXT 46

येऽवशिष्टा रणे तस्मिन् नारदानुमतेन ते ।
बलिं विपन्नमादाय अस्तं गिरिमुपागमन् ।।४६।।

ye 'vaśiṣṭā raṇe tasmin
nāradānumatena te
baliṁ vipannam ādāya
astaṁ girim upāgaman

ye—some of the demons who; *avaśiṣṭāḥ*—remained; *raṇe*—in the fight; *tasmin*—in that; *nārada-anumatena*—by the order of Nārada; *te*—all of them; *balim*—Mahārāja Bali; *vipannam*—in reverses; *ādāya*—taking; *astam*—named Asta; *girim*—to the mountain; *upāgaman*—went.

TRANSLATION

Following the order of Nārada Muni, whatever demons remained on the battlefield took Bali Mahārāja, who was in a precarious condition, to the hill known as Astagiri.

TEXT 47

तत्राविनष्टावयवान् विद्यमानशिरोधरान् ।
उशना जीवयामास संजीवन्या स्वविद्यया ।।४७।।

tatrāvinaṣṭāvayavān
vidyamāna-śirodharān
uśanā jīvayām āsa
sañjīvanyā sva-vidyayā

tatra—on that hill; *avinaṣṭa-avayavān*—the demons who had been killed but whose bodily parts had not been lost; *vidyamāna-śirodharān*—whose heads were still existing on their bodies; *uśanāḥ*—Śukrācārya; *jīvayām āsa*—brought to life; *sañjīvanyā*—by the Sañjīvanī *mantra; sva-vidyayā*—by his own achievement.

TRANSLATION

There, on that hill, Śukrācāyra brought to life all the dead demoniac soldiers who had not lost their heads, trunks and limbs. He achieved this by his own mantra, known as Sañjīvanī.

TEXT 48

बलिश्चोशनसा स्पृष्टः प्रत्यापन्नेन्द्रियस्मृतिः ।
पराजितोऽपि नाखिद्यल्लोकतत्त्वविचक्षणः ॥४८॥

baliś cośanasā spṛṣṭaḥ
pratyāpannendriya-smṛtiḥ
parājito 'pi nākhidyal
loka-tattva-vicakṣaṇaḥ

baliḥ—Mahārāja Bali; *ca*—also; *uśanasā*—by Śukrācārya; *spṛṣṭaḥ*—being touched; *pratyāpanna*—was brought back; *indriya-smṛtiḥ*—realization of the actions of the senses and memory; *parājitaḥ*—he was defeated; *api*—although; *na akhidyat*—he did not lament; *loka-tattva-vicakṣaṇaḥ*—because he was very experienced in universal affairs.

TRANSLATION

Bali Mahārāja was very experienced in universal affairs. When he regained his senses and memory by the grace of Śukrācārya, he could understand everything that had happened. Therefore, although he had been defeated, he did not lament.

PURPORT

It is significant that Bali Mahārāja is here said to be very experienced. Although defeated, he was not at all sorry, for he knew that nothing can take place without the sanction of the Supreme Personality of Godhead. Since he was a devotee, he accepted his defeat without lamentation. As stated by the Supreme Personality of Godhead in *Bhagavad-gītā* (2.47), *karmaṇy evādhikāras te mā phaleṣu kadācana.* Everyone in Kṛṣṇa consciousness should execute his duty, without regard for victory or defeat. One must execute his duty as ordered by Kṛṣṇa or His representative, the spiritual master. *Ānukūlyena kṛṣṇānuśīlanaṁ bhaktir uttamā.* In first-class devotional service, one always abides by the orders and will of Kṛṣṇa.

Thus end the Bhaktivedanta purports of the Eighth Canto, Eleventh Chapter, of the Śrīmad-Bhāgavatam, *entitled "King Indra Annihilates the Demons."*

CHAPTER TWELVE

The Mohinī-mūrti Incarnation Bewilders Lord Śiva

This chapter describes how Lord Śiva was bewildered upon seeing the beautiful Mohinī-mūrti incarnation of the Supreme Personality of Godhead and how he later came to his senses. When Lord Śiva heard about the pastimes performed by the Supreme Personality of Godhead, Hari, in the form of an attractive woman, he mounted his bull and went to see the Lord. Accompanied by his wife, Uma, and his servants, the *bhūta-gaṇa*, or ghosts, he approached the lotus feet of the Lord. Lord Śiva offered obeisances to the Supreme Lord as the all-pervading Lord, the universal form, the supreme controller of creation, the Supersoul, the resting place for everyone, and the completely independent cause of all causes. Thus he offered prayers giving truthful descriptions of the Lord. Then he expressed his desire. The Supreme Personality of Godhead is very kind to His devotees. Therefore, to fulfill the desire of His devotee Lord Śiva, He expanded His energy and manifested Himself in the form of a very beautiful and attractive woman. Upon seeing this form, even Lord Śiva was captivated. Later, by the grace of the Lord, he controlled himself. This demonstrates that by the power of the Lord's external energy, everyone is captivated by the form of woman in this material world. Again, however, by the grace of the Supreme Personality of Godhead, one can overcome the influence of *māyā*. This was evinced by Lord Śiva, the topmost devotee of the Lord. First he was captivated, but later, by the grace of the Lord, he restrained himself. It is declared in this connection that only a pure devotee can restrain himself from the attractive feature of *māyā*. Otherwise, once a living entity is trapped by the external feature of *māya*, he cannot overcome it. After Lord Śiva was graced by the Supreme Lord, he circumambulated the Lord along with his wife, Bhavānī, and his companions, the ghosts. Then he left for his own abode. Śukadeva Gosvāmī concludes this chapter by describing the transcendental qualities of Uttamaśloka, the Supreme Personality of Godhead, and by declaring that one can glorify the Lord by nine kinds of devotional service, beginning with *śravaṇaṁ kīrtanam.*

TEXTS 1–2

श्रीबादरायणिरुवाच

वृषध्वजो निशम्येदं योषिद्रूपेण दानवान् ।
मोहयित्वा सुरगणान्हरिः सोममपाययत् ॥ १ ॥
वृषमारुह्य गिरिशः सर्वभूतगणैर्वृतः ।
सह देव्या ययौ द्रष्टुं यत्रास्ते मधुसूदनः ॥ २ ॥

śrī-bādarāyaṇir uvāca
vṛṣa-dhvajo niśamyedaṁ
yoṣid-rūpeṇa dānavān
mohayitvā sura-gaṇān
hariḥ somam apāyayat

vṛṣam āruhya giriśaḥ
sarva-bhūta-gaṇair vṛtaḥ
saha devyā yayau draṣṭuṁ
yatrāste madhusūdanaḥ

śrī-bādarāyaṇiḥ uvāca—Śrī Śukadeva Gosvāmī said; *vṛṣa-dhvajaḥ*—Lord Śiva, who is carried by a bull; *niśamya*—hearing; *idam*—this (news); *yoṣit-rūpeṇa*—by assuming the form of a woman; *dānavān*—the demons; *mohayitvā*—enchanting; *sura-gaṇān*—unto the demigods; *hariḥ*—the Supreme Personality of Godhead; *somam*—nectar; *apāyayat*—caused to drink; *vṛṣam*—the bull; *āruhya*—mounting; *giriśaḥ*—Lord Śiva; *sarva*—all; *bhūta-gaṇaiḥ*—by the ghosts; *vṛtaḥ*—surrounded; *saha devyā*—with Umā; *yayau*—went; *draṣṭum*—to see; *yatra*—where; *āste*—stays; *madhusūdanaḥ*—Lord Viṣṇu.

TRANSLATION

Śukadeva Gosvāmī said: The Supreme Personality of Godhead, Hari, in the form of a woman, captivated the demons and enabled the demigods to drink the nectar. After hearing of these pastimes,

Lord Śiva, who is carried by a bull, went to the place where Madhusūdana, the Lord, resides. Accompanied by his wife, Umā, and surrounded by his companions, the ghosts, Lord Śiva went there to see the Lord's form as a woman.

TEXT 3

सभाजितो भगवता सादरं सोमया भवः ।
सूपविष्ट उवाचेदं प्रतिपूज्य स्मयन्हरिम् ॥ ३ ॥

sabhājito bhagavatā
sādaraṁ somayā bhavaḥ
sūpaviṣṭa uvācedaṁ
pratipūjya smayan harim

sabhājitaḥ—well received; *bhagavatā*—by the Supreme Personality of Godhead, Viṣṇu; *sa-ādaram*—with great respect (as befitting Lord Śiva); *sa-umayā*—with Umā; *bhavaḥ*—Lord Śambhu (Lord Śiva); *su-upaviṣṭaḥ*—being comfortably situated; *uvāca*—said; *idam*—this; *pratipūjya*—offering respect; *smayan*—smiling; *harim*—unto the Lord.

TRANSLATION

The Supreme Personality of Godhead welcomed Lord Śiva and Umā with great respect, and after being seated comfortably, Lord Śiva duly worshiped the Lord and smilingly spoke as follows.

TEXT 4

श्रीमहादेव उवाच
देवदेव जगद्व्यापिञ्जगदीश जगन्मय ।
सर्वेषामपि भावानां त्वमात्मा हेतुरीश्वरः ॥ ४ ॥

śrī-mahādeva uvāca
deva-deva jagad-vyāpiñ
jagad-īśa jagan-maya
sarveṣām api bhāvānāṁ
tvam ātmā hetur īśvaraḥ

śrī-mahādevaḥ uvāca—Lord Śiva (Mahādeva) said; *deva-deva*—O best demigod among the demigods; *jagat-vyāpin*—O all-pervading Lord; *jagat-īśa*—O master of the universe; *jagat-maya*—O my Lord, who are transformed by Your energy into this creation; *sarveṣām api*—all kinds of; *bhāvānām*—situations; *tvam*—You; *ātmā*—the moving force; *hetuḥ*—because of this; *īśvaraḥ*—the Supreme Lord, Parameśvara.

TRANSLATION

Lord Mahādeva said: O chief demigod among the demigods, O all-pervading Lord, master of the universe, by Your energy You are transformed into the creation. You are the root and efficient cause of everything. You are not material. Indeed, You are the Supersoul or supreme living force of everything. Therefore, You are Parameśvara, the supreme controller of all controllers.

PURPORT

The Supreme Personality of Godhead, Viṣṇu, resides within the material world as the *sattva-guṇa-avatāra*. Lord Śiva is the *tamo-guṇa-avatāra*, and Lord Brahmā is the *rajo-guṇa-avatāra*, but although Lord Viṣṇu is among them, He is not in the same category. Lord Viṣṇu is *deva-deva*, the chief of all the demigods. Since Lord Śiva is in this material world, the energy of the Supreme Lord, Viṣṇu, includes Lord Śiva. Lord Viṣṇu is therefore called *jagad-vyāpī*, "the all-pervading Lord." Lord Śiva is sometimes called Maheśvara, and so people think that Lord Śiva is everything. But here Lord Śiva addresses Lord Viṣṇu as Jagad-īśa, "the master of the universe." Lord Śiva is sometimes called Viśveśvara, but here he addresses Lord Viṣṇu as Jagan-maya, indicating that even Viśveśvara is under Lord Viṣṇu's control. Lord Viṣṇu is the master of the spiritual world, yet He controls the material world also, as stated in *Bhagavad-gītā* (*mayādhyakṣeṇa prakṛtiḥ sūyate sacarācaram*). Lord Brahmā and Lord Śiva are also sometimes called *īśvara*, but the supreme *īśvara* is Lord Viṣṇu, Lord Kṛṣṇa. As stated in *Brahma-saṁhitā*, *īśvaraḥ paramaḥ kṛṣṇaḥ:* the Supreme Lord is Kṛṣṇa, Lord Viṣṇu. Everything in existence works in proper order because of Lord Viṣṇu. *Aṇḍāntara-stha-paramāṇu-cayāntara-stham.* Even *paramāṇu*, the small atoms, work because of Lord Viṣṇu's presence within them.

TEXT 5

आद्यन्तावस्य यन्मध्यमिदमन्यदहं बहिः ।
यतोऽव्ययस्य नैतानि तत् सत्यं ब्रह्म चिद् भवान् ॥५॥

ādy-antāv asya yan madhyam
idaṁ anyad ahaṁ bahiḥ
yato 'vyayasya naitāni
tat satyaṁ brahma cid bhavān

ādi—the beginning; *antau*—and the end; *asya*—of this manifested cosmos or of anything material or visible; *yat*—that which; *madhyam*—between the beginning and the end, the sustenance; *idam*—this cosmic manifestation; *anyat*—anything other than You; *aham*—the wrong mental conception; *bahiḥ*—outside of You; *yataḥ*—because of; *avyayasya*—the inexhaustible; *na*—not; *etāni*—all these differences; *tat*—that; *satyam*—the Absolute Truth; *brahma*—the Supreme; *cit*—spiritual; *bhavān*—Your Lordship.

TRANSLATION

The manifest, the unmanifest, false ego and the beginning, maintenance and annihilation of this cosmic manifestation all come from You, the Supreme Personality of Godhead. But because You are the Absolute Truth, the supreme absolute spirit soul, the Supreme Brahman, such changes as birth, death and sustenance do not exist in You.

PURPORT

According to the Vedic *mantras, yato vā imāni bhūtāni jāyante:* everything is an emanation of the Supreme Personality of Godhead. As stated by the Lord Himself in *Bhagavad-gītā* (7.4):

bhūmir āpo 'nalo vāyuḥ
khaṁ mano buddhir eva ca
ahaṅkāra itīyaṁ me
bhinnā prakṛtir aṣṭadhā

"Earth, water, fire, air, ether, mind, intelligence and false ego—all together these eight comprise My separated material energies." In other words, the ingredients of the cosmic manifestation also consist of the energy of the Supreme Personality of Godhead. This does not mean, however, that because the ingredients come from Him, He is no longer complete. *Pūrṇasya pūrṇam ādāya pūrṇam evāvaśiṣyate:* "Because He is the complete whole, even though so many complete units emanate from Him, He remains the complete balance." Thus the Lord is called *avyaya,* inexhaustible. Unless we accept the Absolute Truth as *acintya-bhedābheda,* simultaneously one and different, we cannot have a clear conception of the Absolute Truth. The Lord is the root of everything. *Aham ādir hi devānām:* He is the original cause of all the *devas,* or demigods. *Ahaṁ sarvasya prabhavaḥ:* everything emanates from Him. In all cases—nominative, objective, positive, negative and so on—whatever we may conceive of in this entire cosmic manifestation is in fact the Supreme Lord. For Him there are no such distinctions as "this is mine, and this belongs to someone else," because He is everything. He is therefore called *avyaya*—changeless and inexhaustible. Because the Supreme Lord is *avyaya,* He is the Absolute Truth, the fully spiritual Supreme Brahman.

TEXT 6

तवैव चरणाम्भोजं श्रेयस्कामा निराशिषः ।
विसृज्योभयतः सङ्गं मुनयः समुपासते ॥ ६ ॥

tavaiva caraṇāmbhojaṁ
śreyas-kāmā nirāśiṣaḥ
visṛjyobhayataḥ saṅgaṁ
munayaḥ samupāsate

tava—Your; *eva*—indeed; *caraṇa-ambhojam*—lotus feet; *śreyaḥ-kāmāḥ*—persons desiring the ultimate auspiciousness, the ultimate goal of life; *nirāśiṣaḥ*—without material desire; *visṛjya*—giving up; *ubhayataḥ*—in this life and the next; *saṅgam*—attachment; *munayaḥ*—great sages; *samupāsate*—worship.

TRANSLATION

Pure devotees or great saintly persons who desire to achieve the highest goal in life and who are completely free from all material

desires for sense gratification engage constantly in the transcendental service of Your lotus feet.

PURPORT

One is in the material world when he thinks, "I am this body, and everything with reference to my body is mine." *Ato gṛha-kṣetra-sutāpta-vittair janasya moho 'yam ahaṁ mameti.* This is the symptom of material life. In the materialistic conception of life, one thinks, "This is my house, this is my land, this is my family, this is my state," and so on. But those who are *munayaḥ,* saintly persons following in the footsteps of Nārada Muni, simply engage in the transcendental loving service of the Lord without any personal desire for sense gratification. *Anyābhilāṣitā-śūnyaṁ jñāna-karmādy-anāvṛtam.* Either in this life or in the next, the only concern of such saintly devotees is to serve the Supreme Personality of Godhead. Thus they are also absolute because they have no other desires. Being freed from the dualities of material desire, they are called *śreyas-kāmāḥ.* In other words, they are not concerned with *dharma* (religiosity), *artha* (economic development), or *kāma* (sense gratification). The only concern of such devotees is *mokṣa,* liberation. This *mokṣa* does not refer to becoming one with the Supreme like the Māyāvādī philosophers. Caitanya Mahāprabhu explained that real *mokṣa* means taking shelter of the lotus feet of the Personality of Godhead. The Lord clearly explained this fact while instructing Sārvabhauma Bhaṭṭācārya. Sārvabhauma Bhaṭṭācārya wanted to correct the word *mukti-pade* in *Śrīmad-Bhāgavatam,* but Caitanya Mahāprabhu informed him that there is no need to correct any word in *Śrīmad-Bhāgavatam.* He explained that *mukti-pade* refers to the lotus feet of the Supreme Personality of Godhead, Viṣṇu, who offers *mukti* and is therefore called Mukunda. A pure devotee is not concerned with material things. He is not concerned with religiosity, economic development or sense gratification. He is interested only in serving the lotus feet of the Lord.

TEXT 7

त्वं ब्रह्म पूर्णममृतं विगुणं विशोक-
मानन्दमात्रमविकारमनन्यदन्यत् ।

विश्वस्य हेतुरुदयस्थितिसंयमाना-
मात्मेश्वरश्च तदपेक्षतयानपेक्षः ॥ ७ ॥

tvaṁ brahma pūrṇam amṛtaṁ viguṇaṁ viśokam
ānanda-mātram avikāram ananyad anyat
viśvasya hetur udaya-sthiti-saṁyamānām
ātmeśvaraś ca tad-apekṣatayānapekṣaḥ

tvam—Your Lordship; *brahma*—the all-pervading Absolute Truth; *pūrṇam*—fully complete; *amṛtam*—never to be vanquished; *viguṇam*—spiritually situated, free from the material modes of nature; *viśokam*—without lamentation; *ānanda-mātram*—always in transcendental bliss; *avikāram*—changeless; *ananyat*—separated from everything; *anyat*—yet You are everything; *viśvasya*—of the cosmic manifestation; *hetuḥ*—the cause; *udaya*—of the beginning; *sthiti*—maintenance; *saṁyamānām*—and of all the directors controlling the various departments of the cosmic manifestation; *ātma-īśvaraḥ*—the Supersoul giving direction to everyone; *ca*—also; *tat-apekṣatayā*—everyone depends upon You; *anapekṣaḥ*—always fully independent.

TRANSLATION

My Lord, You are the Supreme Brahman, complete in everything. Being completely spiritual, You are eternal, free from the material modes of nature, and full of transcendental bliss. Indeed, for You there is no question of lamentation. Since You are the supreme cause, the cause of all causes, nothing can exist without You. Yet we are different from You in a relationship of cause and effect, for in one sense the cause and effect are different. You are the original cause of creation, manifestation and annihilation, and You bestow benedictions upon all living entities. Everyone depends upon You for the results of his activities, but You are always independent.

PURPORT

The Supreme Personality of Godhead says in *Bhagavad-gītā* (9.4):

mayā tatam idaṁ sarvaṁ
jagad avyakta-mūrtinā

mat-sthāni sarva-bhūtāni
na cāhaṁ teṣv avasthitaḥ

"By Me, in My unmanifested form, this entire universe is pervaded. All beings are in Me, but I am not in them." This explains the philosophy of simultaneous oneness and difference, known as *acintya-bhedābheda.* Everything is the Supreme Brahman, the Personality of Godhead, yet the Supreme Person is differently situated from everything. Indeed, because the Lord is differently situated from everything material, He is the Supreme Brahman, the supreme cause, the supreme controller. *Īśvaraḥ paramaḥ kṛṣṇaḥ sac-cid-ānanda-vigrahaḥ.* The Lord is the supreme cause, and His form has nothing to do with the material modes of nature. The devotee prays: "As Your devotee is completely free from all desires, Your Lordship is also completely free from desires. You are fully independent. Although all living entities engage in Your service, You do not depend on the service of anyone. Although this material world is created complete by You, everything depends on Your sanction. As stated in *Bhagavad-gītā, mattaḥ smṛtir jñānam apohanaṁ ca:* remembrance, knowledge and forgetfulness come from You. Nothing can be done independently, yet You act independently of the service rendered by Your servants. The living entities depend on Your mercy for liberation, but when You want to give them liberation, You do not depend on anyone else. Indeed, by Your causeless mercy, You can give liberation to anyone. Those who receive Your mercy are called *kṛpā-siddha.* To reach the platform of perfection takes many, many lives (*bahūnāṁ janmanām ante jñānavān māṁ prapadyate*). Nonetheless, even without undergoing severe austerities, one can attain perfection by Your mercy. Devotional service should be unmotivated and free from impediments (*ahaituky apratihatā yayātmā suprasīdati*). This is the position of *nirāśiṣaḥ,* or freedom from expectations for results. A pure devotee continuously offers transcendental loving service to You, but You may nonetheless offer mercy to anyone, without depending on his service."

TEXT 8

एकस्त्वमेव सदसद् द्वयमद्वयं च
स्वर्णं कृताकृतमिवेह न वस्तुभेदः ।

अज्ञानतस्त्वयि जनैर्विहितो विकल्पो
यस्माद् गुणव्यतिकरो निरुपाधिकस्य ॥ ८ ॥

ekas tvam eva sad asad dvayam advayaṁ ca
svarṇaṁ kṛtākṛtam iveha na vastu-bhedaḥ
ajñānatas tvayi janair vihito vikalpo
yasmād guṇa-vyatikaro nirupādhikasya

ekaḥ—the only one; *tvam*—Your Lordship; *eva*—indeed; *sat*—which is existing, as the effect; *asat*—which is nonexistent, as the cause; *dvayam*—both of them; *advayam*—without duality; *ca*—and; *svarṇam*—gold; *kṛta*—manufactured into different forms; *ākṛtam*—the original source of gold (the gold mine); *iva*—like; *iha*—in this world; *na*—not; *vastu-bhedaḥ*—difference in the substance; *ajñānataḥ*—only because of ignorance; *tvayi*—unto You; *janaiḥ*—by the general mass of people; *vihitaḥ*—it should be done; *vikalpaḥ*—differentiation; *yasmāt*—because of; *guṇa-vyatikaraḥ*—free from the differences created by the material modes of nature; *nirupādhikasya*—without any material designation.

TRANSLATION

My dear Lord, Your Lordship alone is the cause and the effect. Therefore, although You appear to be two, You are the absolute one. As there is no difference between the gold of a golden ornament and the gold in a mine, there is no difference between cause and effect; both of them are the same. Only because of ignorance do people concoct differences and dualities. You are free from material contamination, and since the entire cosmos is caused by You and cannot exist without You, it is an effect of Your transcendental qualities. Thus the conception that Brahman is true and the world false cannot be maintained.

PURPORT

Śrīla Viśvanātha Cakravartī Ṭhākura says that the living entities are representations of the Supreme Personality of Godhead's marginal potency whereas the various bodies accepted by the living entities are products of the material energy. Thus the body is considered material, and the soul is considered spiritual. The origin of them both, however, is the same Supreme Personality of Godhead. As the Lord explains in *Bhagavad-gītā* (7.4–5):

bhūmir āpo 'nalo vāyuḥ
khaṁ mano buddhir eva ca
ahaṅkāra itīyaṁ me
bhinnā prakṛtir aṣṭadhā

apareyam itas tv anyāṁ
prakṛtiṁ viddhi me parām
jīva-bhūtāṁ mahā-bāho
yayedaṁ dhāryate jagat

"Earth, water, fire, air, ether, mind, intelligence and false ego—all together these eight comprise My separated material energies. But besides this inferior nature, O mighty-armed Arjuna, there is a superior energy of Mine, which consists of all living entities who are struggling with material nature and are sustaining the universe." Thus both matter and the living entities are manifestations of energy of the Supreme Lord. Since the energy and the energetic are not different and since the material and marginal energies are both energies of the supreme energetic, the Supreme Lord, ultimately the Supreme Personality of Godhead is everything. In this regard, the example may be given of gold that has not been molded and gold that has been molded into various ornaments. A gold earring and the gold in a mine are different only as cause and effect; otherwise they are the same. The *Vedānta-sūtra* describes that Brahman is the cause of everything. *Janmādy asya yataḥ.* Everything is born of the Supreme Brahman, from which everything emanates as different energies. None of these energies, therefore, should be considered false. The Māyāvādīs' differentiation between Brahman and *māyā* is only due to ignorance.

Śrīmad Vīrarāghava Ācārya, in his *Bhāgavata-candra-candrikā*, describes the Vaiṣṇava philosophy as follows. The cosmic manifestation is described as *sat* and *asat*, as *cit* and *acit.* Matter is *acit*, and the living force is *cit*, but their origin is the Supreme Personality of Godhead, in whom there is no difference between matter and spirit. According to this conception, the cosmic manifestation, consisting of both matter and spirit, is not different from the Supreme Personality of Godhead. *Idaṁ hi viśvaṁ bhagavān ivetaraḥ:* "This cosmic manifestation is also the Supreme Personality of Godhead, although it appears different from Him." In *Bhagavad-gītā* (9.4) the Lord says:

mayā tatam idaṁ sarvaṁ
jagad avyakta-mūrtinā
mat-sthāni sarva-bhūtāni
na cāhaṁ teṣv avasthitaḥ

"By Me, in My unmanifested form, this entire universe is pervaded. All beings are in Me, but I am not in them." Thus although someone may say that the Supreme Person is different from the cosmic manifestation, actually He is not. The Lord says, *mayā tatam idaṁ sarvam:* "In My impersonal feature I am spread throughout the world." Therefore, this world is not different from Him. The difference is a difference in names. For example, whether we speak of gold earrings, gold bangles or gold necklaces, ultimately they are all gold. In a similar way, all the different manifestations of matter and spirit are ultimately one in the Supreme Personality of Godhead. *Ekam evādvitīyaṁ brahma.* This is the Vedic version (*Chāndogya Upaniṣad* 6.2.1). There is oneness because everything emanates from the Supreme Brahman. The example already given is that there is no difference between a golden earring and the gold mine as it is. The Vaiśeṣika philosophers, however, because of their Māyāvāda conception, create differences. They say, *brahma satyaṁ jagan mithyā:* "The Absolute Truth is real, and the cosmic manifestation is false." But why should the *jagat* be considered *mithyā?* The *jagat* is an emanation from Brahman. Therefore the *jagat* is also truth.

Vaiṣṇavas, therefore, do not consider the *jagat* to be *mithyā;* rather, they regard everything as reality in connection with the Supreme Personality of Godhead.

anāsaktasya viṣayān
yathārham upayuñjataḥ
nirbandhaḥ kṛṣṇa-sambandhe
yuktaṁ vairāgyam ucyate

prāpañcikatayā buddhyā
hari-sambandhi-vastunaḥ
mumukṣubhiḥ parityāgo
vairāgyaṁ phalgu kathyate

"Things should be accepted for the Lord's service and not for one's personal sense gratification. If one accepts something without attachment and accepts it because it is related to Kṛṣṇa, one's renunciation is called *yuktaṁ vairāgyam.* Whatever is favorable for the rendering of service to the Lord should be accepted and should not be rejected as a material thing." (*Bhakti-rasāmṛta-sindhu* 1.2.255–256) The *jagat* should not be rejected as *mithyā.* It is truth, and the truth is realized when everything is engaged in the service of the Lord. A flower accepted for one's sense gratification is material, but when the same flower is offered to the Supreme Personality of Godhead by a devotee, it is spiritual. Food taken and cooked for oneself is material, but food cooked for the Supreme Lord is spiritual *prasāda.* This is a question of realization. Actually, everything is given by the Supreme Personality of Godhead, and therefore everything is spiritual, but those who are not advanced in proper knowledge make distinctions because of the interactions of the three modes of material nature. In this regard, Śrīla Jīva Gosvāmī says that although the sun is the only light, the sunshine, which is exhibited in seven colors, and darkness, which is the absence of sunshine, are not different from the sun, for without the existence of the sun such differentiations cannot exist. There may be varied nomenclature because of different conditions, but they are all the sun. The *Purāṇas* therefore say:

eka-deśa-sthitasyāgner
jyotsnā vistāriṇī yathā
parasya brahmaṇaḥ śaktis
tathedam akhilaṁ jagat

"Just as the illumination of a fire, which is situated in one place, is spread all over, the energies of the Supreme Personality of Godhead, Parabrahman, are spread all over this universe." (*Viṣṇu Purāṇa* 1.22.53) Materially, we can directly perceive the sunshine spreading itself according to different names and activities, but ultimately the sun is one. Similarly, *sarvaṁ khalv idaṁ brahma:* everything is an expansion of the Supreme Brahman. Therefore, the Supreme Lord is everything, and He is one without differentiation. There is no existence separate from the Supreme Personality of Godhead.

TEXT 9

त्वां ब्रह्म केचिदवयन्त्युत धर्ममेके
एके परं सदसतोः पुरुषं परेशम् ।
अन्येऽवयन्ति नवशक्तियुतं परं त्वां
केचिन्महापुरुषमव्ययमात्मतन्त्रम् ॥ ९ ॥

tvāṁ brahma kecid avayanty uta dharmam eke
eke paraṁ sad-asatoḥ puruṣaṁ pareśam
anye 'vayanti nava-śakti-yutaṁ paraṁ tvāṁ
kecin mahā-puruṣam avyayam ātma-tantram

tvām—You; *brahma*—the supreme truth, the Absolute Truth, Brahman, *kecit*—some people, namely the group of Māyāvādīs known as the Vedāntists; *avayanti*—consider; *uta*—certainly; *dharmam*—religion; *eke*—some others; *eke*—some others; *param*—transcendental; *sat-asatoḥ*—to both cause and effect; *puruṣam*—the Supreme Person; *pareśam*—the supreme controller; *anye*—others; *avayanti*—describe; *nava-śakti-yutam*—endowed with nine potencies; *param*—transcendental; *tvām*—unto You; *kecit*—some; *mahā-puruṣam*—the Supreme Personality of Godhead; *avyayam*—without loss of energy; *ātma-tantram*—supremely independent.

TRANSLATION

Those who are known as the impersonalist Vedāntists regard You as the impersonal Brahman. Others, known as the Mīmāṁsaka philosophers, regard You as religion. The Sāṅkhya philosophers regard You as the transcendental person who is beyond prakṛti and puruṣa and who is the controller of even the demigods. The followers of the codes of devotional service known as the Pañcarātras regard You as being endowed with nine different

potencies. And the Patañjala philosophers, the followers of Patañjali Muni, regard You as the supreme independent Personality of Godhead, who has no equal or superior.

TEXT 10

नाहं परायुर्ऋषयो न मरीचिमुख्या
जानन्ति यद्विरचितं खलु सत्त्वसर्गाः ।
यन्मायया मुषितचेतस ईश दैत्य-
मर्त्यादयः किमुत शश्वदभद्रवृत्ताः ॥१०॥

nāhaṁ parāyur ṛṣayo na marīci-mukhyā
jānanti yad-viracitaṁ khalu sattva-sargāḥ
yan-māyayā muṣita-cetasa īśa daitya-
martyādayaḥ kim uta śaśvad-abhadra-vṛttāḥ

na—neither; *aham*—I; *para-āyuḥ*—that personality who lives for millions and millions of years (Lord Brahmā); *ṛṣayaḥ*—the seven *ṛṣis* of the seven planets; *na*—nor; *marīci-mukhyāḥ*—headed by Marīci Ṛṣi; *jānanti*—know; *yat*—by whom (the Supreme Lord); *viracitam*—this universe, which has been created; *khalu*—indeed; *sattva-sargāḥ*—although born in the mode of material goodness; *yat-māyayā*—by the influence of whose energy; *muṣita-cetasaḥ*—their hearts are bewildered; *īśa*—O my Lord; *daitya*—the demons; *martya-ādayaḥ*—the human beings and others; *kim uta*—what to speak of; *śaśvat*—always; *abhadra-vṛttāḥ*—influenced by the base qualities of material nature.

TRANSLATION

O my Lord, I, who am considered to be the best of the demigods, and Lord Brahmā and the great ṛṣis, headed by Marīci, are born of the mode of goodness. Nonetheless, we are bewildered by Your illusory energy and cannot understand what this creation is. Aside from us, what is to be said of others, like the demons and human beings, who are in the base modes of material nature [rajo-guṇa and tamo-guṇa]? How will they know You?

PURPORT

Factually speaking, even those who are situated in the material mode of goodness cannot understand the position of the Supreme Personality of Godhead. What then is to be said of those who are situated in *rajo-guṇa* and *tamo-guṇa*, the base qualities of material nature? How can we even imagine the Supreme Personality of Godhead? There are so many philosophers trying to understand the Absolute Truth, but since they are situated in the base qualities of material nature and are addicted to so many bad habits, like drinking, meat-eating, illicit sex and gambling, how can they conceive of the Supreme Personality of Godhead? For them it is impossible. For the present day, the *pāñcarātrikī-vidhi* as enunciated by Nārada Muni is the only hope. Śrīla Rūpa Gosvāmī, therefore, has quoted the following verse from the *Brahma-yāmala:*

śruti-smṛti-purāṇādi-
pañcarātra-vidhiṁ vinā
aikāntikī harer bhaktir
utpātāyaiva kalpate

"Devotional service of the Lord that ignores the authorized Vedic literatures like the *Upaniṣads, Purāṇas* and *Nārada-pañcarātra* is simply an unnecessary disturbance in society." (*Bhakti-rasāmṛta-sindhu* 1.2.101) Those who are very advanced in knowledge and are situated in the mode of goodness follow the Vedic instructions of the *śruti* and *smṛti* and other religious scriptures, including the *pāñcarātrikī-vidhi.* Without understanding the Supreme Personality of Godhead in this way, one only creates a disturbance. In this age of Kali, so many *gurus* have sprung up, and because they do not refer to the *śruti-smṛti-purāṇādi-pañcarātrika-vidhi,* they are creating a great disturbance in the world in regard to understanding the Absolute Truth. However, those who follow the *pāñcarātrikī-vidhi* under the guidance of a proper spiritual master can understand the Absolute Truth. It is said, *pañcarātrasya kṛtsnasya vaktā tu bhagavān svayam:* the *pañcarātra* system is spoken by the Supreme Personality of Godhead, just like *Bhagavad-gītā. Vāsudeva-śaraṇā vidur añjasaiva:* the truth can be understood only by one who has taken shelter of the lotus feet of Vāsudeva.

bahūnāṁ janmanām ante
jñānavān māṁ prapadyate
vāsudevaḥ sarvam iti
sa mahātmā sudurlabhaḥ

"After many births and deaths, he who is actually in knowledge surrenders unto Me, knowing Me to be the cause of all causes and all that is. Such a great soul is very rare." (Bg. 7.19) Only those who have surrendered to the lotus feet of Vāsudeva can understand the Absolute Truth.

vāsudeve bhagavati
bhakti-yogaḥ prayojitaḥ
janayaty āśu vairāgyaṁ
jñānaṁ ca yad ahaitukam

"By rendering devotional service unto the Personality of Godhead, Śrī Kṛṣṇa, one immediately acquires causeless knowledge and detachment from the world." (*Bhāg.* 1.2.7) Therefore, Vāsudeva, Bhagavān Śrī Kṛṣṇa, personally teaches in *Bhagavad-gītā:*

sarva-dharmān parityajya
mām ekaṁ śaraṇaṁ vraja

"Abandon all varieties of religion and just surrender unto Me." (Bg. 18.66)

bhaktyā mām abhijānāti
yāvān yaś cāsmi tattvataḥ

"One can understand the Supreme Personality as He is only by devotional service." (Bg. 18.55) The Supreme Personality of Godhead is not properly understood even by Lord Śiva or Lord Brahmā, what to speak of others, but He can be understood by the process of *bhakti-yoga.*

mayy āsakta-manāḥ pārtha
yogaṁ yuñjan mad-āśrayaḥ
asaṁśayaṁ samagraṁ māṁ
yathā jñāsyasi tac chṛṇu
(Bg. 7.1)

If one practices *bhakti-yoga* by taking shelter of Vāsudeva, Kṛṣṇa, simply by hearing Vāsudeva speak about Himself, one can understand everything about Him. Indeed, one can understand Him completely (*samagram*).

TEXT 11

स त्वं समीहितमदः स्थितिजन्मनाशं
भूतेहितं च जगतो भवबन्धमोक्षौ ।
वायुर्यथा विशति खं च चराचराख्यं
सर्वं तदात्मकतयावगमोऽवरुन्त्से ॥११॥

sa tvaṁ samīhitam adaḥ sthiti-janma-nāśaṁ
bhūtehitaṁ ca jagato bhava-bandha-mokṣau
vāyur yathā viśati khaṁ ca carācarākhyaṁ
sarvaṁ tad-ātmakatayāvagamo 'varuntse

saḥ—Your Lordship; *tvam*—the Supreme Personality of Godhead; *samīhitam*—which has been created (by You); *adaḥ*—of this material cosmic manifestation; *sthiti-janma-nāśam*—creation, maintenance and annihilation; *bhūta*—of the living entities; *īhitam ca*—and the different activities or endeavors; *jagataḥ*—of the whole world; *bhava-bandha-mokṣau*—in being implicated and being liberated from material complications; *vāyuḥ*—the air; *yathā*—as; *viśati*—enters; *kham*—in the vast sky; *ca*—and; *cara-acara-ākhyam*—and everything, moving and nonmoving; *sarvam*—everything; *tat*—that; *ātmakatayā*—because of Your presence; *avagamaḥ*—everything is known to You; *avaruntse*—You are all-pervading and therefore know everything.

TRANSLATION

My Lord, You are the supreme knowledge personified. You know everything about this creation and its beginning, maintenance and annihilation, and You know all the endeavors made by the living entities, by which they are either implicated in this material world or liberated from it. As the air enters the vast sky and also enters the bodies of all moving and nonmoving entities, You are present everywhere, and therefore You are the knower of all.

PURPORT

As stated in the *Brahma-saṁhitā:*

eko 'py asau racayituṁ jagad-aṇḍa-koṭiṁ
yac-chaktir asti jagad-aṇḍa-cayā yad-antaḥ
aṇḍāntara-stha-paramāṇu-cayāntara-sthaṁ
govindam ādi-puruṣaṁ tam ahaṁ bhajāmi

"I worship the Personality of Godhead, Govinda, who by one of His plenary portions enters the existence of every universe and every atomic particle and thus manifests His infinite energy unlimitedly throughout the material creation." (Bs. 5.35)

ānanda-cinmaya-rasa-pratibhāvitābhis
tābhir ya eva nija-rūpatayā kalābhiḥ
goloka eva nivasaty akhilātma-bhūto
govindam ādi-puruṣaṁ tam ahaṁ bhajāmi

"I worship Govinda, the primeval Lord, who resides in His own realm, Goloka, with Rādhā, who resembles His own spiritual figure and who embodies the ecstatic potency [*hlādinī*]. Their companions are Her confidantes, who embody extensions of Her bodily form and who are imbued and permeated with ever-blissful spiritual *rasa.*" (Bs. 5.37)

Although Govinda is always present in His abode (*goloka eva nivasati*), He is simultaneously present everywhere. Nothing is unknown to Him, and nothing can be hidden from Him. The example given here compares the Lord to the air, which is within the vast sky and within every body but still is different from everything.

TEXT 12

अवतारा मया दृष्टा रममाणस्य ते गुणैः ।
सोऽहं तद् द्रष्टुमिच्छामि यत् ते योषिद्वपुर्धृतम् ॥१२॥

avatārā mayā dṛṣṭā
ramamāṇasya te guṇaiḥ

so 'haṁ tad draṣṭum icchāmi
yat te yoṣid-vapur dhṛtam

avatārāḥ—incarnations; *mayā*—by me; *dṛṣṭāḥ*—have been seen; *ramamāṇasya*—while You demonstrate Your various pastimes; *te*—of You; *guṇaiḥ*—by the manifestations of transcendental qualities; *saḥ*—Lord Śiva; *aham*—I; *tat*—that incarnation; *draṣṭum icchāmi*—wish to see; *yat*—which; *te*—of You; *yoṣit-vapuḥ*—the body of a woman; *dhṛtam*—was accepted.

TRANSLATION

My Lord, I have seen all kinds of incarnations You have exhibited by Your transcendental qualities, and now that You have appeared as a beautiful young woman, I wish to see that form of Your Lordship.

PURPORT

When Lord Śiva approached Lord Viṣṇu, Lord Viṣṇu inquired about the purpose for Lord Śiva's coming there. Now Lord Śiva discloses his desire. He wanted to see the recent incarnation of Mohinī-mūrti, which Lord Viṣṇu had assumed to distribute the nectar generated from the churning of the ocean of milk.

TEXT 13

येन सम्मोहिता दैत्याः पायिताश्चामृतं सुराः ।
तद् दिदृक्षव आयाताः परं कौतूहलं हि नः ॥१३॥

yena sammohitā daityāḥ
pāyitāś cāmṛtaṁ surāḥ
tad didṛkṣava āyātāḥ
paraṁ kautūhalaṁ hi naḥ

yena—by such an incarnation; *sammohitāḥ*—were captivated; *daityāḥ*—the demons; *pāyitāḥ*—were fed; *ca*—also; *amṛtam*—nectar; *surāḥ*—the demigods; *tat*—that form; *didṛkṣavaḥ*—desiring to see; *āyātāḥ*—we have come here; *param*—very much; *kautūhalam*—great eagerness; *hi*—indeed; *naḥ*—of ourselves.

TRANSLATION

My Lord, we have come here desiring to see that form of Your Lordship which You showed to the demons to captivate them completely and in this way enable the demigods to drink nectar. I am very eager to see that form.

TEXT 14

श्रीशुक उवाच

एवमभ्यर्थितो विष्णुर्भगवान् शूलपाणिना ।
प्रहस्य भावगम्भीरं गिरिशं प्रत्यभाषत ॥१४॥

śrī-śuka uvāca
evam abhyarthito viṣṇur
bhagavān śūla-pāṇinā
prahasya bhāva-gambhīraṁ
giriśaṁ pratyabhāṣata

śrī-śukaḥ uvāca—Śrī Śukadeva Gosvāmī said; *evam*—in this way; *abhyarthitaḥ*—being requested; *viṣṇuḥ bhagavān*—Lord Viṣṇu, the Supreme Personality of Godhead; *śūla-pāṇinā*—by Lord Śiva, who carries a trident in his hand; *prahasya*—laughing; *bhāva-gambhīram*—with serious gravity; *giriśam*—unto Lord Śiva; *pratyabhāṣata*—replied.

TRANSLATION

Śukadeva Gosvāmī said: When Lord Viṣṇu was thus requested by Lord Śiva, who carries a trident in his hand, He smiled with gravity and replied to Lord Śiva as follows.

PURPORT

The Supreme Personality of Godhead, Viṣṇu, is known as Yogeśvara. *Yatra yogeśvaraḥ kṛṣṇaḥ.* Mystic *yogīs* want to acquire some power by practicing the *yoga* system, but Kṛṣṇa, the Supreme Personality of Godhead, is known as the Supreme Lord of all mystic power. Lord Śiva wanted to see the Mohinī-mūrti, which was captivating the entire world, and Lord Viṣṇu was gravely thinking of how to captivate Lord Śiva also.

Therefore the word *bhāva-gambhīram* is used here. The illusory, material energy is represented by Durgādevī, who is the wife of Giriśa, or Lord Śiva. Durgādevī could not captivate Lord Śiva's mind, but now that Lord Śiva wanted to see Lord Viṣṇu's feminine form, Lord Viṣṇu, by His mystic power, would assume a form that would captivate even Lord Śiva. Therefore Lord Viṣṇu was grave and at the same time was smiling.

TEXT 15

श्रीभगवानुवाच

कौतूहलाय दैत्यानां योषिद्वेषो मया धृतः ।
पश्यता सुरकार्याणि गते पीयूषभाजने ॥१५॥

śrī-bhagavān uvāca
kautūhalāya daityānāṁ
yoṣid-veṣo mayā dhṛtaḥ
paśyatā sura-kāryāṇi
gate pīyūṣa-bhājane

śrī-bhagavān uvāca—the Supreme Personality of Godhead said; *kautūhalāya*—for the bewildering; *daityānām*—of the demons; *yoṣit-veṣaḥ*—the form of a beautiful woman; *mayā*—by Me; *dhṛtaḥ*—assumed; *paśyatā*—seeing that it is necessary for Me; *sura-kāryāṇi*—for executing the interests of the demigods; *gate*—having been taken away; *pīyūṣa-bhājane*—the jug of nectar.

TRANSLATION

The Supreme Personality of Godhead said: When the demons took away the jug of nectar, I assumed the form of a beautiful woman to bewilder them by directly cheating them and thus to act in the interest of the demigods.

PURPORT

When the Supreme Personality of Godhead assumed the form of the beautiful woman Mohinī-mūrti, the demons were certainly captivated, but the demigods present were not. In other words, those who maintain a demoniac mentality are bewildered by the beauty of a woman, but those who are advanced in Kṛṣṇa consciousness, or even those on the platform of goodness, are not bewildered. The Supreme Personality of Godhead knew that because Lord Śiva is not an ordinary person, he cannot be bewildered even by the most beautiful woman. Cupid himself tried to invoke Lord Śiva's lusty desires in the presence of Pārvatī, but Lord Śiva was never agitated. Rather, the blazing fire from Lord Śiva's eyes turned Cupid to ashes. Therefore, Lord Viṣṇu had to think twice about what kind of beautiful form would bewilder even Lord Śiva. Consequently He was smiling gravely, as stated in the previous verse (*prahasya bhāva-gambhīram*). A beautiful woman generally cannot induce Lord Śiva to be lusty, but Lord Viṣṇu was considering whether there was any form of woman who could enchant him.

TEXT 16

तत्तेऽहं दर्शयिष्यामि दिदृक्षोः सुरसत्तम ।
कामिनां बहु मन्तव्यं सङ्कल्पप्रभवोदयम् ॥१६॥

tat te 'haṁ darśayiṣyāmi
didṛkṣoḥ sura-sattama
kāmināṁ bahu mantavyaṁ
saṅkalpa-prabhavodayam

tat—that; *te*—unto you; *aham*—I; *darśayiṣyāmi*—shall show; *didṛkṣoḥ*—desirous of seeing; *sura-sattama*—O best of the demigods; *kāminām*—of persons who are very lusty; *bahu*—very much; *mantavyam*—an object of adoration; *saṅkalpa*—lusty desires; *prabhava-udayam*—causing to be strongly aroused.

TRANSLATION

O best of the demigods, I shall now show you My form that is very much appreciated by those who are lusty. Since you want to see that form, I shall reveal it in your presence.

PURPORT

Lord Śiva's desiring to see Lord Viṣṇu reveal the most attractive and beautiful form of a woman was certainly a joking affair. Lord Śiva knew that he could not be agitated by any so-called beautiful woman. "The Daityas may have been bewildered," he thought, "but since even the demigods could not be agitated, what to speak of me, who am the best of all the demigods?" However, because Lord Śiva wanted to see Lord Viṣṇu's form as a woman, Lord Viṣṇu decided to impersonate a woman and show him a form that would immediately put him in an ocean of lusty desires. In effect, therefore, Lord Viṣṇu told Lord Śiva, "I will show you My form as a woman, and if you become agitated by lusty desires, do not blame Me." The attractive features of a woman are appreciated by those who are affected by lusty desires, but those who are above such desires, who are on the platform of Kṛṣṇa consciousness, are very difficult to bewilder. Nonetheless, by the supreme desire of the Personality of Godhead, everything can be done. This was to be a test of whether Lord Śiva could remain unagitated.

TEXT 17

श्रीशुक उवाच

इति ब्रुवाणो भगवांस्तत्रैवान्तरधीयत ।
सर्वतश्चारयंश्चक्षुर्भव आस्ते सहोमया ॥१७॥

śrī-śuka uvāca
iti bruvāṇo bhagavāṁs
tatraivāntaradhīyata
sarvataś cāryaṁś cakṣur
bhava āste sahomayā

śrī-śukaḥ uvāca—Śrī Śukadeva Gosvāmī said; *iti*—thus; *bruvāṇaḥ*—while speaking; *bhagavān*—Lord Viṣṇu, the Supreme Personality of Godhead; *tatra*—there; *eva*—immediately; *antaradhīyata*—disappeared from the vision of Lord Śiva and his associates; *sarvataḥ*—everywhere; *cārayan*—moving; *cakṣuḥ*—the eyes; *bhavaḥ*—Lord Śiva; *āste*—remained; *saha-umayā*—with his wife, Umā.

TRANSLATION

Śukadeva Gosvāmī continued: After speaking in this way, the Supreme Personality of Godhead, Viṣṇu, immediately disap-

peared, and Lord Śiva remained there with Umā, looking for Him all around with moving eyes.

TEXT 18

ततो ददर्शोपवने वरस्त्रियं
विचित्रपुष्पारुणपल्लवद्रुमे ।
विक्रीडतीं कन्दुकलीलया लसद्-
दुकूलपर्यस्तनितम्बमेखलाम् ॥१८॥

tato dadarśopavane vara-striyaṁ
vicitra-puṣpāruṇa-pallava-drume
vikrīḍatīṁ kanduka-līlayā lasad-
dukūla-paryasta-nitamba-mekhalām

tataḥ—thereafter; *dadarśa*—Lord Śiva saw; *upavane*—in a nice forest; *vara-striyam*—a very beautiful woman; *vicitra*—of many varieties; *puṣpa*—flowers; *aruṇa*—pink; *pallava*—leaves; *drume*—in the midst of the trees; *vikrīḍatīm*—engaged in playing; *kanduka*—with a ball; *līlayā*—by pastimes of playing; *lasat*—shining; *dukūla*—by a sari; *paryasta*—covered; *nitamba*—on her hips; *mekhalām*—dressed with a belt.

TRANSLATION

Thereafter, in a nice forest nearby, full of trees with reddish-pink leaves and varieties of flowers, Lord Śiva saw a beautiful woman playing with a ball. Her hips were covered with a shining sari and ornamented with a belt.

TEXT 19

आवर्तनोद्वर्तनकम्पितस्तन-
प्रकृष्टहारोरुभरैः पदे पदे ।
प्रभज्यमानामिव मध्यतश्चलत्-
पदप्रवालं नयतीं ततस्ततः ॥१९॥

āvartanodvartana-kampita-stana-
prakṛṣṭa-hāroru-bharaiḥ pade pade
prabhajyamānām iva madhyataś calat-
pada-pravālaṁ nayatīṁ tatas tataḥ

āvartana—by the falling down; *udvartana*—and springing up; *kampita*—trembling; *stana*—of the two breasts; *prakṛṣṭa*—beautiful; *hāra*—and of garlands; *uru-bharaiḥ*—because of the heavy load; *pade pade*—at every step; *prabhajyamānām iva*—as if breaking; *madhyataḥ*—in the middle portion of the body; *calat*—moving like that; *pada-pravālam*—feet reddish like coral; *nayatīm*—moving; *tataḥ tataḥ*—here and there.

TRANSLATION

Because the ball was falling down and bouncing up, as She played with it Her breasts trembled, and because of the weight of those breasts and Her heavy flower garlands, Her waist appeared to be all but breaking at every step, as Her two soft feet, which were reddish like coral, moved here and there.

TEXT 20

दिक्षु भ्रमत्कन्दुकचापलैर्भृशं
प्रोद्विग्नतारायतलोललोचनाम् ।
स्वकर्णविभ्राजितकुण्डलोल्लसत्-
कपोलनीलालकमण्डिताननाम् ॥२०॥

dikṣu bhramat-kanduka-cāpalair bhṛśaṁ
prodvigna-tārāyata-lola-locanām
sva-karṇa-vibhrājita-kuṇḍalollasat-
kapola-nīlālaka-maṇḍitānanām

dikṣu—in all directions; *bhramat*—moving; *kanduka*—of the ball; *cāpalaiḥ*—restlessness; *bhṛśam*—now and then; *prodvigna*—full of anxieties; *tāra*—eyes; *āyata*—broad; *lola*—restless; *locanām*—with such eyes; *sva-karṇa*—on Her own two ears; *vibhrājita*—illuminating;

kuṇḍala—earrings; *ullasat*—shining; *kapola*—cheeks; *nīla*—bluish; *alaka*—with hair; *maṇḍita*—was decorated; *ānanām*—face.

TRANSLATION

The woman's face was decorated by broad, beautiful, restless eyes, which moved as the ball bounced here and there from Her hand. The two brilliant earrings on Her ears decorated Her shining cheeks like bluish reflections, and the hair scattered on Her face made Her even more beautiful to see.

TEXT 21

श्लथद् दुकूलं कबरीं च विच्युतां
सन्नह्यतीं वामकरेण वल्गुना ।
विनिघ्नतीमन्यकरेण कन्दुकं
विमोहयन्तीं जगदात्ममायया ॥२१॥

ślathad dukūlaṁ kabarīṁ ca vicyutāṁ
sannahyatīṁ vāma-kareṇa valgunā
vinighnatīm anya-kareṇa kandukaṁ
vimohayantīṁ jagad-ātma-māyayā

ślathat—slipping or slackening; *dukūlam*—the sari; *kabarīm ca*—and the hair on the head; *vicyutām*—being slackened and scattered; *sannahyatīm*—trying to bind; *vāma-kareṇa*—with the left hand; *valgunā*—very beautifully attractive; *vinighnatīm*—striking; *anya-kareṇa*—with the right hand; *kandukam*—the ball; *vimohayantīm*—in this way captivating everyone; *jagat*—the whole world; *ātma-māyayā*—by the spiritual potency, the internal energy.

TRANSLATION

As She played with the ball, the sari covering Her body became loose, and Her hair scattered. She tried to bind Her hair with Her beautiful left hand, and at the same time She played with the ball by striking it with Her right hand. This was so attractive that the

Supreme Lord, by His internal potency, in this way captivated everyone.

PURPORT

In *Bhagavad-gītā* (7.14) it is said, *daivī hy eṣā guṇa-mayī mama māyā duratyayā:* the external potency of the Supreme Personality of Godhead is extremely strong. Indeed, everyone is fully captivated by her activities. Lord Śambhu (Śiva) was not to be captivated by the external potency, but because Lord Viṣṇu wanted to captivate Him also, He exhibited His internal potency to act the way that His external potency acts to captivate ordinary living entities. Lord Viṣṇu can captivate anyone, even such a strong personality as Lord Śambhu.

TEXT 22

तां वीक्ष्य देव इति कन्दुकलीलयेषद्-
व्रीडास्फुटस्मितविसृष्टकटाक्षमुष्टः ।
स्त्रीप्रेक्षणप्रतिसमीक्षणविह्वलात्मा
नात्मानमन्तिक उमां स्वगणांश्च वेद ॥२२॥

tāṁ vīkṣya deva iti kanduka-līlayeṣad-
vrīḍāsphuṭa-smita-visṛṣṭa-kaṭākṣa-muṣṭaḥ
strī-prekṣaṇa-pratisamīkṣaṇa-vihvalātmā
nātmānam antika umāṁ sva-gaṇāṁś ca veda

tām—Her; *vīkṣya*—after observing; *devaḥ*—Lord Śambhu; *iti*—in this way; *kanduka-līlayā*—by playing with the ball; *īṣat*—slight; *vrīḍā*—by bashfulness; *asphuṭa*—not very distinct; *smita*—with smiling; *visṛṣṭa*—sent; *kaṭākṣa-muṣṭaḥ*—defeated by the glances; *strī-prekṣaṇa*—by glancing at that beautiful woman; *pratisamīkṣaṇa*—and by constantly being watched by Her; *vihvala-ātmā*—whose mind was agitated; *na*—not; *ātmānam*—himself; *antike*—(situated) nearby; *umām*—his wife, mother Umā; *sva-gaṇān ca*—and his associates; *veda*—Lord Śiva could understand.

TRANSLATION

While Lord Śiva observed the beautiful woman playing with the ball, She sometimes glanced at him and slightly smiled in bashful-

ness. As he looked at the beautiful woman and She watched him, he forgot both himself and Umā, his most beautiful wife, as well as his associates nearby.

PURPORT

The material bondage of this world is that a beautiful woman can captivate a handsome man and that a handsome man can captivate a beautiful woman. Such are the affairs that began when Lord Śiva observed the beautiful girl playing with the ball. In such activities, the influence of Cupid is very prominent. As both parties move their eyebrows and glance at one another, their lusty desires increase more and more. Such reciprocations of lusty desire took place between Lord Śiva and the beautiful woman, even though Umā and Lord Śiva's associates were by Lord Śiva's side. Such is the attraction between man and woman in the material world. Lord Śiva was supposed to be above all this attraction, but he was victimized by the captivating power of Lord Viṣṇu. Ṛṣabhadeva thus explains the nature of lusty attraction:

puṁsaḥ striyā mithunī-bhāvam etaṁ
tayor mitho hṛdaya-granthim āhuḥ
ato gṛha-kṣetra-sutāpta-vittair
janasya moho 'yam ahaṁ mameti

"The attraction between male and female is the basic principle of material existence. On the basis of this misconception, which ties together the hearts of the male and female, one becomes attracted to his body, home, property, children, relatives and wealth. In this way one increases life's illusions and thinks in terms of 'I and mine.' " (*Bhāg.* 5.5.8) When a man and woman exchange feelings of lust, both of them are victimized, and thus they are bound to this material world in various ways.

TEXT 23

तस्याः कराग्रात् स तु कन्दुको यदा
गतो विदूरं तमनुव्रजत्स्त्रियाः ।
वासः ससूत्रं लघु मारुतोऽहरद्
भवस्य देवस्य किलानुपश्यतः ॥२३॥

tasyāḥ karāgrāt sa tu kanduko yadā
gato vidūraṁ tam anuvrajat-striyāḥ
vāsaḥ sasūtraṁ laghu māruto 'harad
bhavasya devasya kilānupaśyataḥ

tasyāḥ—of the beautiful woman; *kara-agrāt*—from the hand; *saḥ*—that; *tu*—but; *kandukaḥ*—the ball; *yadā*—when; *gataḥ*—had gone; *vidūram*—far off; *tam*—that ball; *anuvrajat*—began to follow; *striyāḥ*—of that woman; *vāsaḥ*—the covering dress; *sa-sūtram*—with the belt; *laghu*—because of being very fine; *mārutaḥ*—the breeze; *aharat*—blew away; *bhavasya*—while Lord Śiva; *devasya*—the chief demigod; *kila*—indeed; *anupaśyataḥ*—was always looking.

TRANSLATION

When the ball leaped from Her hand and fell at a distance, the woman began to follow it, but as Lord Śiva observed these activities, a breeze suddenly blew away the fine dress and belt that covered her.

TEXT 24

एवं तां रुचिरापाङ्गीं दर्शनीयां मनोरमाम् ।
दृष्ट्वा तस्यां मनश्चक्रे विषज्जन्त्यां भवः किल ॥२४॥

evaṁ tāṁ rucirāpāṅgīṁ
darśanīyāṁ manoramām
dṛṣṭvā tasyāṁ manaś cakre
viṣajjantyāṁ bhavaḥ kila

evam—in this way; *tām*—Her; *rucira-apāṅgīm*—possessing all attractive features; *darśanīyām*—pleasing to see; *manoramām*—beautifully formed; *dṛṣṭvā*—seeing; *tasyām*—upon Her; *manaḥ cakre*—thought; *viṣajjantyām*—to be attracted by him; *bhavaḥ*—Lord Śiva; *kila*—indeed.

TRANSLATION

Thus Lord Śiva saw the woman, every part of whose body was beautifully formed, and the beautiful woman also looked at him.

Therefore, thinking that She was attracted to him, Lord Śiva became very much attracted to Her.

PURPORT

Lord Śiva was observing every part of the woman's body, and She was also glancing at him with restless eyes. Thus Śiva thought that She was also attracted to him, and now he wanted to touch Her.

TEXT 25

तयापहृतविज्ञानस्तत्कृतस्मरविह्वलः ।
भवान्या अपि पश्यन्त्या गतह्रीस्तत्पदं ययौ ॥२५॥

tayāpahṛta-vijñānas
tat-kṛta-smara-vihvalaḥ
bhavānyā api paśyantyā
gata-hrīs tat-padaṁ yayau

tayā—by Her; *apahṛta*—taken away; *vijñānaḥ*—good sense; *tat-kṛta*—done by Her; *smara*—by the smiling; *vihvalaḥ*—having become mad for Her; *bhavānyāḥ*—while Bhavānī, the wife of Lord Śiva; *api*—although; *paśyantyāḥ*—was seeing all these incidents; *gata-hrīḥ*—bereft of all shame; *tat-padam*—to the place where She was situated; *yayau*—went.

TRANSLATION

Lord Śiva, his good sense taken away by the woman because of lusty desires to enjoy with Her, became so mad for Her that even in the presence of Bhavānī he did not hesitate to approach Her.

TEXT 26

सा तमायान्तमालोक्य विवस्त्रा व्रीडिता भृशम्।
निलीयमाना वृक्षेषु हसन्ती नान्वतिष्ठत ॥२६॥

sā tam āyāntam ālokya
vivastrā vrīḍitā bhṛśam

nilīyamānā vṛkṣeṣu
hasantī nānvatiṣṭhata

sā—that woman; *tam*—Lord Śiva; *āyāntam*—who was coming near; *ālokya*—seeing; *vivastrā*—She was naked; *vrīḍitā*—very bashful; *bhṛśam*—so much; *nilīyamānā*—was hiding; *vṛkṣeṣu*—among the trees; *hasantī*—smiling; *na*—not; *anvatiṣṭhata*—stood in one place.

TRANSLATION

The beautiful woman was already naked, and when She saw Lord Śiva coming toward Her, She became extremely bashful. Thus She kept smiling, but She hid Herself among the trees and did not stand in one place.

TEXT 27

तामन्वगच्छद् भगवान् भवः प्रमुषितेन्द्रियः ।
कामस्य च वशं नीतः करेणुमिव यूथपः ।।२७।।

tām anvagacchad bhagavān
bhavaḥ pramuṣitendriyaḥ
kāmasya ca vaśaṁ nītaḥ
kareṇum iva yūthapaḥ

tām—Her; *anvagacchat*—followed; *bhagavān*—Lord Śiva; *bhavaḥ*—known as Bhava; *pramuṣita-indriyaḥ*—whose senses were agitated; *kāmasya*—of lusty desires; *ca*—and; *vaśam*—victimized; *nītaḥ*—having become; *kareṇum*—a female elephant; *iva*—just as; *yūthapaḥ*—a male elephant.

TRANSLATION

His senses being agitated, Lord Śiva, victimized by lusty desires, began to follow Her, just as a lusty elephant follows a she-elephant.

TEXT 28

सोऽनुव्रज्यातिवेगेन गृहीत्वानिच्छतीं स्त्रियम् ।
केशबन्ध उपानीय बाहुभ्यां परिषस्वजे ।।२८।।

so 'nuvrajyātivegena
gṛhītvānicchatīṁ striyam
keśa-bandha upānīya
bāhubhyāṁ pariṣasvaje

saḥ—Lord Śiva; *anuvrajya*—following Her; *ati-vegena*—with great speed; *gṛhītvā*—catching; *anicchatīm*—although She was not willing to be caught; *striyam*—the woman; *keśa-bandhe*—on the cluster of hair; *upānīya*—dragging Her near; *bāhubhyām*—with his arms; *pariṣasvaje*—embraced Her.

TRANSLATION

After following Her with great speed, Lord Śiva caught Her by the braid of Her hair and dragged Her near him. Although She was unwilling, he embraced Her with his arms.

TEXTS 29–30

सोपगूढा भगवता करिणा करिणी यथा ।
इतस्ततः प्रसर्पन्ती विप्रकीर्णशिरोरुहा ॥२९॥
आत्मानं मोचयित्वाङ्ग सुरर्षभभुजान्तरात् ।
प्राद्रवत्सा पृथुश्रोणी माया देवविनिर्मिता ॥३०॥

sopagūḍhā bhagavatā
kariṇā kariṇī yathā
itas tataḥ prasarpantī
viprakīrṇa-śiroruhā

ātmānaṁ mocayitvāṅga
surarṣabha-bhujāntarāt
prādravat sā pṛthu-śroṇī
māyā deva-vinirmitā

sā—the woman; *upagūḍhā*—being captured and embraced; *bhagavatā*—by Lord Śiva; *kariṇā*—by a male elephant; *kariṇī*—a she-elephant; *yathā*—as; *itaḥ tataḥ*—here and there; *prasarpantī*—swirling like a snake; *viprakīrṇa*—scattered; *śiroruhā*—all the hair on Her head; *ātmānam*—Herself; *mocayitvā*—releasing; *aṅga*—O King; *sura-ṛṣabha*—of the best of the demigods (Lord Śiva); *bhuja-antarāt*—from the entanglement in the midst of the arms; *prādravat*—began to run very fast; *sā*—She; *pṛthu-śroṇī*—bearing very large hips; *māyā*—internal potency; *deva-vinirmitā*—exhibited by the Supreme Personality of Godhead.

TRANSLATION

Being embraced by Lord Śiva like a female elephant embraced by a male, the woman, whose hair was scattered, swirled like a snake. O King, this woman, who had large, high hips, was a woman of yogamāyā presented by the Supreme Personality of Godhead. She released Herself somehow or other from the fond embrace of Lord Śiva's arms and ran away.

TEXT 31

तस्यासौ पदवीं रुद्रो विष्णोरद्भुतकर्मणः ।
प्रत्यपद्यत कामेन वैरिणेव विनिर्जितः ॥३१॥

tasyāsau padavīṁ rudro
viṣṇor adbhuta-karmaṇaḥ
pratyapadyata kāmena
vairiṇeva vinirjitaḥ

tasya—of He who is the Supreme Lord; *asau*—Lord Śiva; *padavīm*—the place; *rudraḥ*—Lord Śiva; *viṣṇoḥ*—of Lord Viṣṇu; *adbhuta-karmaṇaḥ*—of He who acts very wonderfully; *pratyapadyata*—began to follow; *kāmena*—by lusty desire; *vairiṇā iva*—as if by an enemy; *vinirjitaḥ*—being harassed.

TRANSLATION

As if harassed by an enemy in the form of lusty desires, Lord Śiva followed the path of Lord Viṣṇu, who acts very wonderfully and who had taken the form of Mohinī.

PURPORT

Lord Śiva cannot be victimized by *māyā*. Therefore it is to be understood that Lord Śiva was being thus harassed by Lord Viṣṇu's internal potency. Lord Viṣṇu can perform many wonderful activities through His various potencies.

parāsya śaktir vividhaiva śrūyate
svābhāvikī jñāna-bala-kriyā ca
(*Śvetāśvatara Upaniṣad* 6.8)

The Supreme Lord has various potencies, by which He can act very efficiently. To do anything expertly, He doesn't even need to contemplate. Since Lord Śiva was being harassed by the woman, it is to be understood that this was being done not by a woman but by Lord Viṣṇu Himself.

TEXT 32

तस्यानुधावतो रेतश्चस्कन्दामोघरेतसः ।
शुष्मिणो यूथपस्येव वासितामनुधावतः ॥३२॥

tasyānudhāvato retaś
caskandāmogha-retasaḥ
śuṣmiṇo yūthapasyeva
vāsitām anudhāvataḥ

tasya—of him (Lord Śiva); *anudhāvataḥ*—who was following; *retaḥ*—the semen; *caskanda*—discharged; *amogha-retasaḥ*—of that person whose discharge of semen never goes in vain; *śuṣmiṇaḥ*—mad; *yūthapasya*—of a male elephant; *iva*—just like; *vāsitām*—to a female elephant able to conceive pregnancy; *anudhāvataḥ*—following.

TRANSLATION

Just as a maddened bull elephant follows a female elephant who is able to conceive pregnancy, Lord Śiva followed the beautiful woman and discharged semen, even though his discharge of semen never goes in vain.

TEXT 33

यत्र यत्रापतन्मह्यां रेतस्तस्य महात्मनः ।
तानि रूप्यस्य हेम्नश्च क्षेत्राण्यासन्महीपते ॥३३॥

yatra yatrāpatan mahyāṁ
retas tasya mahātmanaḥ
tāni rūpyasya hemnaś ca
kṣetrāṇy āsan mahī-pate

yatra—wherever; *yatra*—and wherever; *apatat*—fell; *mahyām*—on the surface of the world; *retaḥ*—the semen; *tasya*—of him; *mahā-ātmanaḥ*—of the great personality (Lord Śiva); *tāni*—all those places; *rūpyasya*—of silver; *hemnaḥ*—of gold; *ca*—and; *kṣetrāni*—mines; *āsan*—became; *mahī-pate*—O King.

TRANSLATION

O King, wheresoever on the surface of the globe fell the semen of the great personality of Lord Śiva, mines of gold and silver later appeared.

PURPORT

Śrīla Viśvanātha Cakravartī Ṭhākura comments that those who seek gold and silver can worship Lord Śiva for material opulences. Lord Śiva lives under a bael tree and does not even construct a house in which to dwell, but although he is apparently poverty-stricken, his devotees are sometimes opulently endowed with large quantities of silver and gold. Parīkṣit Mahārāja later asks about this, and Śukadeva Gosvāmī replies.

TEXT 34

सरित्सरःसु शैलेषु वनेषूपवनेषु च ।
यत्र क्व चासन्नृषयस्तत्र संनिहितो हरः ॥३४॥

sarit-saraḥsu śaileṣu
vaneṣūpavaneṣu ca
yatra kva cāsann ṛṣayas
tatra sannihito haraḥ

sarit—near the shores of the rivers; *saraḥsu*—and near the lakes; *śaileṣu*—near the mountains; *vaneṣu*—in the forests; *upavaneṣu*—in the gardens or small forests; *ca*—also; *yatra*—wherever; *kva*—anywhere; *ca*—also; *āsan*—were existing; *ṛṣayaḥ*—great sages; *tatra*—there; *sannihitaḥ*—was present; *haraḥ*—Lord Śiva.

TRANSLATION

Following Mohinī, Lord Śiva went everywhere—near the shores of the rivers and lakes, near the mountains, near the forests, near the gardens, and wherever there lived great sages.

PURPORT

Śrīla Viśvanātha Cakravartī Ṭhākura remarks that Mohinī-mūrti dragged Lord Śiva to so many places, especially to where the great sages lived, to instruct the sages that their Lord Śiva had become mad for a beautiful woman. Thus although they were all great sages and saintly persons, they should not think themselves free, but should remain extremely cautious about beautiful women. No one should think himself liberated in the presence of a beautiful woman. The *śāstras* enjoin:

mātrā svasrā duhitrā vā
nāviviktāsano bhavet
balavān indriya-grāmo
vidvāṁsam api karṣati

"One should not stay in a solitary place with a woman, even if she be his mother, sister or daughter, for the senses are so uncontrollably powerful that in the presence of a woman one may become agitated, even if he is very learned and advanced." (*Bhāg.* 9.19.17)

TEXT 35

स्कन्ने रेतसि सोऽपश्यदात्मानं देवमायया ।
जडीकृतं नृपश्रेष्ठ संन्यवर्तत कश्मलात् ॥३५॥

skanne retasi so 'paśyad
ātmānaṁ deva-māyayā

jaḍīkṛtaṁ nṛpa-śreṣṭha
sannyavartata kaśmalāt

skanne—when fully discharged; *retasi*—the semen; *saḥ*—Lord Śiva; *apaśyat*—saw; *ātmānam*—his own self; *deva-māyayā*—by the *māyā* of the Supreme Personality of Godhead; *jaḍīkṛtam*—had become victimized as a fool; *nṛpa-śreṣṭha*—O best of kings (Mahārāja Parīkṣit); *sannyavartata*—restrained himself further; *kaśmalāt*—from illusion.

TRANSLATION

O Mahārāja Parīkṣit, best of kings, when Lord Śiva had fully discharged semen, he could see how he himself had been victimized by the illusion created by the Supreme Personality of Godhead. Thus he restrained himself from any further māyā.

PURPORT

Once one is agitated by lusty desires upon seeing a woman, those desires increase more and more, but when semen is discharged in the act of sex, the lusty desires diminish. The same principle acted upon Lord Śiva. He was allured by the beautiful woman Mohinī-mūrti, but when his semen had been fully discharged, he came to his senses and realized how he had been victimized as soon as he saw the woman in the forest. If one is trained to protect his semen by observing celibacy, naturally he is not attracted by the beauty of a woman. If one can remain a *brahmacārī,* he saves himself so much trouble in material existence. Material existence means enjoying the pleasure of sexual intercourse (*yan maithunādi-gṛhamedhi-sukham*). If one is educated about sex life and is trained to protect his semen, he is saved from the danger of material existence.

TEXT 36

अथावगतमाहात्म्य आत्मनो जगदात्मनः ।
अपरिज्ञेयवीर्यस्य न मेने तदुहाद्भुतम् ॥३६॥

athāvagata-māhātmya
ātmano jagad-ātmanaḥ

aparijñeya-vīryasya
na mene tad u hādbhutam

atha—thus; *avagata*—being fully convinced about; *māhātmyaḥ*—the greatness; *ātmanaḥ*—of himself; *jagat-ātmanaḥ*—and of the Supreme Personality of Godhead; *aparijñeya-vīryasya*—who has unlimited potency; *na*—not; *mene*—did consider; *tat*—the miraculous activities of the Supreme Personality of Godhead in bewildering him; *u ha*—certainly; *adbhutam*—as wonderful.

TRANSLATION

Thus Lord Śiva could understand his position and that of the Supreme Personality of Godhead, who has unlimited potencies. Having reached this understanding, he was not at all surprised by the wonderful way Lord Viṣṇu had acted upon him.

PURPORT

The Supreme Personality of Godhead is known as all-powerful because no one can excel Him in any activity. In *Bhagavad-gītā* (7.7) the Lord says, *mattaḥ parataraṁ nānyat kiñcid asti dhanañjaya:* "O conqueror of wealth, there is no truth superior to Me." No one can equal the Lord or be greater than Him, for He is the master of everyone. As stated in *Caitanya-caritāmṛta* (*Ādi* 5.142), *ekale īśvara kṛṣṇa, āra saba bhṛtya.* The Supreme Personality of Godhead, Kṛṣṇa, is the only master of everyone, including even Lord Śiva, what to speak of others. Lord Śiva was already aware of the supreme power of Lord Viṣṇu, but when he was actually put into bewilderment, he felt proud to have such an exalted master.

TEXT 37

तमविक्लवमव्रीडमालक्ष्य मधुसूदनः ।
उवाच परमप्रीतो बिभ्रत्स्वां पौरुषीं तनुम् ॥३७॥

tam aviklavam avrīḍam
ālakṣya madhusūdanaḥ

uvāca parama-prīto
bibhrat svāṁ pauruṣīṁ tanum

tam—him (Lord Śiva); *aviklavam*—without being agitated by the incident that had taken place; *avrīḍam*—without being ashamed; *ālakṣya*—seeing; *madhu-sūdanaḥ*—the Supreme Personality of Godhead, who is known as Madhusūdana, the killer of the demon Madhu; *uvāca*—said; *parama-prītaḥ*—being very pleased; *bibhrat*—assuming; *svām*—His own; *pauruṣīm*—original; *tanum*—form.

TRANSLATION

Seeing Lord Śiva unagitated and unashamed, Lord Viṣṇu [Madhusūdana] was very pleased. Thus He resumed His original form and spoke as follows.

PURPORT

Although Lord Śiva was aghast at the potency of Lord Viṣṇu, he did not feel ashamed. Rather, he was proud to be defeated by Lord Viṣṇu. Nothing is hidden from the Supreme Personality of Godhead, for He is in everyone's heart. Indeed, the Lord says in *Bhagavad-gītā* (15.15), *sarvasya cāhaṁ hṛdi sanniviṣṭo mattaḥ smṛtir jñānam apohanaṁ ca:* "I am seated in everyone's heart, and from Me come remembrance, knowledge and forgetfulness." Whatever happened had taken place under the direction of the Supreme Personality of Godhead, and therefore there was no cause to be sorry or ashamed. Although Lord Śiva is never defeated by anyone, when defeated by Lord Viṣṇu he felt proud that he had such an exalted and powerful master.

TEXT 38

श्रीभगवानुवाच
दिष्ट्या त्वं विबुधश्रेष्ठ स्वां निष्ठामात्मना स्थितः ।
यन्मे स्त्रीरूपया स्वैरं मोहितोऽप्यङ्ग मायया ॥३८॥

śrī-bhagavān uvāca
diṣṭyā tvaṁ vibudha-śreṣṭha
svāṁ niṣṭhām ātmanā sthitaḥ

yan me strī-rūpayā svairaṁ
mohito 'py aṅga māyayā

śrī-bhagavān uvāca—the Supreme Personality of Godhead said; *diṣṭyā*—all auspiciousness; *tvam*—unto you; *vibudha-śreṣṭha*—O best of all the demigods; *svām*—in your own; *niṣṭhām*—fixed situation; *ātmanā*—of your own self; *sthitaḥ*—you are situated; *yat*—as; *me*—Mine; *strī-rūpayā*—appearance like a woman; *svairam*—sufficiently; *mohitaḥ*—enchanted; *api*—in spite of; *aṅga*—O Lord Śiva; *māyayā*—by My potency.

TRANSLATION

The Supreme Personality of Godhead said: O best of the demigods, although you have been amply harassed because of My potency in assuming the form of a woman, you are established in your position. Therefore, may all good fortune be upon you.

PURPORT

Since Lord Śiva is the best of the demigods, he is the best of all devotees (*vaiṣṇavānāṁ yathā śambhuḥ*). His exemplary character was therefore praised by the Supreme Personality of Godhead, who gave His benediction by saying, "May all good fortune be upon you." When a devotee becomes a little proud, the Supreme Lord sometimes exhibits His supreme power to dissipate the devotee's misunderstanding. After being amply harassed by Lord Viṣṇu's potency, Lord Śiva resumed his normal, unagitated condition. This is the position of a devotee. A devotee should not be agitated under any circumstances, even in the worst reverses. As confirmed in *Bhagavad-gītā* (6.22), *yasmin sthito na duḥkhena guruṇāpi vicālyate:* because of his full faith in the Supreme Personality of Godhead, a devotee is never agitated, even in the greatest trials. This pridelessness is possible only for the first-class devotees, of whom Lord Śambhu is one.

TEXT 39

को नु मेऽतितरेन्मायां विषक्तस्त्वदृते पुमान् ।
तांस्तान्विसृजतीं भावान्दुस्तरामकृतात्मभिः ॥३९॥

ko nu me 'titaren māyāṁ
viṣaktas tvad-ṛte pumān
tāṁs tān visṛjatīṁ bhāvān
dustarām akṛtātmabhiḥ

kaḥ—what; *nu*—indeed; *me*—My; *atitaret*—can surpass; *māyām*—illusory energy; *viṣaktaḥ*—attached to material sense enjoyment; *tvat-ṛte*—except for you; *pumān*—person; *tān*—such conditions; *tān*—unto the materially attached persons; *visṛjatīm*—in surpassing; *bhāvān*—reactions of material activities; *dustarām*—very difficult to surmount; *akṛta-ātmabhiḥ*—by persons unable to control their senses.

TRANSLATION

My dear Lord Śambhu, who within this material world but you can surpass My illusory energy? People are generally attached to sense enjoyment and conquered by its influence. Indeed, the influence of material nature is very difficult for them to surmount.

PURPORT

Of the three chief demigods—Brahmā, Viṣṇu and Maheśvara—all but Viṣṇu are under the influence of *māyā.* In *Caitanya-caritāmṛta,* they are described as *māyī,* which means "under *māyā's* influence." But even though Lord Śiva associates with *māyā,* he is not influenced. The living entities are affected by *māyā,* but although Lord Śiva apparently associates with *māyā,* he is not affected. In other words, all living entities within this material world except for Lord Śiva are swayed by *māyā.* Lord Śiva is therefore neither *viṣṇu-tattva* nor *jīva-tattva.* He is between the two.

TEXT 40

सेयं गुणमयी माया न त्वामभिभविष्यति ।
मया समेता कालेन कालरूपेण भागशः ॥४०॥

seyaṁ guṇa-mayī māyā
na tvām abhibhaviṣyati

mayā sametā kālena
kāla-rūpeṇa bhāgaśaḥ

sā—that insurmountable; *iyam*—this; *guṇa-mayī*—consisting of the three modes of material nature; *māyā*—illusory energy; *na*—not; *tvām*—you; *abhibhaviṣyati*—will be able to bewilder in the future; *mayā*—with Me; *sametā*—joined; *kālena*—eternal time; *kāla-rūpeṇa*—in the form of time; *bhāgaśaḥ*—with her different parts.

TRANSLATION

The material, external energy [māyā], who cooperates with Me in creation and who is manifested in the three modes of nature, will not be able to bewilder you any longer.

PURPORT

When Lord Śiva was present, his wife, Durgā, was also there. Durgā works in cooperation with the Supreme Personality of Godhead in creating the cosmic manifestation. The Lord says in *Bhagavad-gītā* (9.10), *mayādhyakṣeṇa prakṛtiḥ sūyate sacarācaram:* "The material energy [*prakṛti*] works under My direction, O son of Kuntī, and is producing all moving and unmoving beings." *Prakṛti* is Durgā.

sṛṣṭi-sthiti-pralaya-sādhana-śaktir ekā
chāyeva yasya bhuvanāni bibharti durgā

The entire cosmos is created by Durgā in cooperation with Lord Viṣṇu in the form of *kāla*, time. *Sa īkṣata lokān nu sṛjā. Sa imāl̐ lokān asṛjata.* This is the version of the *Vedas* (*Aitareya Upaniṣad* 1.1.1–2). *Māyā* happens to be the wife of Lord Śiva, and thus Lord Śiva is in association with *māyā*, but Lord Viṣṇu here assures Lord Śiva that this *māyā* will no longer be able to captivate him.

TEXT 41

श्रीशुक उवाच
एवं भगवता राजन् श्रीवत्साङ्केन सत्कृतः ।
आमन्त्र्य तं परिक्रम्य सगणः स्वालयं ययौ ॥४१॥

śrī-śuka uvāca
evaṁ bhagavatā rājan
śrīvatsāṅkena sat-kṛtaḥ
āmantrya taṁ parikramya
sagaṇaḥ svālayaṁ yayau

śrī-śukaḥ uvāca—Śrī Śukadeva Gosvāmī said; *evam*—thus; *bhagavatā*—by the Supreme Personality of Godhead; *rājan*—O King; *śrīvatsa-aṅkena*—who always carries the mark of Śrīvatsa on His breast; *sat-kṛtaḥ*—being very much applauded; *āmantrya*—taking permission from; *tam*—Him; *parikramya*—circumambulating; *sa-gaṇaḥ*—with his associates; *sva-ālayam*—to his own abode; *yayau*—went back.

TRANSLATION

Śukadeva Gosvāmī said: O King, having thus been praised by the Supreme Personality, who bears the mark of Śrīvatsa on His chest, Lord Śiva circumambulated Him. Then, after taking permission from Him, Lord Śiva returned to his abode, Kailāsa, along with his associates.

PURPORT

Śrīla Viśvanātha Cakravartī Ṭhākura remarks that when Lord Śiva was offering obeisances unto Lord Viṣṇu, Lord Viṣṇu arose and embraced him. Therefore the word *śrīvatsāṅkena* is used here. The mark of Śrīvatsa adorns the chest of Lord Viṣṇu, and therefore when Lord Viṣṇu embraced Lord Śiva while being circumambulated, the Śrīvatsa mark touched Lord Śiva's bosom.

TEXT 42

आत्मांशभूतां तां मायां भवानीं भगवान्भवः ।
संमतामृषिमुख्यानां प्रीत्याचष्टाथ भारत ॥४२॥

ātmāṁśa-bhūtāṁ tāṁ māyāṁ
bhavānīṁ bhagavān bhavaḥ
sammatāṁ ṛṣi-mukhyānāṁ
prītyācaṣṭātha bhārata

ātma-aṁśa-bhūtām—a potency of the Supreme Soul; *tām*—unto her; *māyām*—the illusory energy; *bhavānīm*—who is the wife of Lord Śiva; *bhagavān*—the powerful; *bhavaḥ*—Lord Śiva; *sammatām*—accepted; *ṛṣi-mukhyānām*—by the great sages; *prītyā*—in jubilation; *ācaṣṭa*—began to address; *atha*—then; *bhārata*—O Mahārāja Parīkṣit, descendant of Bharata.

TRANSLATION

O descendant of Bharata Mahārāja, Lord Śiva, in jubilation, then addressed his wife, Bhavānī, who is accepted by all authorities as the potency of Lord Viṣṇu.

TEXT 43

अयि व्यपश्यस्त्वमजस्य मायां
परस्य पुंसः परदेवतायाः ।
अहं कलानामृषभोऽपि मुह्ये
यथावशोऽन्ये किमुतास्वतन्त्राः ॥४३॥

ayi vyapaśyas tvam ajasya māyāṁ
parasya puṁsaḥ para-devatāyāḥ
ahaṁ kalānām ṛṣabho 'pi muhye
yayāvaśo 'nye kim utāsvatantrāḥ

ayi—oh; *vyapaśyaḥ*—have seen; *tvam*—you; *ajasya*—of the unborn; *māyām*—the illusory energy; *parasya puṁsaḥ*—of the Supreme Person; *para-devatāyāḥ*—the Absolute Truth; *aham*—myself; *kalānām*—of plenary portions; *ṛṣabhaḥ*—the chief; *api*—although; *muhye*—became bewildered; *yayā*—by her; *avaśaḥ*—imperceptibly; *anye*—others; *kim uta*—what to speak of; *asvatantrāḥ*—fully dependent on *māyā*.

TRANSLATION

Lord Śiva said: O Goddess, you have now seen the illusory energy of the Supreme Personality of Godhead, who is the unborn master of everyone. Although I am one of the principal expansions

of His Lordship, even I was illusioned by His energy. What then is to be said of others, who are fully dependent on māyā?

TEXT 44

यं मामपृच्छस्त्वमुपेत्य योगात्
समासहस्रान्त उपारतं वै ।
स एष साक्षात् पुरुषः पुराणो
न यत्र कालो विशते न वेदः ॥४४॥

yaṁ mām apṛcchas tvam upetya yogāt
samā-sahasrānta upāratam vai
sa eṣa sākṣāt puruṣaḥ purāṇo
na yatra kālo viśate na vedaḥ

yam—about whom; *mām*—from me; *apṛcchaḥ*—inquired; *tvam*—you; *upetya*—coming near me; *yogāt*—from performing mystic *yoga; samā*—years; *sahasra-ante*—at the end of one thousand; *upāratam*—ceasing; *vai*—indeed; *saḥ*—He; *eṣaḥ*—here is; *sākṣāt*—directly; *puruṣaḥ*—the Supreme Person; *purāṇaḥ*—the original; *na*—not; *yatra*—where; *kālaḥ*—eternal time; *viśate*—can enter; *na*—nor; *vedaḥ*—the *Vedas.*

TRANSLATION

When I finished performing mystic yoga for one thousand years, you asked me upon whom I was meditating. Now, here is that Supreme Person to whom time has no entrance and who the Vedas cannot understand.

PURPORT

Eternal time enters anywhere and everywhere, but it cannot enter the kingdom of god. Nor can the *Vedas* understand the Supreme Personality of Godhead. This is an indication of the Lord's being omnipotent, omnipresent and omniscient.

TEXT 45

श्रीशुक उवाच
इति तेऽभिहितस्तात विक्रमः शार्ङ्गधन्वनः ।
सिन्धोर्निर्मथने येन धृतः पृष्ठे महाचलः ॥४५॥

śrī-śuka uvāca
iti te 'bhihitas tāta
vikramaḥ śārṅga-dhanvanaḥ
sindhor nirmathane yena
dhṛtaḥ pṛṣṭhe mahācalaḥ

śrī-śukaḥ uvāca—Śrī Śukadeva Gosvāmī said; *iti*—thus; *te*—unto you; *abhihitaḥ*—explained; *tāta*—my dear King; *vikramaḥ*—prowess; *śārṅga-dhanvanaḥ*—of the Supreme Personality of Godhead, who carries the Śārṅga bow; *sindhoḥ*—of the ocean of milk; *nirmathane*—in the churning; *yena*—by whom; *dhṛtaḥ*—was held; *pṛṣṭhe*—on the back; *mahā-acalaḥ*—the great mountain.

TRANSLATION

Śukadeva Gosvāmī said: My dear King, the person who bore the great mountain on His back for the churning of the ocean of milk is the same Supreme Personality of Godhead, known as Śārṅgadhanvā. I have now described to you His prowess.

TEXT 46

एतन्मुहुः कीर्तयतोऽनुशृण्वतो
न रिष्यते जातु समुद्यमः क्वचित् ।
यदुत्तमश्लोकगुणानुवर्णनं
समस्तसंसारपरिश्रमापहम् ॥४६॥

etan muhuḥ kīrtayato 'nuśṛṇvato
na riṣyate jātu samudyamaḥ kvacit

yad uttamaśloka-guṇānuvarṇanaṁ
samasta-saṁsāra-pariśramāpaham

etat—this narration; *muhuḥ*—constantly; *kīrtayataḥ*—of one who chants; *anuśṛṇvataḥ*—and also hears; *na*—not; *riṣyate*—annihilated; *jātu*—at any time; *samudyamaḥ*—the endeavor; *kvacit*—at any time; *yat*—because; *uttamaśloka*—of the Supreme Personality of Godhead; *guṇa-anuvarṇanam*—describing the transcendental qualities; *samasta*—all; *saṁsāra*—of material existence; *pariśrama*—misery; *apaham*—finishing.

TRANSLATION

The endeavor of one who constantly hears or describes this narration of the churning of the ocean of milk will never be fruitless. Indeed, chanting the glories of the Supreme Personality of Godhead is the only means to annihilate all sufferings in this material world.

TEXT 47

असदविषयमङ्घ्रिं भावगम्यं प्रपन्ना-
नमृतममरवर्यानाशयत् सिन्धुमथ्यम् ।
कपटयुवतिवेषो मोहयन्यः सुरारीं-
स्तमहमुपसृतानां कामपूरं नतोऽस्मि ॥४७॥

asad-aviṣayam aṅghriṁ bhāva-gamyaṁ prapannān
amṛtam amara-varyān āśayat sindhu-mathyam
kapaṭa-yuvati-veṣo mohayan yaḥ surārīṁs
tam aham upasṛtānāṁ kāma-pūraṁ nato 'smi

asat-aviṣayam—not understood by the atheists; *aṅghrim*—unto the lotus feet of the Supreme Personality of Godhead; *bhāva-gamyam*—understood by devotees; *prapannān*—fully surrendered; *amṛtam*—the nectar; *amara-varyān*—only unto the demigods; *āśayat*—gave to drink; *sindhu-mathyam*—produced from the ocean of milk; *kapaṭa-yuvati-veṣaḥ*—appearing as a false young girl; *mohayan*—captivating; *yaḥ*—

He who; *sura-arīn*—the enemies of the demigods; *tam*—unto Him; *aham*—I; *upasṛtānām*—of the devotees; *kāma-pūram*—who fulfills all desires; *nataḥ asmi*—I offer my respectful obeisances.

TRANSLATION

Assuming the form of a young woman and thus bewildering the demons, the Supreme Personality of Godhead distributed to His devotees, the demigods, the nectar produced from the churning of the ocean of milk. Unto that Supreme Personality of Godhead, who always fulfills the desires of His devotees, I offer my respectful obeisances.

PURPORT

The instruction of this narration concerning the churning of the milk ocean is clearly manifested by the Supreme Personality of Godhead. Although He is equal to everyone, because of natural affection He favors His devotees. The Lord says in *Bhagavad-gītā* (9.29):

samo 'haṁ sarva-bhūteṣu
na me dveṣyo 'sti na priyaḥ
ye bhajanti tu māṁ bhaktyā
mayi te teṣu cāpy aham

"I envy no one, nor am I partial to anyone. I am equal to all. But whoever renders service unto Me in devotion is a friend, is in Me, and I am also a friend to him." This partiality of the Supreme Personality of Godhead is natural. A person cares for his children not because of partiality but in a reciprocation of love. The children depend on the father's affection, and the father affectionately maintains the children. Similarly, because devotees do not know anything but the lotus feet of the Lord, the Lord is always prepared to give protection to His devotees and fulfill their desires. He therefore says, *kaunteya pratijānīhi na me bhaktaḥ praṇaśyati:* "O son of Kuntī, declare it boldly that My devotee never perishes."

Thus end the Bhaktivedanta purports of the Eighth Canto, Twelfth Chapter, of the Śrīmad-Bhāgavatam, *entitled "The Mohinī-mūrti Incarnation Bewilders Lord Śiva."*

CHAPTER THIRTEEN

Description of Future Manus

Of the fourteen Manus, six Manus have already been described. Now, this chapter will consecutively describe each Manu from the seventh to the fourteenth.

The seventh Manu, who is the son of Vivasvān, is known as Śrāddhadeva. He has ten sons, named Ikṣvāku, Nabhaga, Dhṛṣṭa, Śaryāti, Nariṣyanta, Nābhāga, Diṣṭa, Tarūṣa, Pṛṣadhra and Vasumān. In this *manvantara,* or reign of Manu, among the demigods are the Ādityas, Vasus, Rudras, Viśvedevas, Maruts, Aśvinī-kumāras and Ṛbhus. The king of heaven, Indra, is known as Purandara, and the seven sages are known as Kaśyapa, Atri, Vasiṣṭha, Viśvāmitra, Gautama, Jamadagni and Bharadvāja. During this period of Manu, the Supreme Personality of Godhead Viṣṇu appears from the womb of Aditi in His incarnation as the son of Kaśyapa.

In the period of the eighth Manu, the Manu is Sāvarṇi. His sons are headed by Nirmoka, and among the demigods are the Sutapās. Bali, the son of Virocana, is Indra, and Gālava and Paraśurāma are among the seven sages. In this age of Manu, the incarnation of the Supreme Personality of Godhead appears as Sārvabhauma, the son of Devaguhya and Sarasvatī.

In the period of the ninth Manu, the Manu is Dakṣa-sāvarṇi. His sons are headed by Bhūtaketu, and among the demigods are the Marīcigarbhas. Adbhuta is Indra, and among the seven sages is Dyutimān. In this period of Manu, the incarnation Ṛṣabha is born of Āyuṣmān and Ambudhārā.

In the period of the tenth Manu, the Manu is Brahma-sāvarṇi. Among his sons is Bhūriṣeṇa, and the seven sages are Haviṣmān and others. Among the demigods are the Suvāsanas, and Śambhu is Indra. The incarnation in this period of Manu is Viṣvaksena, who is a friend of Śambhu and who is born from the womb of Viṣūcī in the house of a *brāhmaṇa* named Viśvasraṣṭā.

In the period of the eleventh Manu, the Manu is Dharma-sāvarṇi, who has ten sons, headed by Satyadharma. Among the demigods are the Vihaṅgamas, Indra is known as Vaidhṛta, and the seven sages are Aruṇa and others. In this *manvantara,* the incarnation is Dharmasetu, who is born of Vaidhṛtā and Āryaka.

In the period of the twelfth Manu, the Manu is Rudra-sāvarṇi, whose sons are headed by Devavān. The demigods are the Haritas and others, Indra is Ṛtadhāmā, and the seven sages are Tapomūrti and others. The incarnation in this *manvantara* is Sudhāmā, or Svadhāmā, who is born from the womb of Sunṛtā. His father's name is Satyasahā.

In the period of the thirteenth Manu, the Manu is Deva-sāvarṇi. Among his sons is Citrasena, the demigods are the Sukarmās and others, Indra is Divaspati, and Nirmoka is among the sages. The *manvantara-avatāra* is Yogeśvara, who is born of Devahotra and Bṛhatī.

In the period of the fourteenth Manu, the Manu is Indra-sāvarṇi. Anong his sons are Uru and Gambhīra, the demigods are the Pavitras and others, Indra is Śuci, and among the sages are Agni and Bāhu. The incarnation of this *manvantara* is known as Bṛhadbhānu. He is born of Satrāyaṇa from the womb of Vitānā.

The total duration of the periods ruled by these Manus is calculated to be one thousand *catur-yugas,* or 4,300,000 times 1,000 years.

TEXT 1

श्रीशुक उवाच

मनुर्विवस्वतः पुत्रः श्राद्धदेव इति श्रुतः ।
सप्तमो वर्तमानो यस्तदपत्यानि मे शृणु ॥ १ ॥

śrī-śuka uvāca
manur vivasvataḥ putraḥ
śrāddhadeva iti śrutaḥ
saptamo vartamāno yas
tad-apatyāni me śṛṇu

śrī-śukaḥ uvāca—Śrī Śukadeva Gosvāmī said; *manuḥ*—Manu; *vivasvataḥ*—of the sun-god; *putraḥ*—son; *śrāddhadevaḥ*—as

Śrāddhadeva; *iti*—thus; *śrutaḥ*—known, celebrated; *saptamaḥ*—seventh; *vartamānaḥ*—at the present moment; *yaḥ*—he who; *tat*—his; *apatyāni*—children; *me*—from me; *śṛṇu*—just hear.

TRANSLATION

Śukadeva Gosvāmī said: The present Manu, who is named Śrāddhadeva, is the son of Vivasvān, the predominating deity on the sun planet. Śrāddhadeva is the seventh Manu. Now please hear from me as I describe his sons.

TEXTS 2–3

इक्ष्वाकुर्नभगश्चैव धृष्टः शर्यातिरेव च ।
नरिष्यन्तोऽथ नाभागः सप्तमो दिष्ट उच्यते ॥ २ ॥
तरूषश्च पृषध्रश्च दशमो वसुमान्स्मृतः ।
मनोर्वैवस्वतस्यैते दशपुत्राः परन्तप ॥ ३ ॥

ikṣvākur nabhagaś caiva
dhṛṣṭaḥ śaryātir eva ca
nariṣyanto 'tha nābhāgaḥ
saptamo diṣṭa ucyate

tarūṣaś ca pṛṣadhraś ca
daśamo vasumān smṛtaḥ
manor vaivasvatasyaite
daśa-putrāḥ parantapa

ikṣvākuḥ—Ikṣvāku; *nabhagaḥ*—Nabhaga; *ca*—also; *eva*—indeed; *dhṛṣṭaḥ*—Dhṛṣṭa; *śaryātiḥ*—Śaryāti; *eva*—certainly; *ca*—also; *nariṣyantaḥ*—Nariṣyanta; *atha*—as well as; *nābhāgaḥ*—Nābhāga; *saptamaḥ*—the seventh one; *diṣṭaḥ*—Diṣṭa; *ucyate*—is so celebrated; *tarūṣaḥ ca*—and Tarūṣa; *pṛṣadhraḥ ca*—and Pṛṣadhra; *daśamaḥ*—the tenth one; *vasumān*—Vasumān; *smṛtaḥ*—known; *manoḥ*—of Manu; *vaivasvatasya*—of Vaivasvata; *ete*—all these; *daśa-putrāḥ*—ten sons; *parantapa*—O King.

TRANSLATION

O King Parīkṣit, among the ten sons of Manu are Ikṣvāku, Nabhaga, Dhṛṣṭa, Śaryāti, Nariṣyanta and Nābhāga. The seventh son is known as Diṣṭa. Then come Tarūṣa and Pṛṣadhra, and the tenth son is known as Vasumān.

TEXT 4

आदित्या वसवो रुद्रा विश्वेदेवा मरुद्गणाः ।
अश्विनावृभवो राजन्निन्द्रस्तेषां पुरन्दरः ॥ ४ ॥

āditya vasavo rudrā
viśvedevā marud-gaṇāḥ
aśvināv ṛbhavo rājann
indras teṣāṁ purandaraḥ

ādityāḥ—the Ādityas; *vasavaḥ*—the Vasus; *rudrāḥ*—the Rudras; *viśvedevāḥ*—the Viśvedevas; *marut-gaṇāḥ*—and the Maruts; *aśvinau*—the two Aśvinī brothers; *ṛbhavaḥ*—the Ṛbhus; *rājan*—O King; *indraḥ*—the king of heaven; *teṣām*—of them; *purandaraḥ*—Purandara.

TRANSLATION

In this manvantara, O King, the Ādityas, the Vasus, the Rudras, the Viśvedevas, the Maruts, the two Aśvinī-kumāra brothers and the Ṛbhus are the demigods. Their head king [Indra] is Purandara.

TEXT 5

कश्यपोऽत्रिर्वसिष्ठश्च विश्वामित्रोऽथ गौतमः ।
जमदग्निर्भरद्वाज इति सप्तर्षयः स्मृताः ॥ ५ ॥

kaśyapo 'trir vasiṣṭhaś ca
viśvāmitro 'tha gautamaḥ
jamadagnir bharadvāja
iti saptarṣayaḥ smṛtāḥ

kaśyapaḥ—Kaśyapa; *atriḥ*—Atri; *vasiṣṭhaḥ*—Vasiṣṭha; *ca*—and; *viśvāmitraḥ*—Viśvāmitra; *atha*—as well as; *gautamaḥ*—Gautama;

jamadagniḥ—Jamadagni; *bharadvājaḥ*—Bharadvāja; *iti*—thus; *saptarṣayaḥ*—the seven sages; *smṛtāḥ*—celebrated.

TRANSLATION

Kaśyapa, Atri, Vasiṣṭha, Viśvāmitra, Gautama, Jamadagni and Bharadvāja are known as the seven sages.

TEXT 6

अत्रापि भगवज्जन्म कश्यपाददितेरभूत् ।
आदित्यानामवरजो विष्णुर्वामनरूपधृक् ॥ ६ ॥

atrāpi bhagavaj-janma
kaśyapād aditer abhūt
ādityānām avarajo
viṣṇur vāmana-rūpa-dhṛk

atra—in this Manu's reign; *api*—certainly; *bhagavat-janma*—appearance of the Supreme Personality of Godhead; *kaśyapāt*—by Kaśyapa Muni; *aditeḥ*—of mother Aditi; *abhūt*—became possible; *ādityānām*—of the Ādityas; *avara-jaḥ*—the youngest; *viṣṇuḥ*—Lord Viṣṇu Himself; *vāmana-rūpa-dhṛk*—appearing as Lord Vāmana.

TRANSLATION

In this manvantara, the Supreme Personality of Godhead appeared as the youngest of all the Ādityas, known as Vāmana, the dwarf. His father was Kaśyapa and His mother Aditi.

TEXT 7

संक्षेपतो मयोक्तानि सप्तमन्वन्तराणि ते ।
भविष्याण्यथ वक्ष्यामि विष्णोः शक्त्यान्वितानि च ॥७॥

saṅkṣepato mayoktāni
sapta-manvantarāṇi te
bhaviṣyāṇy atha vakṣyāmi
viṣṇoḥ śaktyānvitāni ca

saṅkṣepataḥ—in brief; *mayā*—by me; *uktāni*—explained; *sapta*—seven; *manu-antarāṇi*—changes of Manu; *te*—unto you; *bhaviṣyāṇi*—the future Manus; *atha*—also; *vakṣyāmi*—I shall speak; *viṣṇoḥ*—of Lord Viṣṇu; *śaktyā anvitāni*—empowered by the energy; *ca*—also.

TRANSLATION

I have briefly explained to you the position of the seven Manus. Now I shall describe the future Manus, along with the incarnations of Lord Viṣṇu.

TEXT 8

विवस्वतश्च द्वे जाये विश्वकर्मसुते उभे ।
संज्ञा छाया च राजेन्द्र ये प्रागभिहिते तव ॥ ८ ॥

vivasvataś ca dve jāye
viśvakarma-sute ubhe
saṁjñā chāyā ca rājendra
ye prāg abhihite tava

vivasvataḥ—of Vivasvān; *ca*—also; *dve*—two; *jāye*—wives; *viśvakarma-sute*—the two daughters of Viśvakarmā; *ubhe*—both of them; *saṁjñā*—Saṁjñā; *chāyā*—Chāyā; *ca*—and; *rāja-indra*—O King; *ye*—both of whom; *prāk*—before; *abhihite*—described; *tava*—unto you.

TRANSLATION

O King, I have previously described [in the Sixth Canto] the two daughters of Viśvakarmā, named Saṁjñā and Chāyā, who were the first two wives of Vivasvān.

TEXT 9

तृतीयां वडवामेके तासां संज्ञासुतास्त्रयः ।
यमो यमी श्राद्धदेवश्छायायाश्च सुतान्छृणु ॥ ९ ॥

tṛtīyāṁ vaḍavām eke
tāsāṁ saṁjñā-sutās trayaḥ

yamo yamī śrāddhadevaś
chāyāyāś ca sutāñ chṛṇu

tṛtīyām—the third wife; *vaḍavām*—Vaḍavā; *eke*—some people; *tāsām*—of all three wives; *saṁjñā-sutāḥ trayaḥ*—three issues of Saṁjñā; *yamaḥ*—one son named Yama; *yamī*—Yamī, a daughter; *śrāddhadevaḥ*—Śrāddhadeva, another son; *chāyāyāḥ*—of Chāyā; *ca*—and; *sutān*—the sons; *śṛṇu*—just hear about.

TRANSLATION

It is said that the sun-god had a third wife, named Vaḍavā. Of the three wives, the wife named Saṁjñā had three children—Yama, Yamī and Śrāddhadeva. Now let me describe the children of Chāyā.

TEXT 10

सावर्णिस्तपती कन्या भार्या संवरणस्य या ।
शनैश्चरस्तृतीयोऽभूदश्विनौ वडवात्मजौ ॥१०॥

sāvarṇis tapatī kanyā
bhāryā saṁvaraṇasya yā
śanaiścaras tṛtīyo 'bhūd
aśvinau vaḍavātmajau

sāvarṇiḥ—Sāvarṇi; *tapatī*—Tapatī; *kanyā*—the daughter; *bhāryā*—the wife; *saṁvaraṇasya*—of King Saṁvaraṇa; *yā*—she who; *śanaiścaraḥ*—Śanaiścara; *tṛtīyaḥ*—the third issue; *abhūt*—took birth; *aśvinau*—the two Aśvinī-kumāras; *vaḍavā-ātma-jau*—the sons of the wife known as Vaḍavā.

TRANSLATION

Chāyā had a son named Sāvarṇi and a daughter named Tapatī, who later became the wife of King Saṁvaraṇa. Chāyā's third child is known as Śanaiścara [Saturn]. Vaḍavā gave birth to two sons, namely the Aśvinī brothers.

TEXT 11

अष्टमेऽन्तर आयाते सावर्णिर्भविता मनुः ।
निर्मोकविरजस्काद्याः सावर्णितनया नृप ॥११॥

aṣṭame 'ntara āyāte
sāvarṇir bhavitā manuḥ
nirmoka-virajaskādyāḥ
sāvarṇi-tanayā nṛpa

aṣṭame—the eighth; *antare*—Manu's period; *āyāte*—when arrived; *sāvarṇiḥ*—Sāvarṇi; *bhavitā*—will become; *manuḥ*—the eighth Manu; *nirmoka*—Nirmoka; *virajaska-ādyāḥ*—Virajaska and others; *sāvarṇi*—of Sāvarṇi; *tanayāḥ*—the sons; *nṛpa*—O King.

TRANSLATION

O King, when the period of the eighth Manu arrives, Sāvarṇi will become the Manu. Nirmoka and Virajaska will be among his sons.

PURPORT

The present reign is that of Vaivasvata Manu. According to astronomical calculations, we are now in the twenth-eighth *yuga* of Vaivasvata Manu. Each Manu lives for seventy-one *yugas*, and fourteen such Manus rule in one day of Lord Brahmā. We are now in the period of Vaivasvata Manu, the seventh Manu, and the eighth Manu will come into existence after many millions of years. But Śukadeva Gosvāmī, having heard from authorities, foretells that the eighth Manu will be Sāvarṇi and that Nirmoka and Virajaska will be among his sons. *Śāstra* can foretell what will happen millions and millions of years in the future.

TEXT 12

तत्र देवाः सुतपसो विरजा अमृतप्रभाः ।
तेषां विरोचनसुतो बलिरिन्द्रो भविष्यति ॥१२॥

tatra devāḥ sutapaso
virājā amṛtaprabhāḥ

teṣāṁ virocana-suto
balir indro bhaviṣyati

tatra—in that period of Manu; *devāḥ*—the demigods; *sutapasaḥ*—the Sutapās; *virajāḥ*—the Virajas; *amṛtaprabhāḥ*—the Amṛtaprabhas; *teṣām*—of them; *virocana-sutaḥ*—the son of Virocana; *baliḥ*—Mahārāja Bali; *indraḥ*—the king of heaven; *bhaviṣyati*—will become.

TRANSLATION

In the period of the eighth Manu, among the demigods will be the Sutapās, the Virajas and the Amṛtaprabhas. The king of the demigods, Indra, will be Bali Mahārāja, the son of Virocana.

TEXT 13

दत्त्वेमां याचमानाय विष्णवे यः पदत्रयम् ।
राद्धमिन्द्रपदं हित्वा ततः सिद्धिमवाप्स्यति ॥१३॥

dattvemāṁ yācamānāya
viṣṇave yaḥ pada-trayam
rāddham indra-padaṁ hitvā
tataḥ siddhim avāpsyati

dattvā—giving in charity; *imām*—this entire universe; *yācamānāya*—who was begging from him; *viṣṇave*—unto Lord Viṣṇu; *yaḥ*—Bali Mahārāja; *pada-trayam*—three paces of land; *rāddham*—achieved; *indra-padam*—the post of Indra; *hitvā*—giving up; *tataḥ*—thereafter; *siddhim*—perfection; *avāpsyati*—will achieve.

TRANSLATION

Bali Mahārāja gave a gift of three paces of land to Lord Viṣṇu, and because of this charity he lost all the three worlds. Later, however, when Lord Viṣṇu is pleased because of Bali's giving everything to Him, Bali Mahārāja will achieve the perfection of life.

PURPORT

In *Bhagavad-gītā* (7.3) it is stated, *manuṣyāṇāṁ sahasreṣu kaścid yatati siddhaye:* out of many millions of people, one may attempt to achieve success in life. This success is explained here. *Rāddham indra-padaṁ hitvā tataḥ siddhim avāpsyati. Siddhi* consists of achieving the favor of Lord Viṣṇu, not the *yoga-siddhis.* The *yoga-siddhis—aṇimā, laghimā, mahimā, prāpti, prākāmya, īśitva, vaśitva* and *kāmā-vasāyitā*—are temporary. The ultimate *siddhi* is to achieve the favor of Lord Viṣṇu.

TEXT 14

योऽसौ भगवता बद्धः प्रीतेन सुतले पुनः ।
निवेशितोऽधिके स्वर्गादधुनास्ते स्वराडिव ॥१४॥

yo 'sau bhagavatā baddhaḥ
prītena sutale punaḥ
niveśito 'dhike svargād
adhunāste sva-rāḍ iva

yaḥ—Bali Mahārāja; *asau*—he; *bhagavatā*—by the Personality of Godhead; *baddhaḥ*—bound; *prītena*—because of favor; *sutale*—in the kingdom of Sutala; *punaḥ*—again; *niveśitaḥ*—situated; *adhike*—more opulent; *svargāt*—than the heavenly planets; *adhunā*—at the present moment; *āste*—is situated; *sva-rāṭ iva*—equal to the position of Indra.

TRANSLATION

With great affection, the Personality of Godhead bound Bali and then installed him in the kingdom of Sutala, which is more opulent than the heavenly planets. Mahārāja Bali now resides on that planet and is more comfortably situated than Indra.

TEXTS 15–16

गालवो दीप्तिमान्रामो द्रोणपुत्रः कृपस्तथा ।
ऋष्यशृङ्गः पितास्माकं भगवान्बादरायणः ॥१५॥

इमे सप्तर्षयस्तत्र भविष्यन्ति स्वयोगतः ।
इदानीमासते राजन् स्वे स्व आश्रममण्डले ॥१६॥

gālavo dīptimān rāmo
droṇa-putraḥ kṛpas tathā
ṛṣyaśṛṅgaḥ pitāsmākaṁ
bhagavān bādarāyaṇaḥ

ime saptarṣayas tatra
bhaviṣyanti sva-yogataḥ
idānīm āsate rājan
sve sva āśrama-maṇḍale

gālavaḥ—Gālava; *dīptimān*—Dīptimān; *rāmaḥ*—Paraśurāma; *droṇa-putraḥ*—the son of Droṇācārya, namely Aśvatthāmā; *kṛpaḥ*—Kṛpācārya; *tathā*—as well; *ṛṣyaśṛṅgaḥ*—Ṛṣyaśṛṅga; *pitā asmākam*—our father; *bhagavān*—the incarnation of Godhead; *bādarāyaṇaḥ*—Vyāsadeva; *ime*—all of them; *sapta-ṛṣayaḥ*—the seven sages; *tatra*—in the eighth *manvantara; bhaviṣyanti*—will become; *sva-yogataḥ*—as a result of their service to the Lord; *idānīm*—at the present moment; *āsate*—they are all existing; *rājan*—O King; *sve sve*—in their own; *āśrama-maṇḍale*—different hermitages.

TRANSLATION

O King, during the eighth manvantara, the great personalities Gālava, Dīptimān, Paraśurāma, Aśvatthāmā, Kṛpācārya, Ṛṣyaśṛṅga and our father, Vyāsadeva, the incarnation of Nārāyaṇa, will be the seven sages. For the present, they are all residing in their respective āśramas.

TEXT 17

देवगुह्यात्सरस्वत्यां सार्वभौम इति प्रभुः ।
स्थानं पुरन्दराद्धृत्वा बलये दास्यतीश्वरः ॥१७॥

devaguhyāt sarasvatyāṁ
sārvabhauma iti prabhuḥ

sthānaṁ purandarād dhṛtvā
balaye dāsyatīśvaraḥ

devaguhyāt—from His father, Devaguhya; *sarasvatyām*—in the womb of Sarasvatī; *sārvabhaumaḥ*—Sārvabhauma; *iti*—thus; *prabhuḥ*—the master; *sthānam*—place; *purandarāt*—from Lord Indra; *hṛtvā*—taking away by force; *balaye*—unto Bali Mahārāja; *dāsyati*—will give; *īśvaraḥ*—the master.

TRANSLATION

In the eighth manvantara, the greatly powerful Personality of Godhead Sārvabhauma will take birth. His father will be Devaguhya, and His mother will be Sarasvatī. He will take the kingdom away from Purandara [Lord Indra] and give it to Bali Mahārāja.

TEXT 18

नवमो दक्षसावर्णिर्मनुर्वरुणसम्भवः ।
भूतकेतुर्दीप्तकेतुरित्याद्यास्तत्सुता नृप ॥१८॥

navamo dakṣa-sāvarṇir
manur varuṇa-sambhavaḥ
bhūtaketur dīptaketur
ity ādyās tat-sutā nṛpa

navamaḥ—ninth; *dakṣa-sāvarṇiḥ*—Dakṣa-sāvarṇi; *manuḥ*—the Manu; *varuṇa-sambhavaḥ*—born as the son of Varuṇa; *bhūtaketuḥ*—Bhūtaketu; *dīptaketuḥ*—Dīptaketu; *iti*—thus; *ādyāḥ*—and so on; *tat*—his; *sutāḥ*—sons; *nṛpa*—O King.

TRANSLATION

O King, the ninth Manu will be Dakṣa-sāvarṇi, who is born of Varuṇa. Among his sons will be Bhūtaketu, and Dīptaketu.

TEXT 19

पारामरीचिगर्भाद्या देवा इन्द्रोऽद्भुतः स्मृतः ।
द्युतिमत्प्रमुखास्तत्र भविष्यन्त्यृषयस्ततः ॥१९॥

pārā-marīcigarbhādyā
devā indro 'dbhutaḥ smṛtaḥ
dyutimat-pramukhās tatra
bhaviṣyanty ṛṣayas tataḥ

pārā—the Pāras; *marīcigarbha*—the Marīcigarbhas; *ādyāḥ*—like that; *devāḥ*—the demigods; *indraḥ*—the king of heaven; *adbhutaḥ*—Adbhuta; *smṛtaḥ*—known; *dyutimat*—Dyutimān; *pramukhāḥ*—headed by; *tatra*—in that ninth period of Manu; *bhaviṣyanti*—will become; *ṛṣayaḥ*—the seven *ṛṣis; tataḥ*—then.

TRANSLATION

In this ninth manvantara, the Pāras and Marīcigarbhas will be among the demigods. The king of heaven, Indra, will be named Adbhuta, and Dyutimān will be among the seven sages.

TEXT 20

आयुष्मतोऽम्बुधारायामृषभो भगवत्कला ।
भविता येन संराद्धां त्रिलोकीं भोक्ष्यतेऽद्भुतः ॥२०॥

āyuṣmato 'mbudhārāyām
ṛṣabho bhagavat-kalā
bhavitā yena saṁrāddhāṁ
tri-lokīṁ bhokṣyate 'dbhutaḥ

āyuṣmataḥ—of the father, Āyuṣmān; *ambudhārāyām*—in the womb of the mother, Ambudhārā; *ṛṣabhaḥ*—Ṛṣabha; *bhagavat-kalā*—a partial incarnation of the Supreme Personality of Godhead; *bhavitā*—will be; *yena*—by whom; *saṁrāddhām*—all-opulent; *tri-lokīm*—the three worlds; *bhokṣyate*—will enjoy; *adbhutaḥ*—the Indra of the name Adbhuta.

TRANSLATION

Ṛṣabhadeva, a partial incarnation of the Supreme Personality of Godhead, will take birth from his father, Āyuṣmān, and his mother, Ambudhārā. He will enable the Indra named Adbhuta to enjoy the opulence of the three worlds.

TEXT 21

दशमो ब्रह्मसावर्णिरुपश्लोकसुतो मनुः ।
तत्सुता भूरिषेणाद्या हविष्मत्प्रमुखा द्विजाः ॥२१॥

daśamo brahma-sāvarṇir
upaśloka-suto manuḥ
tat-sutā bhūriṣeṇādyā
haviṣmat pramukhā dvijāḥ

daśamaḥ—the tenth Manu; *brahma-sāvarṇiḥ*—Brahma-sāvarṇi; *upaśloka-sutaḥ*—born of Upaśloka; *manuḥ*—will be Manu; *tat-sutāḥ*—his sons; *bhūriṣeṇa-ādyāḥ*—Bhūriṣeṇa and others; *haviṣmat*—Haviṣmān; *pramukhāḥ*—headed by; *dvijāḥ*—the seven sages.

TRANSLATION

The son of Upaśloka known as Brahma-sāvarṇi will be the tenth Manu. Bhūriṣeṇa will be among his sons, and the brāhmaṇas headed by Haviṣmān will be the seven sages.

TEXT 22

हविष्मान्सुकृतः सत्यो जयो मूर्तिस्तदा द्विजाः ।
सुवासनविरुद्धाद्या देवाः शम्भुः सुरेश्वरः ॥२२॥

haviṣmān sukṛtaḥ satyo
jayo mūrtis tadā dvijāḥ
suvāsana-viruddhādyā
devāḥ śambhuḥ sureśvaraḥ

haviṣmān—Haviṣmān; *sukṛtaḥ*—Sukṛta; *satyaḥ*—Satya; *jayaḥ*—Jaya; *mūrtiḥ*—Mūrti; *tadā*—at that time; *dvijāḥ*—the seven sages;

suvāsana—the Suvāsanas; *viruddha*—the Viruddhas; *ādyāḥ*—and so on; *devāḥ*—the demigods; *śambhuḥ*—Śambhu; *sura-īśvaraḥ*—Indra, king of the demigods.

TRANSLATION

Haviṣmān, Sukṛta, Satya, Jaya, Mūrti and others will be the seven sages, the Suvāsanas and Viruddhas will be among the demigods, and Śambhu will be their king, Indra.

TEXT 23

विष्वक्सेनो विषूच्यां तु शम्भोः सख्यं करिष्यति ।
जातः स्वांशेन भगवान्गृहे विश्वसृजो विभुः ॥२३॥

viṣvakseno viṣūcyāṁ tu
śambhoḥ sakhyaṁ kariṣyati
jātaḥ svāṁśena bhagavān
gṛhe viśvasṛjo vibhuḥ

viṣvaksenaḥ—Viṣvaksena; *viṣūcyām*—in the womb of Viṣūcī; *tu*—then; *śambhoḥ*—of Śambhu; *sakhyam*—friendship; *kariṣyati*—will create; *jātaḥ*—being born; *sva-aṁśena*—by a plenary portion; *bhagavān*—the Supreme Personality of Godhead; *gṛhe*—in the home; *viśvasṛjaḥ*—of Viśvasraṣṭā; *vibhuḥ*—the supremely powerful Lord.

TRANSLATION

In the home of Viśvasraṣṭā, a plenary portion of the Supreme Personality of Godhead will appear from the womb of Viṣūcī as the incarnation known as Viṣvaksena. He will make friends with Śambhu.

TEXT 24

मनुर्वै धर्मसावर्णिरेकादशम आत्मवान् ।
अनागतास्तत्सुताश्च सत्यधर्मादयो दश ॥२४॥

manur vai dharma-sāvarṇir
ekādaśama ātmavān

anāgatās tat-sutāś ca
satyadharmādayo daśa

manuḥ—the Manu; *vai*—indeed; *dharma-sāvarṇiḥ*—Dharma-sāvarṇi; *ekādaśamaḥ*—eleventh; *ātmavān*—the controller of the senses; *anāgatāḥ*—will come in the future; *tat*—his; *sutāḥ*—sons; *ca*—and; *satyadharma-ādayaḥ*—Satyadharma and others; *daśa*—ten.

TRANSLATION

In the eleventh manvantara, the Manu will be Dharma-sāvarṇi, who will be extremely learned in spiritual knowledge. From him there will come ten sons, headed by Satyadharma.

TEXT 25

विहङ्गमाः कामगमा निर्वाणरुचयः सुराः ।
इन्द्रश्च वैधृतस्तेषामृषयश्चारुणादयः ॥२५॥

vihaṅgamāḥ kāmagamā
nirvāṇarucayaḥ surāḥ
indraś ca vaidhṛtas teṣām
ṛṣayaś cāruṇādayaḥ

vihaṅgamāḥ—the Vihaṅgamas; *kāmagamāḥ*—the Kāmagamas; *nirvāṇarucayaḥ*—the Nirvāṇarucis; *surāḥ*—the demigods; *indraḥ*—the king of heaven, Indra; *ca*—also; *vaidhṛtaḥ*—Vaidhṛta; *teṣām*—of them; *ṛṣayaḥ*—the seven sages; *ca*—also; *aruṇa-ādayaḥ*—headed by Aruṇa.

TRANSLATION

The Vihaṅgamas, Kāmagamas, Nirvāṇarucis and others will be the demigods. The king of the demigods, Indra, will be Vaidhṛta, and the seven sages will be headed by Aruṇa.

TEXT 26

आर्यकस्य सुतस्तत्र धर्मसेतुरिति स्मृतः ।
वैधृतायां हरेरंशस्त्रिलोकीं धारयिष्यति ॥२६॥

āryakasya sutas tatra
dharmasetur iti smṛtaḥ
vaidhṛtāyāṁ harer aṁśas
tri-lokīṁ dhārayiṣyati

āryakasya—of Āryaka; *sutaḥ*—the son; *tatra*—in that period (the eleventh *manvantara*); *dharmasetuḥ*—Dharmasetu; *iti*—thus; *smṛtaḥ*—celebrated; *vaidhṛtāyām*—from the mother, Vaidhṛtā; *hareḥ*—of the Supreme Personality of Godhead; *aṁśaḥ*—a partial incarnation; *tri-lokīm*—the three worlds; *dhārayiṣyati*—will rule.

TRANSLATION

The son of Āryaka known as Dharmasetu, a partial incarnation of the Supreme Personality of Godhead, will appear from the womb of Vaidhṛtā, the wife of Āryaka, and will rule the three worlds.

TEXT 27

भविता रुद्रसावर्णी राजन्द्वादशमो मनुः ।
देववानुपदेवश्च देवश्रेष्ठादयः सुताः ॥२७॥

bhavitā rudra-sāvarṇī
rājan dvādaśamo manuḥ
devavān upadevaś ca
devaśreṣṭhādayaḥ sutāḥ

bhavitā—will appear; *rudra-sāvarṇiḥ*—Rudra-sāvarṇi; *rājan*—O King; *dvādaśamaḥ*—the twelfth; *manuḥ*—Manu; *devavān*—Devavān; *upadevaḥ*—Upadeva; *ca*—and; *devaśreṣṭha*—Devaśreṣṭha; *ādayaḥ*—such persons; *sutāḥ*—sons of the Manu.

TRANSLATION

O King, the twelfth Manu will be named Rudra-sāvarṇi. Devavān, Upadeva and Devaśreṣṭha will be among his sons.

TEXT 28

ऋतधामा च तत्रेन्द्रो देवाश्च हरितादयः ।
ऋषयश्च तपोमूर्तिस्तपस्व्याग्नीध्रकादयः ॥२८॥

ṛtadhāmā ca tatrendro
devāś ca haritādayaḥ
ṛṣayaś ca tapomūrtis
tapasvy āgnīdhrakādayaḥ

ṛtadhāmā—Ṛtadhāmā; *ca*—also; *tatra*—in that period; *indraḥ*—the king of heaven; *devāḥ*—the demigods; *ca*—and; *harita-ādayaḥ*—headed by the Haritas; *ṛṣayaḥ ca*—and the seven sages; *tapomūrtiḥ*—Tapomūrti; *tapasvī*—Tapasvī; *āgnīdhraka*—Āgnīdhraka; *ādayaḥ*—and so on.

TRANSLATION

In this manvantara, the name of Indra will be Ṛtadhāmā, and the demigods will be headed by the Haritas. Among the sages will be Tapomūrti, Tapasvī and Āgnīdhraka.

TEXT 29

स्वधामाख्यो हरेरंशः साधयिष्यति तन्मनोः ।
अन्तरं सत्यसहसः सुनृतायाः सुतो विभुः ॥२९॥

svadhāmākhyo harer aṁśaḥ
sādhayiṣyati tan-manoḥ
antaraṁ satyasahasaḥ
sunṛtāyāḥ suto vibhuḥ

svadhāmā-ākhyaḥ—Svadhāmā; *hareḥ aṁśaḥ*—a partial incarnation of the Supreme Personality of Godhead; *sādhayiṣyati*—will rule; *tat-manoḥ*—of that Manu; *antaram*—the *manvantara; satyasahasaḥ*—of Satyasahā; *sunṛtāyāḥ*—of Sunṛtā; *sutaḥ*—the son; *vibhuḥ*—most powerful.

TRANSLATION

From the mother named Sunṛtā and the father named Satyasahā will come Svadhāmā, a partial incarnation of the Supreme Personality of Godhead. He will rule that manvantara.

TEXT 30

मनुस्त्रयोदशो भाव्यो देवसावर्णिरात्मवान् ।
चित्रसेनविचित्राद्या देवसावर्णिदेहजाः ॥३०॥

manus trayodaśo bhāvyo
deva-sāvarṇir ātmavān
citrasena-vicitrādyā
deva-sāvarṇi-dehajāḥ

manuḥ—the Manu; *trayodaśaḥ*—thirteenth; *bhāvyaḥ*—will become; *deva-sāvarṇiḥ*—Deva-sāvarṇi; *ātmavān*—well advanced in spiritual knowledge; *citrasena*—Citrasena; *vicitra-ādyāḥ*—and others, like Vicitra; *deva-sāvarṇi*—of Deva-sāvarṇi; *deha-jāḥ*—sons.

TRANSLATION

The thirteenth Manu will be named Deva-sāvarṇi, and he will be very advanced in spiritual knowledge. Among his sons will be Citrasena and Vicitra.

TEXT 31

देवाः सुकर्मसुत्रामसंज्ञा इन्द्रो दिवस्पतिः ।
निर्मोकतत्त्वदर्शाद्या भविष्यन्त्यृषयस्तदा ॥३१॥

devāḥ sukarma-sutrāma-
saṁjñā indro divaspatiḥ
nirmoka-tattvadarśādyā
bhaviṣyanty ṛṣayas tadā

devāḥ—the demigods; *sukarma*—the Sukarmās; *sutrāma-saṁjñāḥ*—and the Sutrāmas; *indraḥ*—the king of heaven; *divaspatiḥ*—Divaspati;

nirmoka—Nirmoka; *tattvadarśa-ādyāḥ*—and others, like Tattvadarśa; *bhaviṣyanti*—will become; *ṛṣayaḥ*—the seven sages; *tadā*—at that time.

TRANSLATION

In the thirteenth manvantara, the Sukarmās and Sutrāmās will be among the demigods, Divaspati will be the king of heaven, and Nirmoka and Tattvadarśa will be among the seven sages.

TEXT 32

देवहोत्रस्य तनय उपहर्ता दिवस्पतेः ।
योगेश्वरो हरेरंशो बृहत्यां सम्भविष्यति ॥३२॥

devahotrasya tanaya
upahartā divaspateḥ
yogeśvaro harer aṁśo
bṛhatyāṁ sambhaviṣyati

devahotrasya—of Devahotra; *tanayaḥ*—the son; *upahartā*—the benefactor; *divaspateḥ*—of Divaspati, the Indra at that time; *yoga-īśvaraḥ*—Yogeśvara, the master of mystic powers; *hareḥ aṁśaḥ*—a partial representation of the Supreme Personality of Godhead; *bṛhatyām*—in the womb of his mother, Bṛhatī; *sambhaviṣyati*—will appear.

TRANSLATION

The son of Devahotra known as Yogeśvara will appear as a partial incarnation of the Supreme Personality of Godhead. His mother's name will be Bṛhatī. He will perform activities for the welfare of Divaspati.

TEXT 33

मनुर्वा इन्द्रसावर्णिश्चतुर्दशम एष्यति ।
उरुगम्भीरबुदाद्या इन्द्रसावर्णिवीर्यजाः ॥३३॥

manur vā indra-sāvarṇiś
caturdaśama eṣyati

uru-gambhīra-budhādyā
indra-sāvarṇi-vīryajāḥ

manuḥ—the Manu; *vā*—either; *indra-sāvarṇiḥ*—Indra-sāvarṇi; *caturdaśamaḥ*—fourteenth; *eṣyati*—will become; *uru*—Uru; *gambhīra*—Gambhīra; *budha-ādyāḥ*—and others, such as Budha; *indra-sāvarṇi*—of Indra-sāvarṇi; *vīrya-jāḥ*—born of the semen.

TRANSLATION

The name of the fourteenth Manu will be Indra-sāvarṇi. He will have sons like Uru, Gambhīra and Budha.

TEXT 34

पवित्राश्चाक्षुषा देवाः शुचिरिन्द्रो भविष्यति ।
अग्निर्बाहुः शुचिः शुद्धो मागधाद्यास्तपस्विनः ॥३४॥

pavitrāś cākṣuṣā devāḥ
śucir indro bhaviṣyati
agnir bāhuḥ śuciḥ śuddho
māgadhādyās tapasvinaḥ

pavitrāḥ—the Pavitras; *cākṣuṣāḥ*—the Cākṣuṣas; *devāḥ*—the demigods; *śuciḥ*—Śuci; *indraḥ*—the king of heaven; *bhaviṣyati*—will become; *agniḥ*—Agni; *bāhuḥ*—Bāhu; *śuciḥ*—Śuci; *śuddhaḥ*—Śuddha; *māgadha*—Māgadha; *ādyāḥ*—and so on; *tapasvinaḥ*—the sages.

TRANSLATION

The Pavitras and Cākṣuṣas will be among the demigods, and Śuci will be Indra, the king of heaven. Agni, Bāhu, Śuci, Śuddha, Māgadha and others of great austerity will be the seven sages.

TEXT 35

सत्रायणस्य तनयो बृहद्भानुस्तदा हरिः ।
वितानायां महाराज क्रियातन्तून्वितायिता ॥३५॥

satrāyaṇasya tanayo
bṛhadbhānus tadā hariḥ
vitānāyāṁ mahārāja
kriyā-tantūn vitāyitā

satrāyaṇasya—of Satrāyaṇa; *tanayaḥ*—the son; *bṛhadbhānuḥ*—Bṛhadbhānu; *tadā*—at that time; *hariḥ*—the Supreme Personality of Godhead; *vitānāyām*—in the womb of Vitānā; *mahā-rāja*—O King; *kriyā-tantūn*—all spiritual activities; *vitāyitā*—will perform.

TRANSLATION

O King Parīkṣit, in the fourteenth manvantara the Supreme Personality of Godhead will appear from the womb of Vitānā, and His father's name will be Satrāyaṇa. This incarnation will be celebrated as Bṛhadbhānu, and He will administer spiritual activities.

TEXT 36

राजंश्चतुर्दशैतानि त्रिकालानुगतानि ते ।
प्रोक्तान्येभिर्मितः कल्पो युगसाहस्रपर्ययः ॥३६॥

rājaṁś caturdaśaitāni
tri-kālānugatāni te
proktāny ebhir mitaḥ kalpo
yuga-sāhasra-paryayaḥ

rājan—O King; *caturdaśa*—fourteen; *etāni*—all these; *tri-kāla*—the three periods of time (past, present and future); *anugatāni*—covering; *te*—to you; *proktāni*—described; *ebhiḥ*—by these; *mitaḥ*—estimated; *kalpaḥ*—one day of Brahmā; *yuga-sāhasra*—one thousand cycles of four *yugas; paryayaḥ*—consisting of.

TRANSLATION

O King, I have now described to you the fourteen Manus appearing in the past, present and future. The total duration of time

ruled by these Manus is one thousand yuga cycles. This is called a kalpa, or one day of Lord Brahmā.

Thus end the Bhaktivedanta purports of the Eighth Canto, Thirteenth Chapter, of the Śrīmad-Bhāgavatam, *entitled "Description of Future Manus."*

CHAPTER FOURTEEN

The System of Universal Management

This chapter describes the duties allotted to Manu by the Supreme Personality of Godhead. All the Manus, as well as their sons, the sages, the demigods and the Indras, act under the orders of various incarnations of the Supreme Personality of Godhead. At the end of every *catur-yuga*, consisting of Satya-yuga, Dvāpara-yuga, Tretā-yuga and Kali-yuga, the sages, acting under the orders of the Supreme Personality of Godhead, distribute the Vedic knowledge and thus reinstate eternal religious principles. Manu's duty is to reestablish the system of religion. Manu's sons execute Manu's orders, and thus the entire universe is maintained by Manu and his descendants. The Indras are various rulers of the heavenly planets. Assisted by the demigods, they rule the three worlds. The Supreme Personality of Godhead also appears as incarnations in different *yugas*. He appears as Sanaka, Sanātana, Yājñavalkya, Dattātreya and others, and thus He gives instructions in spiritual knowledge, prescribed duties, principles of mystic *yoga*, and so on. As Marīci and others, He creates progeny; as the king, He punishes the miscreants; and in the form of time, He annihilates the creation. One may argue, "If the all-powerful Supreme Personality of Godhead can do anything simply by His will, why has He arranged for so many personalities to manage?" How and why He does this cannot be understood by those who are under the clutches of *māyā*.

TEXT 1

श्रीराजोवाच

मन्वन्तरेषु भगवन्यथा मन्वादयस्त्विमे ।
यस्मिन्कर्मणि ये येन नियुक्तास्तद्वदस्व मे ॥ १ ॥

śrī-rājovāca
manvantareṣu bhagavan
yathā manv-ādayas tv ime

yasmin karmaṇi ye yena
niyuktās tad vadasva me

śrī-rājā uvāca—King Parīkṣit said; *manvantareṣu*—in the reign of each Manu; *bhagavan*—O great sage; *yathā*—as; *manu-ādayaḥ*—the Manus and others; *tu*—but; *ime*—these; *yasmin*—in which; *karmaṇi*—activities; *ye*—which persons; *yena*—by whom; *niyuktāḥ*—appointed; *tat*—that; *vadasva*—kindly describe; *me*—to me.

TRANSLATION

Mahārāja Parīkṣit inquired: O most opulent Śukadeva Gosvāmī, please explain to me how Manu and the others in each manvantara are engaged in their respective duties, and by whose order they are so engaged.

TEXT 2

श्रीऋषिरुवाच
मनवो मनुपुत्राश्च मुनयश्च महीपते ।
इन्द्राः सुरगणाश्चैव सर्वे पुरुषशासनाः ॥ २ ॥

śrī-ṛṣir uvāca
manavo manu-putrāś ca
munayaś ca mahī-pate
indrāḥ sura-gaṇāś caiva
sarve puruṣa-śāsanāḥ

śrī-ṛṣiḥ uvāca—Śrī Śukadeva Gosvāmī said; *manavaḥ*—all the Manus; *manu-putrāḥ*—all the sons of Manu; *ca*—and; *munayaḥ*—all the great sages; *ca*—and; *mahī-pate*—O King; *indrāḥ*—all the Indras; *sura-gaṇāḥ*—the demigods; *ca*—and; *eva*—certainly; *sarve*—all of them; *puruṣa-śāsanāḥ*—under the rule of the Supreme Person.

TRANSLATION

Śukadeva Gosvāmī said: The Manus, the sons of Manu, the great sages, the Indras and all the demigods, O King, are appointed by

the Supreme Personality of Godhead in His various incarnations such as Yajña.

TEXT 3

यज्ञादयो याः कथिताः पौरुष्यस्तनवो नृप ।
मन्वादयो जगद्यात्रां नयन्त्याभिः प्रचोदिताः॥ ३ ॥

yajñādayo yāḥ kathitāḥ
pauruṣyas tanavo nṛpa
manv-ādayo jagad-yātrāṁ
nayanty ābhiḥ pracoditāḥ

yajña-ādayaḥ—the Lord's incarnation known as Yajña and others; *yāḥ*—who; *kathitāḥ*—already spoken of; *pauruṣyaḥ*—of the Supreme Person; *tanavaḥ*—incarnations; *nṛpa*—O King; *manu-ādayaḥ*—the Manus and others; *jagat-yātrām*—universal affairs; *nayanti*—conduct; *ābhiḥ*—by the incarnations; *pracoditāḥ*—being inspired.

TRANSLATION

O King, I have already described to you various incarnations of the Lord, such as Yajña. The Manus and others are chosen by these incarnations, under whose direction they conduct the universal affairs.

PURPORT

The Manus execute the orders of the Supreme Personality of Godhead in His various incarnations.

TEXT 4

चतुर्युगान्ते कालेन ग्रस्ताञ्छ्रुतिगणान्यथा ।
तपसा ऋषयोऽपश्यन्यतो धर्मः सनातनः ॥ ४ ॥

catur-yugānte kālena
grastāñ chruti-gaṇān yathā
tapasā ṛṣayo 'paśyan
yato dharmaḥ sanātanaḥ

catuḥ-yuga-ante—at the end of every four *yugas* (Satya, Dvāpara, Tretā and Kali); *kālena*—in due course of time; *grastān*—lost; *śruti-gaṇān*—the Vedic instruction; *yathā*—as; *tapasā*—by austerity; *ṛṣayaḥ*—great saintly persons; *apaśyan*—by seeing misuse; *yataḥ*—wherefrom; *dharmaḥ*—occupational duties; *sanātanaḥ*—eternal.

TRANSLATION

At the end of every four yugas, the great saintly persons, upon seeing that the eternal occupational duties of mankind have been misused, reestablish the principles of religion.

PURPORT

In this verse, the words *dharmaḥ* and *sanātanaḥ* are very important. *Sanātana* means "eternal," and *dharma* means "occupational duties." From Satya-yuga to Kali-yuga, the principles of religion and occupational duty gradually deteriorate. In Satya-yuga, the religious principles are observed in full, without deviation. In Tretā-yuga, however, these principles are somewhat neglected, and only three fourths of the religious duties continue. In Dvāpara-yuga only half of the religious principles continue, and in Kali-yuga only one fourth of the religious principles, which gradually disappear. At the end of Kali-yuga, the principles of religion, or the occupational duties of humanity, are almost lost. Indeed, in this Kali-yuga we have passed through only five thousand years, yet the decline of *sanātana-dharma* is very prominent. The duty of saintly persons, therefore, is to take up seriously the cause of *sanātana-dharma* and try to reestablish it for the benefit of the entire human society. The Kṛṣṇa consciousness movement has been started according to this principle. As stated in *Śrīmad-Bhāgavatam* (12.3.51):

kaler doṣa-nidhe rājann
asti hy eko mahān guṇaḥ
kīrtanād eva kṛṣṇasya
mukta-saṅgaḥ paraṁ vrajet

The entire Kali-yuga is full of faults. It is like an unlimited ocean of faults. But the Kṛṣṇa consciousness movement is very authorized.

Therefore, following in the footsteps of Śrī Caitanya Mahāprabhu, who five hundred years ago inaugurated the movement of *saṅkīrtana, kṛṣṇa-kīrtana,* we are trying to introduce this movement, according to superior orders, all over the world. Now, if the inaugurators of this movement strictly follow the regulative principles and spread this movement for the benefit of all human society, they will certainly usher in a new way of life by reestablishing *sanātana-dharma,* the eternal occupational duties of humanity. The eternal occupational duty of the human being is to serve Kṛṣṇa. *Jīvera 'svarūpa' haya—kṛṣṇera 'nitya-dāsa.'* This is the purport of *sanātana-dharma. Sanātana* means *nitya,* or "eternal," and *kṛṣṇa-dāsa* means "servant of Kṛṣṇa." The eternal occupational duty of the human being is to serve Kṛṣṇa. This is the sum and substance of the Kṛṣṇa consciousness movement.

TEXT 5

ततो धर्मं चतुष्पादं मनवो हरिणोदिताः ।
युक्ताः सञ्चारयन्त्यद्धा स्वे स्वे काले महीं नृप ॥ ५ ॥

tato dharmaṁ catuṣpādaṁ
manavo hariṇoditāḥ
yuktāḥ sañcārayanty addhā
sve sve kāle mahīṁ nṛpa

tataḥ—thereafter (at the end of Kali-yuga); *dharmam*—the religious principle; *catuḥ-pādam*—in four parts; *manavaḥ*—all the Manus; *hariṇā*—by the Supreme Personality of Godhead; *uditāḥ*—being instructed; *yuktāḥ*—being engaged; *sañcārayanti*—reestablish; *addhā*—directly; *sve sve*—in their own; *kāle*—time; *mahīm*—within this world; *nṛpa*—O King.

TRANSLATION

Thereafter, O King, the Manus, being fully engaged according to the instructions of the Supreme Personality of Godhead, directly reestablish the principles of occupational duty in its full four parts.

PURPORT

Dharma, or occupational duty, can be established in its full four parts as explained in *Bhagavad-gītā*. In *Bhagavad-gītā* (4.1) the Lord says:

imaṁ vivasvate yogaṁ
proktavān aham avyayam
vivasvān manave prāha
manur ikṣvākave 'bravīt

"I instructed this imperishable science of *yoga* to the sun-god, Vivasvān, and Vivasvān instructed it to Manu, the father of mankind, and Manu in turn instructed it to Ikṣvāku." This is the process of disciplic succession. Following the same process, the Kṛṣṇa consciousness movement is teaching the principles of *Bhagavad-gītā* as it is, without deviation, all over the world. If the fortunate people of this time accept the instructions of Lord Kṛṣṇa, they will certainly be happy in Śrī Caitanya Mahāprabhu's mission. Caitanya Mahāprabhu wanted everyone, at least in India, to become a preacher of this mission. In other words, one should become a *guru* and preach the Lord's instructions all over the world for the peace and prosperity of humanity.

TEXT 6

पालयन्ति प्रजापाला यावदन्तं विभागशः ।
यज्ञभागभुजो देवा ये च तत्रान्विताश्च तैः ॥ ६ ॥

pālayanti prajā-pālā
yāvad antaṁ vibhāgaśaḥ
yajña-bhāga-bhujo devā
ye ca tatrānvitāś ca taiḥ

pālayanti—execute the order; *prajā-pālāḥ*—the rulers of the world, namely the sons and grandsons of Manu; *yāvat antam*—unto the end of Manu's reign; *vibhāgaśaḥ*—in divisions; *yajña-bhāga-bhujaḥ*—the enjoyers of the result of *yajñas; devāḥ*—the demigods; *ye*—others; *ca*—also; *tatra anvitāḥ*—engaged in that business; *ca*—also; *taiḥ*—by them.

TRANSLATION

To enjoy the results of sacrifices [yajñas], the rulers of the world, namely the sons and grandsons of Manu, discharge the orders of the Supreme Personality of Godhead until the end of Manu's reign. The demigods also share the results of these sacrifices.

PURPORT

As stated in *Bhagavad-gītā* (4.2):

evaṁ paramparā-prāptam
imaṁ rājarṣayo viduḥ

"This supreme science was thus received through the chain of disciplic succession, and the saintly kings understood it in that way." This *paramparā* system extends from Manu to Ikṣvāku and from Ikṣvāku to his sons and grandsons. The rulers of the world in the line of hierarchy execute the order of the Supreme Personality of Godhead in the *paramparā* system. Anyone interested in peaceful life must participate in this *paramparā* system and perform *yajñas.* As Gauḍīya Vaiṣṇavas in the *paramparā* system of Śrī Caitanya Mahāprabhu, we must perform *saṅkīrtana-yajña* all over the world (*yajñaiḥ saṅkīrtana-prāyair yajanti hi sumedhasaḥ*). Śrī Caitanya Mahāprabhu is the incarnation of the Supreme Personality of Godhead in this age of Kali, and He will be easily satisfied if the *saṅkīrtana* movement is spread vigorously all over the world. This will also make people happy without a doubt.

TEXT 7

इन्द्रो भगवता दत्तां त्रैलोक्यश्रियमूर्जिताम् ।
भुञ्जानः पाति लोकांस्त्रीन् कामं लोके प्रवर्षति ॥ ७ ॥

indro bhagavatā dattāṁ
trailokya-śriyam ūrjitām
bhuñjānaḥ pāti lokāṁs trīn
kāmaṁ loke pravarṣati

indraḥ—the King of heaven; *bhagavatā*—by the Supreme Personality of Godhead; *dattām*—given; *trailokya*—of the three worlds; *śriyam ūrjitām*—the great opulences; *bhuñjānaḥ*—enjoying; *pāti*—maintains; *lokān*—all the planets; *trīn*—within the three worlds; *kāmam*—as much as necessary; *loke*—within the world; *pravarṣati*—pours rain.

TRANSLATION

Indra, King of heaven, receiving benedictions from the Supreme Personality of Godhead and thus enjoying highly developed opulences, maintains the living entities all over the three worlds by pouring sufficient rain on all the planets.

TEXT 8

ज्ञानं चानुयुगं ब्रूते हरिः सिद्धस्वरूपधृक् ।
ऋषिरूपधरः कर्म योगं योगेशरूपधृक् ॥ ८ ॥

jñānaṁ cānuyugaṁ brūte
hariḥ siddha-svarūpa-dhṛk
ṛṣi-rūpa-dharaḥ karma
yogaṁ yogeśa-rūpa-dhṛk

jñānam—transcendental knowledge; *ca*—and; *anuyugam*—according to the age; *brūte*—explains; *hariḥ*—the Supreme Personality of Godhead; *siddha-svarūpa-dhṛk*—assuming the form of liberated persons like Sanaka and Sanātana; *ṛṣi-rūpa-dharaḥ*—assuming the form of great saintly persons like Yājñavalkya; *karma*—*karma; yogam*—the mystic *yoga* system; *yoga-īśa-rūpa-dhṛk*—by assuming the form of a great *yogī* like Dattātreya.

TRANSLATION

In every yuga, the Supreme Personality of Godhead, Hari, assumes the form of Siddhas such as Sanaka to preach transcendental knowledge, He assumes the form of great saintly persons such as Yājñavalkya to teach the way of karma, and He assumes the form of great yogīs such as Dattātreya to teach the system of mystic yoga.

PURPORT

For the benefit of all human society, not only does the Lord assume the form of Manu as an incarnation to rule the universe properly, but He also assumes the forms of a teacher, *yogī*, *jñānī* and so on, for the benefit of human society. The duty of human society, therefore, is to accept the path of action enunciated by the Supreme Lord. In the present age, the sum and substance of all Vedic knowledge is to be found in *Bhagavad-gītā*, which is personally taught by the Supreme Personality of Godhead, and the same Supreme Godhead, assuming the form of Śrī Caitanya Mahāprabhu, expands the teachings of *Bhagavad-gītā* all over the world. In other words, the Supreme Personality of Godhead, Hari, is so kind and merciful to human society that He is always anxious to take the fallen souls back home, back to Godhead.

TEXT 9

सर्गं प्रजेशरूपेण दस्यून्हन्यात् स्वराड्वपुः ।
कालरूपेण सर्वेषामभावाय पृथग्गुणः ॥ ९ ॥

sargaṁ prajeśa-rūpeṇa
dasyūn hanyāt svarāḍ-vapuḥ
kāla-rūpeṇa sarveṣām
abhāvāya pṛthag guṇaḥ

sargam—creation of progeny; *prajā-īśa-rūpeṇa*—in the form of the Prajāpati Marīci and others; *dasyūn*—thieves and rogues; *hanyāt*—kills; *sva-rāṭ-vapuḥ*—in the form of the king; *kāla-rūpeṇa*—in the form of time; *sarveṣām*—of everything; *abhāvāya*—for the annihilation; *pṛthak*—different; *guṇaḥ*—possessing qualities.

TRANSLATION

In the form of Prajāpati Marīci, the Supreme Personality of Godhead creates progeny; becoming the king, He kills the thieves and rogues; and in the form of time, He annihilates everything. All the different qualities of material existence should be understood to be qualities of the Supreme Personality of Godhead.

TEXT 10

स्तूयमानो जनैरेभिर्मायया नामरूपया ।
विमोहितात्मभिर्नानादर्शनैर्न च दृश्यते ॥१०॥

stūyamāno janair ebhir
māyayā nāma-rūpayā
vimohitātmabhir nānā-
darśanair na ca dṛśyate

stūyamānaḥ—being sought; *janaiḥ*—by people in general; *ebhiḥ*—by all of them; *māyayā*—under the influence of *māyā; nāma-rūpayā*—possessing different names and forms; *vimohita*—bewildered; *ātmabhiḥ*—by illusion; *nānā*—various; *darśanaiḥ*—by philosophical approaches; *na*—not; *ca*—and; *dṛśyate*—the Supreme Personality of Godhead can be found.

TRANSLATION

People in general are bewildered by the illusory energy, and therefore they try to find the Absolute Truth, the Supreme Personality of Godhead, through various types of research and philosophical speculation. Nonetheless, they are unable to see the Supreme Lord.

PURPORT

Whatever actions and reactions take place for the creation, maintenance and annihilation of this material world are actually brought about by the one Supreme Person. There are many varieties of philosophers trying to search for the ultimate cause under different names and forms, but they are unable to find the Supreme Personality of Godhead, Kṛṣṇa, who explains in *Bhagavad-gītā* that He is the origin of everything and the cause of all causes (*ahaṁ sarvasya prabhavaḥ*). This inability is due to the illusory energy of the Supreme Lord. Devotees, therefore, accept the Supreme Personality of Godhead as He is and remain happy simply by chanting the glories of the Lord.

TEXT 11

एतत् कल्पविकल्पस्य प्रमाणं परिकीर्तितम् ।
यत्र मन्वन्तराण्याहुश्चतुर्दश पुराविदः ॥११॥

etat kalpa-vikalpasya
pramāṇaṁ parikīrtitam
yatra manvantarāṇy āhuś
caturdaśa purāvidaḥ

etat—all these; *kalpa*—in one day of Lord Brahmā; *vikalpasya*—of the changes in a *kalpa*, such as the change of Manus; *pramāṇam*—evidences; *parikīrtitam*—described (by me); *yatra*—wherein; *manvantarāṇi*—periods of Manu; *āhuḥ*—said; *caturdaśa*—fourteen; *purā-vidaḥ*—learned scholars.

TRANSLATION

In one kalpa, or one day of Brahmā, there take place the many changes called vikalpas. O King, all of these have been previously described to you by me. Learned scholars who know the past, present and future have ascertained that in one day of Brahmā there are fourteen Manus.

Thus end the Bhaktivedanta purports of the Eighth Canto, Fourteenth Chapter, of the Śrīmad-Bhāgavatam, *entitled "The System of Universal Management."*

CHAPTER FIFTEEN

Bali Mahārāja Conquers the Heavenly Planets

This chapter describes how Bali, after performing the Viśvajit-yajña, received the benediction of a chariot and various kinds of paraphernalia for war, with which he attacked the King of heaven. All the demigods, being afraid of him, left the heavenly planets and went away, following the instructions of their *guru.*

Mahārāja Parīkṣit wanted to understand how Lord Vāmanadeva, on the plea of taking three paces of land from Bali Mahārāja, took everything away from him and arrested him. Śukadeva Gosvāmī responded to this inquiry with the following explanation. In the fight between the demons and the demigods, as described in the Eleventh Chapter of this canto, Bali was defeated, and he died in the fight, but by the grace of Śukrācārya he regained his life. Thus he engaged himself in the service of Śukrācārya, his spiritual master. The descendants of Bhṛgu, being pleased with him, engaged him in the Viśvajit-yajña. When this *yajña* was performed, from the fire of *yajña* came a chariot, horses, a flag, a bow, armor and two quivers of arrows. Mahārāja Prahlāda, Bali Mahārāja's grandfather, gave Bali an eternal garland of flowers, and Śukrācārya gave him a conchshell. Bali Mahārāja, after offering obeisances to Prahlāda, the *brāhmaṇas* and his spiritual master, Śukrācārya, equipped himself to fight with Indra and went to Indrapurī with his soldiers. Blowing his conchshell, he attacked the outskirts of Indra's kingdom. When Indra saw Bali Mahārāja's prowess, he went to his own spiritual master, Bṛhaspati, told him about Bali's strength, and inquired about his duty. Bṛhaspati informed the demigods that because Bali had been endowed with extraordinary power by the *brāhmaṇas,* the demigods could not fight with him. Their only hope was to gain the favor of the Supreme Personality of Godhead. Indeed, there was no alternative. Under the circumstances, Bṛhaspati advised the demigods to leave the heavenly planets and keep themselves somewhere invisible. The demigods followed his orders, and Bali Mahārāja, along with his associates, gained the entire kingdom of Indra. The descendants of Bhṛgu Muni, being very affectionate to their disciple Bali Mahārāja, engaged him in performing one hundred *aśvamedha-yajñas.* In this way, Bali enjoyed the opulences of the heavenly planets.

TEXTS 1–2

श्रीराजोवाच

बलेः पदत्रयं भूमेः कस्माद्धरिरयाचत ।
भूतेश्वरः कृपणवल्लब्धार्थोऽपि बबन्ध तम् ॥ १ ॥
एतद् वेदितुमिच्छामो महत् कौतूहलं हि नः ।
याच्ञेश्वरस्य पूर्णस्य बन्धनं चाप्यनागसः ॥ २ ॥

śrī-rājovāca
baleḥ pada-trayaṁ bhūmeḥ
kasmād dharir ayācata
bhūteśvaraḥ kṛpaṇa-val
labdhārtho 'pi babandha tam

etad veditum icchāmo
mahat kautūhalaṁ hi naḥ
yācñeśvarasya pūrṇasya
bandhanaṁ cāpy anāgasaḥ

śrī-rājā uvāca—the King said; *baleḥ*—of Bali Mahārāja; *pada-trayam*—three steps; *bhūmeḥ*—of land; *kasmāt*—why; *hariḥ*—the Supreme Personality of Godhead (in the form of Vāmana); *ayācata*—begged; *bhūtva-īśvaraḥ*—the proprietor of all the universe; *kṛpaṇa-vat*—like a poor man; *labdha-arthaḥ*—He got the gift; *api*—although; *babandha*—arrested; *tam*—him (Bali); *etat*—all this; *veditum*—to understand; *icchāmaḥ*—we desire; *mahat*—very great; *kautūhalam*—eagerness; *hi*—indeed; *naḥ*—our; *yācñā*—begging; *īśvarasya*—of the Supreme Personality of Godhead; *pūrṇasya*—who is full in everything;

bandhanam—arresting; *ca*—also; *api*—although; *anāgasaḥ*—of he who was faultless.

TRANSLATION

Mahārāja Parīkṣit inquired: The Supreme Personality of Godhead is the proprietor of everything. Why did He beg three paces of land from Bali Mahārāja like a poor man, and when He got the gift for which He had begged, why did He nonetheless arrest Bali Mahārāja? I am very much anxious to know the mystery of these contradictions.

TEXT 3

श्रीशुक उवाच

पराजितश्रीरसुभिश्च हापितो
हीन्द्रेण राजन्भृगुभिः स जीवितः ।
सर्वात्मना तानभजद् भृगून्बलिः
शिष्यो महात्मार्थनिवेदनेन ॥ ३ ॥

śrī-śuka uvāca
parājita-śrīr asubhiś ca hāpito
hīndreṇa rājan bhṛgubhiḥ sa jīvitaḥ
sarvātmanā tān abhajad bhṛgūn baliḥ
śiṣyo mahātmārtha-nivedanena

śrī-śukaḥ uvāca—Śrī Śukadeva Gosvāmī said; *parājita*—being defeated; *śrīḥ*—opulences; *asubhiḥ ca*—of life also; *hāpitaḥ*—deprived; *hi*—indeed; *indreṇa*—by King Indra; *rājan*—O King; *bhṛgubhiḥ*—by the descendants of Bhṛgu Muni; *saḥ*—he (Bali Mahārāja); *jīvitaḥ*—brought back to life; *sarva-ātmanā*—in full submission; *tān*—them; *abhajat*—worshiped; *bhṛgūn*—the descendants of Bhṛgu Muni; *baliḥ*—Mahārāja Bali; *śiṣyaḥ*—a disciple; *mahātmā*—the great soul; *artha-nivedanena*—by giving them everything.

TRANSLATION

Śukadeva Gosvāmī said: O King, when Bali Mahārāja lost all his opulence and died in the fight, Śukrācārya, a descendant of Bhṛgu

Muni, brought him back to life. Because of this, the great soul Bali Mahārāja became a disciple of Śukrācārya and began to serve him with great faith, offering everything he had.

TEXT 4

तं ब्राह्मणा भृगवः प्रीयमाणा
अयाजयन्विश्वजिता त्रिणाकम् ।
जिगीषमाणं विधिनाभिषिच्य
महाभिषेकेण महानुभावाः ॥ ४ ॥

taṁ brāhmaṇā bhṛgavaḥ prīyamāṇā
ayājayan viśvajitā tri-ṇākam
jigīṣamāṇaṁ vidhinābhiṣicya
mahābhiṣekeṇa mahānubhāvāḥ

tam—upon him (Bali Mahārāja); *brāhmaṇāḥ*—all the *brāhmaṇas; bhṛgavaḥ*—the descendants of Bhṛgu Muni; *prīyamāṇāḥ*—being very pleased; *ayājayan*—engaged him in performing a sacrifice; *viśvajitā*—known as Viśvajit; *tri-nākam*—the heavenly planets; *jigīṣamāṇam*—desiring to conquer; *vidhinā*—according to regulative principles; *abhiṣicya*—after purifying; *mahā-abhiṣekeṇa*—by bathing him in a great *abhiṣeka* ceremony; *mahā-anubhāvāḥ*—the exalted *brāhmaṇas.*

TRANSLATION

The brāhmaṇa descendants of Bhṛgu Muni were very pleased with Bali Mahārāja, who desired to conquer the kingdom of Indra. Therefore, after purifying him and properly bathing him according to regulative principles, they engaged him in performing the yajña known as Viśvajit.

TEXT 5

ततो रथः काञ्चनपट्टनद्धो
हयाश्च हर्यश्वतुरङ्गवर्णाः ।

ध्वजश्च सिंहेन विराजमानो
हुताशनादास हविर्भिरिष्टात् ॥ ५ ॥

tato rathaḥ kāñcana-paṭṭa-naddho
hayāś ca haryaśva-turaṅga-varṇāḥ
dhvajaś ca siṁhena virājamāno
hutāśanād āsa havirbhir iṣṭāt

tataḥ—thereafter; *rathaḥ*—a chariot; *kāñcana*—with gold; *paṭṭa*—and silk garments; *naddhaḥ*—wrapped; *hayāḥ ca*—horses also; *haryaśva-turaṅga-varṇāḥ*—exactly of the same color as the horses of Indra (yellow); *dhvajaḥ ca*—a flag also; *siṁhena*—with the mark of a lion; *virājamānaḥ*—existing; *huta-aśanāt*—from the blazing fire; *āsa*—there was; *havirbhiḥ*—by offerings of clarified butter; *iṣṭāt*—worshiped.

TRANSLATION

When ghee [clarified butter] was offered in the fire of sacrifice, there appeared from the fire a celestial chariot covered with gold and silk. There also appeared yellow horses like those of Indra, and a flag marked with a lion.

TEXT 6

धनुश्च दिव्यं पुरटोपनद्धं
तूणावरिक्तौ कवचं च दिव्यम् ।
पितामहस्तस्य ददौ च माला-
मम्लानपुष्पां जलजं च शुक्रः ॥ ६ ॥

dhanuś ca divyaṁ puraṭopanaddhaṁ
tūṇāv ariktau kavacaṁ ca divyam
pitāmahas tasya dadau ca mālām
amlāna-puṣpāṁ jalajaṁ ca śukraḥ

dhanuḥ—a bow; *ca*—also; *divyam*—uncommon; *puraṭa-upanaddham*—covered with gold; *tūṇau*—two quivers; *ariktau*—infallible; *kavacam ca*—and armor; *divyam*—celestial; *pitāmahaḥ tasya*—his grandfather, namely Prahlāda Mahārāja; *dadau*—gave; *ca*—and; *mālām*—a garland; *amlāna-puṣpām*—made of flowers that do not fade away; *jala-jam*—a conchshell (which is born in water); *ca*—as well as; *śukraḥ*—Śukrācārya.

TRANSLATION

A gilded bow, two quivers of infallible arrows, and celestial armor also appeared. Bali Mahārāja's grandfather Prahlāda Mahārāja offered Bali a garland of flowers that would never fade, and Śukrācārya gave him a conchshell.

TEXT 7

एवं स विप्रार्जितयोधनार्थ-
स्तैः कल्पितस्वस्त्ययनोऽथ विप्रान् ।
प्रदक्षिणीकृत्य कृतप्रणामः
प्रह्लादमामन्त्र्य नमश्चकार ॥ ७ ॥

evaṁ sa viprārjita-yodhanārthas
taiḥ kalpita-svastyayano 'tha viprān
pradakṣiṇī-kṛtya kṛta-praṇāmaḥ
prahrādam āmantrya namaś-cakāra

evam—in this way; *saḥ*—he (Bali Mahārāja); *vipra-arjita*—gained by the grace of the *brāhmaṇas; yodhana-arthaḥ*—possessing equipment for fighting; *taiḥ*—by them (the *brāhmaṇas*); *kalpita*—advice; *svastyayanaḥ*—ritualistic performance; *atha*—as; *viprān*—all the *brāhmaṇas* (Śukrācārya and others); *pradakṣiṇī-kṛtya*—circumambulating; *kṛta-praṇāmaḥ*—offered his respectful obeisances; *prahrādam*—unto Prahlāda Mahārāja; *āmantrya*—addressing; *namaḥ-cakāra*—offered him obeisances.

TRANSLATION

When Mahārāja Bali had thus performed the special ritualistic ceremony advised by the brāhmaṇas and had received, by their grace, the equipment for fighting, he circumambulated the

brāhmaṇas and offered them obeisances. He also saluted Prahlāda Mahārāja and offered obeisances to him.

TEXTS 8–9

अथारुह्य रथं दिव्यं भृगुदत्तं महारथः ।
सुस्रग्धरोऽथ संनह्य धन्वी खड्गी धृतेषुधिः ॥ ८ ॥
हेमाङ्गदलसद्बाहुः स्फुरन्मकरकुण्डलः ।
रराज रथमारूढो धिष्ण्यस्थ इव हव्यवाट् ॥ ९ ॥

athāruhya rathaṁ divyaṁ
bhṛgu-dattaṁ mahārathaḥ
susrag-dharo 'tha sannahya
dhanvī khaḍgī dhṛteṣudhiḥ

hemāṅgada-lasad-bāhuḥ
sphuran-makara-kuṇḍalaḥ
rarāja ratham ārūḍho
dhiṣṇya-stha iva havyavāṭ

atha—thereupon; *āruhya*—getting on; *ratham*—the chariot; *divyam*—celestial; *bhṛgu-dattam*—given by Śukrācārya; *mahā-rathaḥ*—Bali Mahārāja, the great charioteer; *su-srak-dharaḥ*—decorated with a nice garland; *atha*—thus; *sannahya*—covering his body with armor; *dhanvī*—equipped with a bow; *khaḍgī*—taking a sword; *dhṛta-iṣudhiḥ*—taking a quiver of arrows; *hema-aṅgada-lasat-bāhuḥ*—decorated with golden bangles on his arms; *sphurat-makara-kuṇḍalaḥ*—decorated with brilliant earrings resembling sapphires; *rarāja*—was illuminating; *ratham ārūḍhaḥ*—getting on the chariot; *dhiṣṇya-sthaḥ*—situated on the altar of sacrifice; *iva*—like; *havya-vāṭ*—worshipable fire.

TRANSLATION

Then, after getting on the chariot given by Śukrācārya, Bali Mahārāja, decorated with a nice garland, put protective armor on his body, equipped himself with a bow, and took up a sword and a

quiver of arrows. When he sat down on the seat of the chariot, his arms decorated with golden bangles and his ears with sapphire earrings, he shone like a worshipable fire.

TEXTS 10–11

तुल्यैश्वर्यबलश्रीभिः स्वयूथैर्दैत्ययूथपैः ।
पिबद्भिरिव खं दृग्भिर्दहद्भिः परिधीनिव ॥१०॥
वृतो विकर्षन् महतीमासुरीं ध्वजिनीं विभुः ।
ययाविन्द्रपुरीं स्वृद्धां कम्पयन्निव रोदसी ॥११॥

tulyaiśvarya-bala-śrībhiḥ
sva-yūthair daitya-yūthapaiḥ
pibadbhir iva khaṁ dṛgbhir
dahadbhiḥ paridhīn iva

vṛto vikarṣan mahatīm
āsurīṁ dhvajinīṁ vibhuḥ
yayāv indra-purīṁ svṛddhāṁ
kampayann iva rodasī

tulya-aiśvarya—equal in opulence; *bala*—strength; *śrībhiḥ*—and in beauty; *sva-yūthaiḥ*—by his own men; *daitya-yūtha-paiḥ*—and by the chiefs of the demons; *pibadbhiḥ*—drinking; *iva*—as if; *kham*—the sky; *dṛgbhiḥ*—with the sight; *dahadbhiḥ*—burning; *paridhīn*—all directions; *iva*—as if; *vṛtaḥ*—surrounded; *vikarṣan*—attracting; *mahatīm*—very great; *āsurīm*—demoniac; *dhvajinīm*—soldiers; *vibhuḥ*—most powerful; *yayau*—went; *indra-purīm*—to the capital of King Indra; *su-ṛddhām*—very opulent; *kampayan*—causing to tremble; *iva*—as if; *rodasī*—the complete surface of the world.

TRANSLATION

When he assembled with his own soldiers and the demon chiefs, who were equal to him in strength, opulence and beauty, they appeared as if they would swallow the sky and burn all directions with their vision. After thus gathering the demoniac soldiers, Bali

Mahārāja departed for the opulent capital of Indra. Indeed, he seemed to make the entire surface of the world tremble.

TEXT 12

रम्यामुपवनोद्यानैः श्रीमद्भिर्नन्दनादिभिः ।
कूजद्विहङ्गमिथुनैर्गायन्मत्तमधुव्रतैः ।
प्रवालफलपुष्पोरुभारशाखामरद्रुमैः ॥१२॥

ramyām upavanodyānaiḥ
śrīmadbhir nandanādibhiḥ
kūjad-vihaṅga-mithunair
gāyan-matta-madhuvrataiḥ
pravāla-phala-puṣporu-
bhāra-śākhāmara-drumaiḥ

ramyām—very pleasing; *upavana*—with orchards; *udyānaiḥ*—and gardens; *śrīmadbhiḥ*—very beautiful to see; *nandana-ādibhiḥ*—such as Nandana; *kūjat*—chirping; *vihaṅga*—birds; *mithunaiḥ*—with pairs; *gāyat*—singing; *matta*—mad; *madhu-vrataiḥ*—with bees; *pravāla*—of leaves; *phala-puṣpa*—fruits and flowers; *uru*—very great; *bhāra*—bearing the weight; *śākhā*—whose branches; *amara-drumaiḥ*—with eternal trees.

TRANSLATION

King Indra's city was full of pleasing orchards and gardens, such as the Nandana garden. Because of the weight of the flowers, leaves and fruit, the branches of the eternally existing trees were bending down. The gardens were visited by pairs of chirping birds and singing bees. The entire atmosphere was celestial.

TEXT 13

हंससारसचक्राह्वकारण्डवकुलाकुलाः ।
नलिन्यो यत्र क्रीडन्ति प्रमदाः सुरसेविताः ॥१३॥

haṁsa-sārasa-cakrāhva-
kāraṇḍava-kulākulāḥ
nalinyo yatra krīḍanti
pramadāḥ sura-sevitāḥ

haṁsa—of swans; *sārasa*—cranes; *cakrāhva*—birds known as *cakravākas; kāraṇḍava*—and water fowl; *kula*—by groups; *ākulāḥ*—congested; *nalinyaḥ*—lotus flowers; *yatra*—where; *krīḍanti*—enjoyed sporting; *pramadāḥ*—beautiful women; *sura-sevitāḥ*—protected by the demigods.

TRANSLATION

Beautiful women protected by the demigods sported in the gardens, which had lotus ponds full of swans, cranes, cakravākas and ducks.

TEXT 14

आकाशगङ्गया देव्या वृतां परिखभूतया ।
प्राकारेणाग्निवर्णेन साट्टालेनोन्नतेन च ॥१४॥

ākāśa-gaṅgayā devyā
vṛtāṁ parikha-bhūtayā
prākāreṇāgni-varṇena
sāṭṭālenonnatena ca

ākāśa-gaṅgayā—by Ganges water known as Ākāśa-gaṅgā; *devyā*—the always-worshipable goddess; *vṛtām*—surrounded; *parikha-bhūtayā*—as a trench; *prākāreṇa*—by ramparts; *agni-varṇena*—resembling fire; *sa-aṭṭālena*—with places for fighting; *unnatena*—very high; *ca*—and.

TRANSLATION

The city was surrounded by trenches full of Ganges water, known as Ākāśa-gaṅgā, and by a high wall, which was the color of fire. Upon this wall were parapets for fighting.

TEXT 15

रुक्मपट्टकपाटैश्च द्वारैः स्फटिकगोपुरैः ।
जुष्टां विभक्तप्रपथां विश्वकर्मविनिर्मिताम् ॥१५॥

rukma-paṭṭa-kapāṭaiś ca
dvāraiḥ sphaṭika-gopuraiḥ
juṣṭāṁ vibhakta-prapathāṁ
viśvakarma-vinirmitām

rukma-paṭṭa—possessing plates made of gold; *kapāṭaiḥ*—the doors of which; *ca*—and; *dvāraiḥ*—with entrances; *sphaṭika-gopuraiḥ*—with gates made of excellent marble; *juṣṭām*—linked; *vibhakta-prapathām*—with many different public roads; *viśvakarma-vinirmitam*—constructed by Viśvakarmā, the heavenly architect.

TRANSLATION

The doors were made of solid gold plates, and the gates were of excellent marble. These were linked by various public roads. The entire city had been constructed by Viśvakarmā.

TEXT 16

सभाचत्वररथ्याढ्यां विमानैर्न्यर्बुदैर्युताम् ।
शृङ्गाटकैर्मणिमयैर्वज्रविद्रुमवेदिभिः ॥१६॥

sabhā-catvara-rathyāḍhyāṁ
vimānair nyārbudair yutām
śṛṅgāṭakair maṇimayair
vajra-vidruma-vedibhiḥ

sabhā—with assembly houses; *catvara*—courtyards; *rathya*—and public roads; *āḍhyām*—opulent; *vimānaiḥ*—by airplanes; *nyārbudaiḥ*—not less than ten crores (one hundred million); *yutām*—endowed; *śṛṅga-ātakaiḥ*—with crossroads; *maṇi-mayaiḥ*—made of pearls; *vajra*—made of diamonds; *vidruma*—and coral; *vedibhiḥ*—with places to sit.

TRANSLATION

The city was full of courtyards, wide roads, assembly houses, and not less than one hundred million airplanes. The crossroads were made of pearl, and there were sitting places made of diamond and coral.

TEXT 17

यत्र नित्यवयोरूपाः श्यामा विरजवाससः ।
भ्राजन्ते रूपवन्नार्यो ह्यर्चिर्भिरिव वह्नयः ॥१७॥

yatra nitya-vayo-rūpāḥ
śyāmā viraja-vāsasaḥ
bhrājante rūpavan-nāryo
hy arcirbhir iva vahnayaḥ

yatra—in that city; *nitya-vayaḥ-rūpāḥ*—who were ever beautiful and young; *śyāmāḥ*—possessing the quality of *śyāmā; viraja-vāsasaḥ*—always dressed with clean garments; *bhrājante*—glitter; *rūpa-vat*—well decorated; *nāryaḥ*—women; *hi*—certainly; *arcirbhiḥ*—with many flames; *iva*—like; *vahnayaḥ*—fires.

TRANSLATION

Everlastingly beautiful and youthful women, who were dressed with clean garments, glittered in the city like fires with flames. They all possessed the quality of śyāmā.

PURPORT

Śrīla Viśvanātha Cakravartī Ṭhākura gives a hint of the quality of the *śyāmā* woman.

śīta-kāle bhaved uṣṇā
uṣma-kāle suśītalāḥ
stanau sukaṭhinau yāsāṁ
tāḥ śyāmāḥ parikīrtitāḥ

A woman whose body is very warm during the winter and cool during the summer and who generally has very firm breasts is called *śyāmā*.

TEXT 18

सुरस्त्रीकेशविभ्रष्टनवसौगन्धिकस्रजाम् ।
यत्रामोदमुपादाय मार्ग आवाति मारुतः ॥१८॥

sura-strī-keśa-vibhraṣṭa-
nava-saugandhika-srajām
yatrāmodam upādāya
mārga āvāti mārutaḥ

sura-strī—of the women of the demigods; *keśa*—from the hair; *vibhraṣṭa*—fallen; *nava-saugandhika*—made of fresh, fragrant flowers; *srajām*—of the flower garlands; *yatra*—wherein; *āmodam*—the fragrance; *upādāya*—carrying; *mārge*—on the roads; *āvāti*—blows; *mārutaḥ*—the breeze.

TRANSLATION

The breezes blowing in the streets of the city bore the fragrance of the flowers falling from the hair of the women of the demigods.

TEXT 19

हेमजालाक्षनिर्गच्छद्धूमेनागुरुगन्धिना ।
पाण्डुरेण प्रतिच्छन्नमार्गे यान्ति सुरप्रियाः ॥१९॥

hema-jālākṣa-nirgacchad-
dhūmenāguru-gandhinā
pāṇḍureṇa praticchanna-
mārge yānti sura-priyāḥ

hema-jāla-akṣa—from dainty little windows made of networks of gold; *nirgacchat*—emanating; *dhūmena*—by smoke; *aguru-gandhinā*—fragrant due to burning incense known as *aguru; pāṇḍureṇa*—very white; *praticchanna*—covered; *mārge*—on the street; *yānti*—pass; *sura-priyāḥ*—beautiful public women known as Apsarās, celestial girls.

TRANSLATION

Apsarās passed on the streets, which were covered with the white, fragrant smoke of aguru incense emanating from windows with golden filigree.

TEXT 20

मुक्तावितानैर्मणिहेमकेतुभि-
र्नानापताकावलभीभिरावृताम् ।
शिखण्डिपारावतभृङ्गनादितां
वैमानिकस्त्रीकलगीतमङ्गलाम् ॥२०॥

muktā-vitānair maṇi-hema-ketubhir
nānā-patākā-valabhībhir āvṛtām
śikhaṇḍi-pārāvata-bhṛṅga-nāditāṁ
vaimānika-strī-kala-gīta-maṅgalām

muktā-vitānaiḥ—by canopies decorated with pearls; *maṇi-hema-ketubhiḥ*—with flags made with pearls and gold; *nānā-patākā*—possessing various kinds of flags; *valabhībhiḥ*—with the domes of the palaces; *āvṛtām*—covered; *śikhaṇḍi*—of birds like peacocks; *pārāvata*—pigeons; *bhṛṅga*—bees; *nāditām*—vibrated by the respective sounds; *vaimānika*—getting on airplanes; *strī*—of women; *kala-gīta*—from the choral singing; *maṅgalām*—full of auspiciousness.

TRANSLATION

The city was shaded by canopies decorated with pearls, and the domes of the palaces had flags of pearl and gold. The city always resounded with the vibrations of peacocks, pigeons and bees, and above the city flew airplanes full of beautiful women who constantly chanted auspicious songs that were very pleasing to the ear.

TEXT 21

मृदङ्गशङ्खानकदुन्दुभिस्वनैः
सतालवीणामुरजेष्टवेणुभिः ।

नृत्यैः सवाद्यैरुपदेवगीतकै-
मनोरमां स्वप्रभया जितप्रभाम् ॥२१॥

mṛdaṅga-śaṅkhānaka-dundubhi-svanaiḥ
satāla-vīṇā-murajeṣṭa-veṇubhiḥ
nṛtyaiḥ savādyair upadeva-gītakair
manoramāṁ sva-prabhayā jita-prabhām

mṛdaṅga—of drums; *śaṅkha*—conchshells; *ānaka-dundubhi*—and kettledrums; *svanaiḥ*—by the sounds; *sa-tāla*—in perfect tune; *vīṇā*—a stringed instrument; *muraja*—a kind of drum; *iṣṭa-veṇubhiḥ*—accompanied by the very nice sound of the flute; *nṛtyaiḥ*—with dancing; *savādyaiḥ*—with concert instruments; *upadeva-gītakaiḥ*—with singing by the secondary demigods like the Gandharvas; *manoramām*—beautiful and pleasing; *sva-prabhayā*—by its own brilliance; *jita-prabhām*—the personification of beauty was conquered.

TRANSLATION

The city was filled with the sounds of mṛdaṅgas, conchshells, kettledrums, flutes and well-tuned stringed instruments all playing in concert. There was constant dancing and the Gandharvas sang. The combined beauty of Indrapurī defeated beauty personified.

TEXT 22

यां न व्रजन्त्यधर्मिष्ठाः खला भूतद्रुहः शठाः ।
मानिनः कामिनो लुब्धा एभिर्हीना व्रजन्ति यत् ॥ २२॥

yāṁ na vrajanty adharmiṣṭhāḥ
khalā bhūta-druhaḥ śaṭhāḥ
māninaḥ kāmino lubdhā
ebhir hīnā vrajanti yat

yām—in the streets of the city; *na*—not; *vrajanti*—pass; *adharmiṣṭhāḥ*—irreligious persons; *khalāḥ*—envious persons; *bhūta-druhaḥ*—persons violent toward other living entities; *śaṭhāḥ*—cheaters;

māninaḥ—falsely prestigious; *kāminaḥ*—lusty; *lubdhāḥ*—greedy; *ebhiḥ*—these; *hīnāḥ*—completely devoid of; *vrajanti*—walk; *yat*—on the street.

TRANSLATION

No one who was sinful, envious, violent toward other living entities, cunning, falsely proud, lusty or greedy could enter that city. The people who lived there were all devoid of these faults.

TEXT 23

तां देवधानीं स वरूथिनीपति-
बहिः समन्ताद् रुरुधे पृतन्यया ।
आचार्यदत्तं जलजं महास्वनं
दध्मौ प्रयुञ्जन्भयमिन्द्रयोषिताम् ॥२३॥

tāṁ deva-dhānīṁ sa varūthinī-patir
bahiḥ samantād rurudhe pṛtanyayā
ācārya-dattaṁ jalajaṁ mahā-svanaṁ
dadhmau prayuñjan bhayam indra-yoṣitām

tām—that; *deva-dhānīm*—place where Indra lived; *saḥ*—he (Bali Mahārāja); *varūthinī-patiḥ*—the commander of the soldiers; *bahiḥ*—outside; *samantāt*—in all directions; *rurudhe*—attacked; *pṛtanyayā*—by soldiers; *ācārya-dattam*—given by Śukrācārya; *jala-jam*—the conchshell; *mahā-svanam*—a loud sound; *dadhmau*—resounded; *prayuñjan*—creating; *bhayam*—fear; *indra-yoṣitām*—of all the ladies protected by Indra.

TRANSLATION

Bali Mahārāja, who was the commander of numberless soldiers, gathered his soldiers outside this abode of Indra and attacked it from all directions. He sounded the conchshell given him by his spiritual master, Śukrācārya, thus creating a fearful situation for the women protected by Indra.

TEXT 24

मघवांस्तमभिप्रेत्य बलेः परममुद्यमम् ।
सर्वदेवगणोपेतो गुरुमेतदुवाच ह ॥२४॥

maghavāṁs tam abhipretya
baleḥ paramam udyamam
sarva-deva-gaṇopeto
gurum etad uvāca ha

maghavān—Indra; *tam*—the situation; *abhipretya*—understanding; *baleḥ*—of Bali Mahārāja; *paramam udyamam*—great enthusiasm; *sarva-deva-gaṇa*—by all the demigods; *upetaḥ*—accompanied; *gurum*—unto the spiritual master; *etat*—the following words; *uvāca*—said; *ha*—indeed.

TRANSLATION

Seeing Bali Mahārāja's indefatigable endeavor and understanding his motive, King Indra, along with the other demigods, approached his spiritual master, Bṛhaspati, and spoke as follows.

TEXT 25

भगवन्नुद्यमो भूयान्बलेर्नः पूर्ववैरिणः ।
अविषह्यमिमं मन्ये केनासीत्तेजसोर्जितः ॥२५॥

bhagavann udyamo bhūyān
baler naḥ pūrva-vairiṇaḥ
aviṣahyam imaṁ manye
kenāsīt tejasorjitaḥ

bhagavan—O my lord; *udyamaḥ*—enthusiasm; *bhūyān*—great; *baleḥ*—of Bali Mahārāja; *naḥ*—our; *pūrva-vairiṇaḥ*—past enemy; *aviṣahyam*—unbearable; *imam*—this; *manye*—I think; *kena*—by whom; *āsīt*—got; *tejasā*—prowess; *ūrjitaḥ*—achieved.

TRANSLATION

My lord, our old enemy Bali Mahārāja now has new enthusiasm, and he has obtained such astonishing power that we think that perhaps we cannot resist his prowess.

TEXT 26

नैनं कश्चित् कुतो वापि प्रतिव्योढुमधीश्वरः ।
पिबन्निव मुखेनेदं लिहन्निव दिशो दश ।
दहन्निव दिशो दृग्भिः संवर्ताग्निरिवोत्थितः ॥२६॥

nainaṁ kaścit kuto vāpi
prativyoḍhum adhīśvaraḥ
pibann iva mukhenedaṁ
lihann iva diśo daśa
dahann iva diśo dṛgbhiḥ
saṁvartāgnir ivotthitaḥ

na—not; *enam*—this arrangement; *kaścit*—anyone; *kutaḥ*—from anywhere; *vā api*—either; *prativyoḍhum*—to counteract; *adhīśvaraḥ*—capable; *piban iva*—as if drinking; *mukhena*—by the mouth; *idam*—this (world); *lihan iva*—as if licking up; *diśaḥ daśa*—all ten directions; *dahan iva*—as if burning; *diśaḥ*—all directions; *dṛgbhiḥ*—by his vision; *saṁvarta-agniḥ*—the fire known as *saṁvarta; iva*—like; *utthitaḥ*—now arisen.

TRANSLATION

No one anywhere can counteract this military arrangement of Bali's. It now appears that Bali is trying to drink up the entire universe with his mouth, lick up the ten directions with his tongue, and raise fire in every direction with his eyes. Indeed, he has arisen like the annihilating fire known as saṁvartaka.

TEXT 27

ब्रूहि कारणमेतस्य दुर्धर्षत्वस्य मद्रिपोः ।
ओजः सहो बलं तेजो यत एतत्समुद्यमः ॥२७॥

brūhi kāraṇam etasya
durdharṣatvasya mad-ripoḥ
ojaḥ saho balaṁ tejo
yata etat samudyamaḥ

brūhi—kindly inform us; *kāraṇam*—the cause; *etasya*—of all this; *durdharṣatvasya*—of the formidableness; *mat-ripoḥ*—of my enemy; *ojaḥ*—prowess; *sahaḥ*—energy; *balam*—strength; *tejaḥ*—influence; *yataḥ*—wherefrom; *etat*—all this; *samudyamaḥ*—endeavor.

TRANSLATION

Kindly inform me. What is the cause for Bali Mahārāja's strength, endeavor, influence and victory? How has he become so enthusiastic?

TEXT 28

श्रीगुरुरुवाच
जानामि मघवञ्छत्रोरुन्नतेरस्य कारणम् ।
शिष्यायोपभृतं तेजो भृगुभिर्ब्रह्मवादिभिः ॥२८॥

śrī-gurur uvāca
jānāmi maghavañ chatror
unnater asya kāraṇam
śiṣyāyopabhṛtaṁ tejo
bhṛgubhir brahma-vādibhiḥ

śrī-guruḥ uvāca—Bṛhaspati said; *jānāmi*—I know; *maghavan*—O Indra; *śatroḥ*—of the enemy; *unnateḥ*—of the elevation; *asya*—of him; *kāraṇam*—the cause; *śiṣyāya*—unto the disciple; *upabhṛtam*—endowed; *tejaḥ*—power; *bhṛgubhiḥ*—by the descendants of Bhṛgu; *brahma-vādibhiḥ*—all-powerful *brāhmaṇas.*

TRANSLATION

Bṛhaspati, the spiritual master of the demigods, said: O Indra, I know the cause for your enemy's becoming so powerful. The

brāhmaṇa descendants of Bhṛgu Muni, being pleased by Bali Mahārāja, their disciple, endowed him with such extraordinary power.

PURPORT

Bṛhaspati, the spiritual master of the demigods, informed Indra, "Ordinarily, Bali and his forces could not achieve such strength, but it appears that the *brāhmaṇa* descendants of Bhṛgu Muni, being pleased with Bali Mahārāja, endowed them with this spiritual power." In other words, Bṛhaspati informed Indra that Bali Mahārāja's prowess was not his own but that of his exalted *guru*, Śukrācārya. We sing in our daily prayers, *yasya prasādād bhagavat-prasādo yasyāprasādān na gatiḥ kuto 'pi.* By the pleasure of the spiritual master, one can get extraordinary power, especially in spiritual advancement. The blessings of the spiritual master are more powerful than one's personal endeavor for such advancement. Narottama dāsa Ṭhākura therefore says:

guru-mukha-padma-vākya, cittete kariyā aikya,
āra nā kariha mane āśā

Especially for spiritual advancement, one should carry out the bona fide order of the spiritual master. By the *paramparā* system, one can thus be endowed with the original spiritual power coming from the Supreme Personality of Godhead (*evaṁ paramparā-prāptam imaṁ rājarṣayo viduḥ*).

TEXT 29

ओजस्विनं बलिं जेतुं न समर्थोऽस्ति कश्चन ।
भवद्विधो भवान्वापि वर्जयित्वेश्वरं हरिम् ।
विजेष्यति न कोऽप्येनं ब्रह्मतेजःसमेधितम् ।
नास्य शक्तः पुरः स्थातुं कृतान्तस्य यथा जनाः ॥२९॥

ojasvinaṁ baliṁ jetuṁ
na samartho 'sti kaścana
bhavad-vidho bhavān vāpi
varjayitveśvaraṁ harim

vijeṣyati na ko 'py enaṁ
brahma-tejaḥ-samedhitam
nāsya śaktaḥ puraḥ sthātuṁ
kṛtāntasya yathā janāḥ

ojasvinam—so powerful; *balim*—Bali Mahārāja; *jetum*—to conquer; *na*—not; *samarthaḥ*—able; *asti*—is; *kaścana*—anyone; *bhavat-vidhaḥ*—like you; *bhavān*—you yourself; *vā api*—either; *varjayitvā*—excepting; *īśvaram*—the supreme controller; *harim*—the Supreme Personality of Godhead; *vijeṣyati*—will conquer; *na*—not; *kaḥ api*—anyone; *enam*—him (Bali Mahārāja); *brahma-tejaḥ-samedhitam*—now empowered with *brahma-tejas,* extraordinary spiritual power; *na*—not; *asya*—of him; *śaktaḥ*—is able; *puraḥ*—in front; *sthātum*—to stay; *kṛta-antasya*—of Yamarāja; *yathā*—as; *janāḥ*—people.

TRANSLATION

Neither you nor your men can conquer the most powerful Bali. Indeed, no one but the Supreme Personality of Godhead can conquer him, for he is now equipped with the supreme spiritual power [brahma-tejas]. As no one can stand before Yamarāja, no one can now stand before Bali Mahārāja.

TEXT 30

तस्मान्निलयमुत्सृज्य यूयं सर्वे त्रिविष्टपम् ।
यात कालं प्रतीक्षन्तो यतः शत्रोर्विपर्ययः ॥३०॥

tasmān nilayam utsṛjya
yūyaṁ sarve tri-viṣṭapam
yāta kālaṁ pratīkṣanto
yataḥ śatror viparyayaḥ

tasmāt—therefore; *nilayam*—not visible; *utsṛjya*—giving up; *yūyam*—you; *sarve*—all; *tri-viṣṭapam*—the heavenly kingdom; *yāta*—go somewhere else; *kālam*—time; *pratīkṣantaḥ*—waiting for; *yataḥ*—whereof; *śatroḥ*—of your enemy; *viparyayaḥ*—the reverse condition arrives.

TRANSLATION

Therefore, waiting until the situation of your enemies is reversed, you should all leave this heavenly planet and go elsewhere, where you will not be seen.

TEXT 31

एष विप्रबलोदर्कः सम्प्रत्यूर्जितविक्रमः ।
तेषामेवापमानेन सानुबन्धो विनङ्क्ष्यति ॥३१॥

eṣa vipra-balodarkaḥ
sampraty ūrjita-vikramaḥ
teṣām evāpamānena
sānubandho vinaṅkṣyati

eṣaḥ—this (Bali Mahārāja); *vipra-bala-udarkaḥ*—flourishing because of the brahminical power invested in him; *samprati*—at the present moment; *ūrjita-vikramaḥ*—extremely powerful; *teṣām*—of the same *brāhmaṇas; eva*—indeed; *apamānena*—by insult; *sa-anubandhaḥ*—with friends and assistants; *vinaṅkṣyati*—will be vanquished.

TRANSLATION

Bali Mahārāja has now become extremely powerful because of the benedictions given him by the brāhmaṇas, but when he later insults the brāhmaṇas, he will be vanquished, along with his friends and assistants.

PURPORT

Bali Mahārāja and Indra were enemies. Therefore, when Bṛhaspati, the spiritual master of the demigods, predicted that Bali Mahārāja would be vanquished when he insulted the *brāhmaṇas* by whose grace he had become so powerful, Bali Mahārāja's enemies were naturally anxious to know when that opportune moment would come. To pacify King Indra, Bṛhaspati assured him that the time would certainly come, for Bṛhaspati could see that in the future Bali Mahārāja would defy the orders of Śukrācārya in order to pacify Lord Viṣṇu, Vāmanadeva. Of course, to advance in Kṛṣṇa consciousness, one can take all risks. To please

Vāmanadeva, Bali Mahārāja risked defying the orders of his spiritual master, Śukrācārya. Because of this, he would lose all his property, yet because of devotional service to the Lord, he would get more than he expected, and in the future, in the eighth *manvantara*, he would occupy the throne of Indra again.

TEXT 32

एवं सुमन्त्रितार्थास्ते गुरुणार्थानुदर्शिना ।
हित्वा त्रिविष्टपं जग्मुर्गीर्वाणाः कामरूपिणः ॥३२॥

evaṁ sumantritārthās te
guruṇārthānudarśinā
hitvā tri-viṣṭapaṁ jagmur
gīrvāṇāḥ kāma-rūpiṇaḥ

evam—thus; *su-mantrita*—being well advised; *arthāḥ*—about duties; *te*—they (the demigods); *guruṇā*—by their spiritual master; *artha-anudarśinā*—whose instructions were quite befitting; *hitvā*—giving up; *tri-viṣṭapam*—the heavenly kingdom; *jagmuḥ*—went; *gīrvāṇāḥ*—the demigods; *kāma-rūpiṇaḥ*—who could assume any form they liked.

TRANSLATION

Śukadeva Gosvāmī continued: The demigods, being thus advised by Bṛhaspati for their benefit, immediately accepted his words. Assuming forms according to their desire, they left the heavenly kingdom and scattered, without being observed by the demons.

PURPORT

The word *kāma-rūpiṇaḥ* indicates that the demigods, the inhabitants of the heavenly planets, can assume any form they desire. Thus it was not at all difficult for them to remain incognito before the eyes of the demons.

TEXT 33

देवेष्वथ निलीनेषु बलिर्वैरोचनः पुरीम् ।
देवधानीमधिष्ठाय वशं निन्ये जगत्त्रयम् ॥३३॥

deveṣv atha nilīneṣu
balir vairocanaḥ purīm
deva-dhānīm adhiṣṭhāya
vaśaṁ ninye jagat-trayam

deveṣu—all the demigods; *atha*—in this way; *nilīneṣu*—when they disappeared; *baliḥ*—Bali Mahārāja; *vairocanaḥ*—the son of Virocana; *purīm*—the heavenly kingdom; *deva-dhānīm*—the residence of the demigods; *adhiṣṭhāya*—taking possession of; *vaśam*—under control; *ninye*—brought; *jagat-trayam*—the three worlds.

TRANSLATION

When the demigods had disappeared, Bali Mahārāja, the son of Virocana, entered the heavenly kingdom, and from there he brought the three worlds under his control.

TEXT 34

तं विश्वजयिनं शिष्यं भृगवः शिष्यवत्सलाः ।
शतेन हयमेधानामनुव्रतमयाजयन् ॥३४॥

taṁ viśva-jayinaṁ śiṣyaṁ
bhṛgavaḥ śiṣya-vatsalāḥ
śatena hayamedhānām
anuvratam ayājayan

tam—unto him (Bali Mahārāja); *viśva-jayinam*—the conqueror of the entire universe; *śiṣyam*—because of his being a disciple; *bhṛgavaḥ*—the *brāhmaṇas,* descendants of Bhṛgu like Śukrācārya; *śiṣya-vatsalāḥ*—being very pleased with the disciple; *śatena*—by one hundred; *haya-medhānām*—sacrifices known as *aśvamedha; anuvratam*—following the instruction of the *brāhmaṇas; ayājayan*—caused to execute.

TRANSLATION

The brāhmaṇa descendants of Bhṛgu, being very pleased with their disciple, who had conquered the entire universe, now engaged him in performing one hundred aśvamedha sacrifices.

PURPORT

We have seen in the dispute between Mahārāja Pṛthu and Indra that when Mahārāja Pṛthu wanted to perform one hundred *aśvamedha-yajñas*, Indra wanted to impede him, for it is because of such great sacrifices that Indra was made King of heaven. Here the *brāhmaṇa* descendants of Bhṛgu decided that although Mahārāja Bali was situated on the throne of Indra, he would not be able to stay there unless he performed such sacrifices. Therefore they advised Mahārāja Bali to perform at least as many *aśvamedha-yajñas* as Indra. The word *ayājayan* indicates that all the *brāhmaṇas* induced Bali Mahārāja to perform such sacrifices.

TEXT 35

ततस्तदनुभावेन भुवनत्रयविश्रुताम् ।
कीर्तिं दिक्षु वितन्वानः स रेज उडुराडिव ॥३५॥

tatas tad-anubhāvena
bhuvana-traya-viśrutām
kīrtiṁ dikṣu vitanvānaḥ
sa reja uḍurāḍ iva

tataḥ—thereafter; *tat-anubhāvena*—because of performing such great sacrifices; *bhuvana-traya*—throughout the three worlds; *viśrutām*—celebrated; *kīrtim*—reputation; *dikṣu*—in all directions; *vitanvānaḥ*—spreading; *saḥ*—he (Bali Mahārāja); *reje*—became effulgent; *uḍurāṭ*—the moon; *iva*—like.

TRANSLATION

When Bali Mahārāja performed these sacrifices, he gained a great reputation in all directions, throughout the three worlds. Thus he shone in his position, like the brilliant moon in the sky.

TEXT 36

बुभुजे च श्रियं स्वृद्धां द्विजदेवोपलम्भिताम् ।
कृतकृत्यमिवात्मानं मन्यमानो महामनाः ॥३६॥

bubhuje ca śriyaṁ svṛddhāṁ
dvija-devopalambhitām
kṛta-kṛtyam ivātmānaṁ
manyamāno mahāmanāḥ

bubhuje—enjoyed; *ca*—also; *śriyam*—opulence; *su-ṛddhām*—prosperity; *dvija*—of the *brāhmaṇas; deva*—as good as the demigods; *upalambhitām*—achieved because of the favor; *kṛta-kṛtyam*—very satisfied by his activities; *iva*—like that; *ātmānam*—himself; *manyamānaḥ*—thinking; *mahā-manāḥ*—the great-minded.

TRANSLATION

Because of the favor of the brāhmaṇas, the great soul Bali Mahārāja, thinking himself very satisfied, became very opulent and prosperous and began to enjoy the kingdom.

PURPORT

The *brāhmaṇas* are called *dvija-deva,* and *kṣatriyas* are generally called *nara-deva.* The word *deva* actually refers to the Supreme Personality of Godhead. The *brāhmaṇas* guide human society in becoming happy by satisfying Lord Viṣṇu, and according to their advice, the *kṣatriyas,* who are called *nara-deva,* keep law and order so that other people, namely the *vaiśyas* and *śūdras,* may properly follow regulative principles. In this way, people are gradually elevated to Kṛṣṇa consciousness.

Thus end the Bhaktivedanta purports of the Eighth Canto, Fifteenth Chapter, of the Śrīmad-Bhāgavatam, *entitled "Bali Mahārāja Conquers the Heavenly Planets."*

CHAPTER SIXTEEN

Executing the Payo-vrata Process of Worship

As described in this chapter, because Aditi, the mother of the demigods, was very afflicted, her husband, Kaśyapa Muni, told her how to observe vows in austerities for the benefit of her sons.

Since the demigods were not visible in the heavenly kingdom, their mother, Aditi, because of separation from them, was very much aggrieved. One day after many, many years, the great sage Kaśyapa emerged from a trance of meditation and returned to his *āśrama.* He saw that the *āśrama* was no longer beautiful and that his wife was very morose. Everywhere in the *āśrama,* he saw signs of lamentation. The great sage therefore inquired from his wife about the well-being of the *āśrama* and asked her why she looked so morose. After Aditi informed Kaśyapa Muni about the *āśrama's* well-being, she told him that she was lamenting for the absence of her sons. She then requested him to tell her how her sons could return and reoccupy their positions. She wanted all good fortune for her sons. Moved by Aditi's request, Kaśyapa Muni instructed her in the philosophy of self-realization, the difference between matter and spirit, and how to be unaffected by material loss. But when he saw that Aditi was not satisfied even after he had given these instructions, he advised her to worship Vāsudeva, Janārdana. He assured her that only Lord Vāsudeva could satisfy her and fulfill all her desires. When Aditi then expressed her desire to worship Lord Vāsudeva, Prajāpati Kaśyapa told her about a process of worship known as *payo-vrata,* which is executed in twelve days. Lord Brahmā had instructed him how to satisfy Lord Kṛṣṇa by this process, and thus he advised his wife to observe this vow and its regulative principles.

TEXT 1

श्रीशुक उवाच

एवं पुत्रेषु नष्टेषु देवमातादितिस्तदा ।
हृते त्रिविष्टपे दैत्यैः पर्यतप्यदनाथवत् ॥ १ ॥

śrī-śuka uvāca
evaṁ putreṣu naṣṭeṣu
deva-mātāditis tadā
hṛte tri-viṣṭape daityaiḥ
paryatapyad anāthavat

śrī-śukaḥ uvāca—Śrī Śukadeva Gosvāmī said; *evam*—in this way; *putreṣu*—when her sons; *naṣṭeṣu*—disappearing from their position; *deva-mātā*—the mother of the demigods; *aditiḥ*—Aditi; *tadā*—at that time; *hṛte*—because of being lost; *tri-viṣṭape*—the kingdom of heaven; *daityaiḥ*—by the influence of the demons; *paryatapyat*—began to lament; *anātha-vat*—as if she had no protector.

TRANSLATION

Śukadeva Gosvāmī said: O King, when Aditi's sons, the demigods, had thus disappeared from heaven and the demons had occupied their places, Aditi began lamenting, as if she had no protector.

TEXT 2

एकदा कश्यपस्तस्या आश्रमं भगवानगात् ।
निरुत्सवं निरानन्दं समाधेर्विरतश्चिरात् ॥ २ ॥

ekadā kaśyapas tasyā
āśramaṁ bhagavān agāt
nirutsavaṁ nirānandaṁ
samādher virataś cirāt

ekadā—one day; *kaśyapaḥ*—the great sage Kaśyapa Muni; *tasyāḥ*—of Aditi; *āśramam*—to the shelter; *bhagavān*—greatly powerful; *agāt*—went; *nirutsavam*—without enthusiasm; *nirānandam*—without jubilation; *samādheḥ*—his trance; *virataḥ*—stopping; *cirāt*—after a long time.

TRANSLATION

After many, many days, the great powerful sage Kaśyapa Muni arose from a trance of meditation and returned home to see the āśrama of Aditi neither jubilant nor festive.

TEXT 3

स पत्नीं दीनवदनां कृतासनपरिग्रहः ।
सभाजितो यथान्यायमिदमाह कुरूद्वह ॥ ३ ॥

sa patnīṁ dīna-vadanāṁ
kṛtāsana-parigrahaḥ
sabhājito yathā-nyāyam
idam āha kurūdvaha

saḥ—Kaśyapa Muni; *patnīm*—unto his wife; *dīna-vadanām*—having a dry face; *kṛta-āsana-parigrahaḥ*—after accepting a sitting place; *sabhājitaḥ*—being honored by Aditi; *yathā-nyāyam*—according to time and place; *idam āha*—spoke as follows; *kuru-udvaha*—O Mahārāja Parīkṣit, the best of the Kurus.

TRANSLATION

O best of the Kurus, when Kaśyapa Muni had been properly received and welcomed, he took his seat and then spoke as follows to his wife, Aditi, who was very morose.

TEXT 4

अप्यभद्रं न विप्राणां भद्रे लोकेऽधुनागतम् ।
न धर्मस्य न लोकस्य मृत्योश्छन्दानुवर्तिनः ॥ ४ ॥

apy abhadraṁ na viprāṇāṁ
bhadre loke 'dhunāgatam
na dharmasya na lokasya
mṛtyoś chandānuvartinaḥ

api—whether; *abhadram*—ill fortune; *na*—not; *viprāṇām*—of the *brāhmaṇas; bhadre*—O most gentle Aditi; *loke*—in this world; *adhunā*—at the present moment; *āgatam*—has come; *na*—not; *dharmasya*—of religious principles; *na*—not; *lokasya*—of the people in general; *mṛtyoḥ*—death; *chanda-anuvartinaḥ*—who are followers of the whims of death.

TRANSLATION

O most gentle one, I wonder whether anything inauspicious has now taken place in regard to religious principles, the brāhmaṇas or the people in general, who are subject to the whims of death.

PURPORT

There are prescribed duties for all the inhabitants of this material world, especially for the *brāhmaṇas* but also for the people in general, who are subject to the whims of death. Kaśyapa Muni wondered whether the regulative principles, which are meant for the well-being of everyone, had been disobeyed. He accordingly continued his inquiries for seven verses.

TEXT 5

अपि वाकुशलं किञ्चिद् गृहेषु गृहमेधिनि ।
धर्मस्यार्थस्य कामस्य यत्र योगो ह्ययोगिनाम् ॥ ५ ॥

api vākuśalaṁ kiñcid
gṛheṣu gṛha-medhini
dharmasyārthasya kāmasya
yatra yogo hy ayoginām

api—I am wondering; *vā*—either; *akuśalam*—inauspiciousness; *kiñcit*—some; *gṛheṣu*—at home; *gṛha-medhini*—O my wife, who are attached to household life; *dharmasya*—of the principles of religion; *arthasya*—of the economic condition; *kāmasya*—of satisfaction of desires; *yatra*—at home; *yogaḥ*—the result of meditation; *hi*—indeed; *ayoginām*—even of those who are not transcendentalists.

TRANSLATION

O my wife, who are very much attached to household life, if the principles of religion, economic development and satisfaction of the senses are properly followed in household life, one's activities are as good as those of a transcendentalist. I wonder whether there have been any discrepancies in following these principles.

PURPORT

In this verse, Aditi has been addressed by her husband, Kaśyapa Muni, as *gṛha-medhini*, which means "one who is satisfied in household life for sense gratification." Generally, those who are in household life pursue sense gratification in the field of activities performed for material results. Such *gṛhamedhīs* have only one aim in life—sense gratification. Therefore it is said, *yan maithunādi-gṛhamedhi-sukhaṁ hi tuccham:* the householder's life is based on sense gratification, and therefore the happiness derived from it is very meager. Nonetheless, the Vedic process is so comprehensive that even in householder life one can adjust his activities according to the regulative principles of *dharma, artha, kāma* and *mokṣa.* One's aim should be to achieve liberation, but because one cannot at once give up sense gratification, in the *śāstras* there are injunctions prescribing how to follow the principles of religion, economic development and sense gratification. As explained in *Śrīmad-Bhāgavatam* (1.2.9), *dharmasya hy āpavargyasya nārtho 'rthāyopakalpate:* "All occupational engagements are certainly meant for ultimate liberation. They should never be performed for material gain." Those who are in household life should not think that religion is meant to improve the process of the householder's sense gratification. Household life is also meant for advancement in spiritual understanding, by which one can ultimately gain liberation from the material clutches. One should remain in household life with the aim of understanding the ultimate goal of life (*tattva-jijñāsā*). Then household life is as good as the life of a *yogī.* Kaśyapa Muni therefore inquired from his wife whether the principles of religion, economic development and sense gratification were being properly followed in terms of the śāstric injunctions. As soon as one deviates from the injunctions of the *śāstra,* the purpose of household life is immediately lost in confusion.

TEXT 6

अपि वातिथयोऽभ्येत्य कुटुम्बासक्तया त्वया ।
गृहादपूजिता याताः प्रत्युत्थानेन वा क्वचित् ॥ ६ ॥

api vātithayo 'bhyetya
kuṭumbāsaktayā tvayā

gṛhād apūjitā yātāḥ
pratyutthānena vā kvacit

api—whether; *vā*—either; *atithayaḥ*—guests who come without an invitation; *abhyetya*—coming to the home; *kuṭumba-āsaktayā*—who were too attached to the family members; *tvayā*—by you; *gṛhāt*—from the house; *apūjitāḥ*—without being properly welcomed; *yātāḥ*—went away; *pratyutthānena*—by standing up; *vā*—either; *kvacit*—sometimes.

TRANSLATION

I wonder whether because of being too attached to the members of your family, you failed to properly receive uninvited guests, who therefore were not welcomed and went away.

PURPORT

It is the duty of a householder to receive guests, even if a guest be an enemy. When a guest comes to one's home, one should properly receive him by standing up and offering him a seat. It is enjoined, *gṛhe śatrum api prāptaṁ viśvastam akutobhayam:* if even an enemy comes to one's home, one should receive him in such a way that the guest will forget that his host is an enemy. According to one's position, one should properly receive anyone who comes to one's home. At least a seat and a glass of water should be offered, so that the guest will not be displeased. Kaśyapa Muni inquired from Aditi whether disrespect had been shown to such guests, or *atithis*. The word *atithi* refers to one who comes without an invitation.

TEXT 7

गृहेषु येष्वतिथयो नार्चिताः सलिलैरपि ।
यदि निर्यान्ति ते नूनं फेरुराजगृहोपमाः ॥ ७ ॥

gṛheṣu yeṣv atithayo
nārcitāḥ salilair api
yadi niryānti te nūnaṁ
pherurāja-gṛhopamāḥ

gṛheṣu—at home; *yeṣu*—which; *atithayaḥ*—uninvited guests; *na*—not; *arcitāḥ*—welcomed; *salilaiḥ api*—even by offering a glass of water; *yadi*—if; *niryānti*—they go away; *te*—such houschold life; *nūnam*—indeed; *pheru-rāja*—of jackals; *gṛha*—the homes; *upamāḥ*—like.

TRANSLATION

Homes from which guests go away without having been received even with an offering of a little water are like those holes in the field which are the homes of jackals.

PURPORT

In a field there may be holes made by snakes and mice, but when there are very big holes, it may be supposed that jackals live there. Certainly no one goes to take shelter in such homes. Thus the homes of human beings where *atithis*, uninvited guests, are not properly received are like the homes of jackals.

TEXT 8

अप्यग्नयस्तु वेलायां न हुता हविषा सति ।
त्वयोद्विग्नधिया भद्रे प्रोषिते मयि कर्हिचित् ॥ ८ ॥

apy agnayas tu velāyāṁ
na hutā haviṣā sati
tvayodvigna-dhiyā bhadre
proṣite mayi karhicit

api—whether; *agnayaḥ*—fires; *tu*—indeed; *velāyām*—in the fire sacrifice; *na*—not; *hutāḥ*—offered; *haviṣā*—by ghee; *sati*—O chaste woman; *tvayā*—by you; *udvigna-dhiyā*—because of some anxiety; *bhadre*—O auspicious woman; *proṣite*—was away from home; *mayi*—when I; *karhicit*—sometimes.

TRANSLATION

O chaste and auspicious woman, when I left home for other places, were you in so much anxiety that you did not offer oblations of ghee into the fire?

TEXT 9

यत्पूजया कामदुघान्याति लोकान्गृहान्वितः ।
ब्राह्मणोऽग्निश्च वै विष्णोः सर्वदेवात्मनो मुखम् ॥ ९ ॥

yat-pūjayā kāma-dughān
yāti lokān gṛhānvitaḥ
brāhmaṇo 'gniś ca vai viṣṇoḥ
sarva-devātmano mukham

yat-pūjayā—by worshiping the fire and *brāhmaṇas; kāma-dughān*—which fulfill one's desires; *yāti*—one goes; *lokān*—to the destination of the higher planetary system; *gṛha-anvitaḥ*—a person attached to household life; *brāhmaṇaḥ*—the *brāhmaṇas; agniḥ ca*—and the fire; *vai*—indeed; *viṣṇoḥ*—of Lord Viṣṇu; *sarva-deva-ātmanaḥ*—the soul of all the demigods; *mukham*—the mouth.

TRANSLATION

By worshiping the fire and the brāhmaṇas, a householder can achieve the desired goal of residing in the higher planets, for the sacrificial fire and the brāhmaṇas are to be considered the mouth of Lord Viṣṇu, who is the Supersoul of all the demigods.

PURPORT

According to the Vedic system, a fire sacrifice is held in order to offer oblations of ghee, grains, fruits, flowers and so on, so that Lord Viṣṇu may eat and be satisfied. The Lord says in *Bhagavad-gītā* (9.26):

patraṁ puṣpaṁ phalaṁ toyaṁ
yo me bhaktyā prayacchati
tad ahaṁ bhakty-upahṛtam
aśnāmi prayatātmanaḥ

"If one offers Me with love and devotion a leaf, a flower, fruit or water, I will accept it." Therefore, all these items may be offered in the sacrificial fire, and Lord Viṣṇu will be satisfied. Similarly, *brāhmaṇa-bhojana*, feeding of the *brāhmaṇas*, is also recommended, for when the *brāhmaṇas* eat sumptuous remnants of food after *yajña*, this is another way that Lord Viṣṇu Himself eats. Therefore the Vedic principles recommend that in every festival or ceremony one offer oblations to the fire and give sumptuous food for the *brāhmaṇas* to eat. By such activities, a householder may be elevated to the heavenly planets and similar places in the higher planetary systems.

TEXT 10

अपि सर्वे कुशलिनस्तव पुत्रा मनस्विनि ।
लक्षयेऽस्वस्थमात्मानं भवत्या लक्षणैरहम् ॥१०॥

api sarve kuśalinas
tava putrā manasvini
lakṣaye 'svastham ātmānaṁ
bhavatyā lakṣaṇair aham

api—whether; *sarve*—all; *kuśalinaḥ*—in full auspiciousness; *tava*—your; *putrāḥ*—sons; *manasvini*—O great-minded lady; *lakṣaye*—I see; *asvastham*—not in tranquillity; *ātmānam*—the mind; *bhavatyāḥ*—of you; *lakṣaṇaiḥ*—by symptoms; *aham*—I.

TRANSLATION

O great-minded lady, are all your sons faring well? Seeing your withered face, I can perceive that your mind is not tranquil. How is this so?

TEXT 11

श्रीअदितिरुवाच
भद्रं द्विजगवां ब्रह्मन्धर्मस्यास्य जनस्य च ।
त्रिवर्गस्य परं क्षेत्रं गृहमेधिन्गृहा इमे ॥११॥

śrī-aditir uvāca
bhadraṁ dvija-gavāṁ brahman
dharmasyāsya janasya ca

tri-vargasya paraṁ kṣetraṁ
gṛhamedhin gṛhā ime

śrī-aditiḥ uvāca—Śrīmatī Aditi said; *bhadram*—all auspiciousness; *dvija-gavām*—of the *brāhmaṇas* and the cows; *brahman*—O *brāhmaṇa; dharmasya asya*—of the religious principles mentioned in *śāstra; janasya*—of the people in general; *ca*—and; *tri-vargasya*—of the three processes of elevation (*dharma, artha* and *kāma*); *param*—the supreme; *kṣetram*—field; *gṛhamedhin*—O my husband, who are attached to household life; *gṛhāḥ*—your home; *ime*—all these things.

TRANSLATION

Aditi said: O my respected brāhmaṇa husband, all is well with the brāhmaṇas, the cows, religion and the welfare of other people. O master of the house, the three principles of dharma, artha and kāma flourish in household life, which is consequently full of good fortune.

PURPORT

In household life one can develop the three principles of religion, economic development and sense gratification according to the regulations given in the *śāstras*, but to attain liberation one must give up household life and place himself in the transcendental renounced order. Kaśyapa Muni was not in the renounced order of life. Therefore he is addressed here once as *brahman* and another time as *gṛhamedhin*. Aditi, his wife, assured him that as far as household life was concerned, everything was going nicely, and the *brāhmaṇas* and cows were being honored and protected. In other words, there were no disturbances; household life was duly progressing.

TEXT 12

अग्नयोऽतिथयो भृत्या भिक्षवो ये च लिप्सवः ।
सर्वं भगवतो ब्रह्मन्नुध्यानान्न रिष्यति ॥१२॥

agnayo 'tithayo bhṛtyā
bhikṣavo ye ca lipsavaḥ

sarvaṁ bhagavato brahmann
anudhyānān na riṣyati

agnayaḥ—worshiping the fires; *atithayaḥ*—receiving the guests; *bhṛtyāḥ*—satisfying the servants; *bhikṣavaḥ*—pleasing the beggars; *ye*—all of them who; *ca*—and; *lipsavaḥ*—as they desire (are taken care of); *sarvam*—all of them; *bhagavataḥ*—of you, my lord; *brahman*—O *brāhmaṇa; anudhyānāt*—from always thinking; *na riṣyati*—nothing is missed (everything is properly done).

TRANSLATION

O beloved husband, the fires, guests, servants and beggars are all being properly cared for by me. Because I always think of you, there is no possibility that any of the religious principles will be neglected.

TEXT 13

को नु मे भगवन्कामो न सम्पद्येत मानसः ।
यस्या भवान्प्रजाध्यक्ष एवं धर्मान्प्रभाषते ॥१३॥

ko nu me bhagavan kāmo
na sampadyeta mānasaḥ
yasyā bhavān prajādhyakṣa
evaṁ dharmān prabhāṣate

kaḥ—what; *nu*—indeed; *me*—my; *bhagavan*—O lord; *kāmaḥ*—desire; *na*—not; *sampadyeta*—can be fulfilled; *mānasaḥ*—within my mind; *yasyāḥ*—of me; *bhavān*—your good self; *prajā-adhyakṣaḥ*—Prajāpati; *evam*—thus; *dharmān*—religious principles; *prabhāṣate*—talks.

TRANSLATION

O my lord, since you are a Prajāpati and are personally my instructor in the principles of religion, where is the possibility that all my desires will not be fulfilled?

TEXT 14

तवैव मारीच मनःशरीरजाः
प्रजा इमाः सत्त्वरजस्तमोजुषः ।
समो भवांस्तास्वसुरादिषु प्रभो
तथापि भक्तं भजते महेश्वरः ॥१४॥

tavaiva mārīca manaḥ-śarīrajāḥ
prajā imāḥ sattva-rajas-tamo-juṣaḥ
samo bhavāṁs tāsv asurādiṣu prabho
tathāpi bhaktaṁ bhajate maheśvaraḥ

tava—your; *eva*—indeed; *mārīca*—O son of Marīci; *manaḥ-śarīra-jāḥ*—born either of your body or of your mind (all the demons and demigods); *prajāḥ*—born of you; *imāḥ*—all of them; *sattva-rajaḥ-tamaḥ-juṣaḥ*—infected with *sattva-guṇa, rajo-guṇa* or *tamo-guṇa; samaḥ*—equal; *bhavān*—your good self; *tāsu*—to every one of them; *asura-ādiṣu*—beginning with the *asuras; prabho*—O my lord; *tathā api*—still; *bhaktam*—unto the devotees; *bhajate*—takes care of; *mahā-īśvaraḥ*—the Supreme Personality of Godhead, the supreme controller.

TRANSLATION

O son of Marīci, because you are a great personality you are equal toward all the demons and demigods, who are born either from your body or from your mind and who possess one or another of the three qualities—sattva-guṇa, rajo-guṇa or tamo-guṇa. But although the Supreme Personality of Godhead, the supreme controller, is equal toward all living entities, He is especially favorable to the devotees.

PURPORT

In *Bhagavad-gītā* (9.29) the Lord says:

samo 'haṁ sarva-bhūteṣu
na me dveṣyo 'sti na priyaḥ

ye bhajanti tu māṁ bhaktyā
mayi te teṣu cāpy aham

Although the Supreme Personality of Godhead is equal toward everyone, He is especially inclined toward those who engage in His devotional service. The Lord says, *kaunteya pratijānīhi na me bhaktaḥ praṇaśyati:* "My dear son of Kuntī, please declare that My devotee will never be vanquished." Elsewhere, Kṛṣṇa also says:

ye yathā māṁ prapadyante
tāṁs tathaiva bhajāmy aham
mama vartmānuvartante
manuṣyāḥ pārtha sarvaśaḥ
(Bg. 4.11)

Actually, everyone is trying to please the Supreme Personality of Godhead in various ways, but according to their methods of approach, the Supreme Lord endows them with different benedictions. Thus Aditi appealed to her husband by saying that since even the supreme controller favors His devotees and since Indra, Kaśyapa's devoted son, was in difficulty, Kaśyapa should bestow his favor upon Indra.

TEXT 15

तस्मादीश भजन्त्या मे श्रेयश्चिन्तय सुव्रत ।
हृतश्रियो हृतस्थानान्सपत्नैः पाहि नः प्रभो ॥१५॥

tasmād īśa bhajantyā me
śreyaś cintaya suvrata
hṛta-śriyo hṛta-sthānān
sapatnaiḥ pāhi naḥ prabho

tasmāt—therefore; *īśa*—O powerful controller; *bhajantyāḥ*—of your servitor; *me*—me; *śreyaḥ*—auspiciousness; *cintaya*—just consider; *suvrata*—O most gentle one; *hṛta-śriyaḥ*—bereft of all opulence; *hṛta-sthānān*—bereft of a residence; *sapatnaiḥ*—by the competitors; *pāhi*—please protect; *naḥ*—us; *prabho*—O my lord.

TRANSLATION

Therefore, most gentle lord, kindly favor your maidservant. We have now been deprived of our opulence and residence by our competitors, the demons. Kindly give us protection.

PURPORT

Aditi, the mother of the demigods, appealed to Kaśyapa Muni to give the demigods protection. When we speak of the demigods, this also includes their mother.

TEXT 16

परैर्विवासिता साहं मग्ना व्यसनसागरे ।
ऐश्वर्यं श्रीर्यशः स्थानं हृतानि प्रबलैर्मम ॥१६॥

parair vivāsitā sāhaṁ
magnā vyasana-sāgare
aiśvaryaṁ śrīr yaśaḥ sthānaṁ
hṛtāni prabalair mama

paraiḥ—by our enemies; *vivāsitā*—taken away from our residential quarters; *sā*—the same; *aham*—I; *magnā*—drowned; *vyasana-sāgare*—in an ocean of trouble; *aiśvaryam*—opulence; *śrīḥ*—beauty; *yaśaḥ*—reputation; *sthānam*—place; *hṛtāni*—all taken away; *prabalaiḥ*—very powerful; *mama*—my.

TRANSLATION

The demons, our formidably powerful enemies, have taken away our opulence, our beauty, our fame and even our residence. Indeed, we have now been exiled, and we are drowning in an ocean of trouble.

TEXT 17

यथा तानि पुनः साधो प्रपद्येरन् ममात्मजाः ।
तथा विधेहि कल्याणं धिया कल्याणकृत्तम ॥१७॥

yathā tāni punaḥ sādho
prapadyeran mamātmajāḥ

tathā vidhehi kalyāṇaṁ
dhiyā kalyāṇa-kṛttama

yathā—as; *tāni*—all of our lost things; *punaḥ*—again; *sādho*—O great saintly person; *prapadyeran*—can regain; *mama*—my; *ātma-jāḥ*—offspring (sons); *tathā*—so; *vidhehi*—kindly do; *kalyāṇam*—auspiciousness; *dhiyā*—by consideration; *kalyāṇa-kṛt-tama*—O you who are the best person to act for our welfare.

TRANSLATION

O best of sages, best of all those who grant auspicious benedictions, please consider our situation and bestow upon my sons the benedictions by which they can regain what they have lost.

TEXT 18

श्रीशुक उवाच
एवमभ्यर्थितोऽदित्या कस्तामाह स्मयन्निव ।
अहो मायाबलं विष्णोः स्नेहबद्धमिदं जगत् ॥१८॥

śrī-śuka uvāca
evam abhyarthito 'dityā
kas tām āha smayann iva
aho māyā-balaṁ viṣṇoḥ
sneha-baddham idaṁ jagat

śrī-śukaḥ uvāca—Śrī Śukadeva Gosvāmī said; *evam*—in this way; *abhyarthitaḥ*—being requested; *adityā*—by Aditi; *kaḥ*—Kaśyapa Muni; *tām*—unto her; *āha*—said; *smayan*—smiling; *iva*—just like; *aho*—alas; *māyā-balam*—the influence of the illusory energy; *viṣṇoḥ*—of Lord Viṣṇu; *sneha-baddham*—influenced by this affection; *idam*—this; *jagat*—whole world.

TRANSLATION

Śukadeva Gosvāmī continued: When Kaśyapa Muni was thus requested by Aditi, he slightly smiled. "Alas," he said, "how

powerful is the illusory energy of Lord Viṣṇu, by which the entire world is bound by affection for children!"

PURPORT

Kaśyapa Muni was surely sympathetic to his wife's affliction, yet he was surprised at how the whole world is influenced by affection.

TEXT 19

क्व देहो भौतिकोऽनात्मा क्व चात्मा प्रकृतेः परः ।
कस्य के पतिपुत्राद्या मोह एव हि कारणम् ॥१९॥

kva deho bhautiko 'nātmā
kva cātmā prakṛteḥ paraḥ
kasya ke pati-putrādyā
moha eva hi kāraṇam

kva—where is; *dehaḥ*—this material body; *bhautikaḥ*—made of five elements; *anātmā*—not the spirit soul; *kva*—where is; *ca*—also; *ātmā*—the spirit soul; *prakṛteḥ*—to the material world; *paraḥ*—transcendental; *kasya*—of whom; *ke*—who is; *pati*—husband; *putra-ādyāḥ*—or son and so on; *mohaḥ*—illusion; *eva*—indeed; *hi*—certainly; *kāraṇam*—cause.

TRANSLATION

Kaśyapa Muni continued: What is this material body, made of five elements? It is different from the spirit soul. Indeed, the spirit soul is completely different from the material elements from which the body is made. But because of bodily attachment, one is regarded as a husband or son. These illusory relationships are caused by misunderstanding.

PURPORT

The spirit soul (*ātmā* or *jīva*) is certainly different from the body, which is a combination of five material elements. This is a simple fact, but it is not understood unless one is spiritually educated. Kaśyapa Muni met his wife, Aditi, in the heavenly planets, but the same misconception extends throughout the entire universe and is also here on earth. There are different grades of living entities, but all of them are more or less under the impression of the bodily conception of life. In other words, all living entities in this material world are more or less devoid of spiritual education. The Vedic civilization, however, is based on spiritual education, and spiritual education is the special basis on which *Bhagavad-gītā* was spoken to Arjuna. In the beginning of *Bhagavad-gītā*, Kṛṣṇa instructed Arjuna to understand that the spirit soul is different from the body.

dehino 'smin yathā dehe
kaumāraṁ yauvanaṁ jarā
tathā dehāntara-prāptir
dhīras tatra na muhyati

"As the embodied soul continually passes, in this body, from boyhood to youth to old age, the soul similarly passes into another body at death. The self-realized soul is not bewildered by such a change." (Bg. 2.13) Unfortunately, this spiritual education is completely absent from modern human civilization. No one understands his real self-interest, which lies with the spirit soul, not with the material body. Education means spiritual education. To work hard in the bodily conception of life, without spiritual education, is to live like an animal. *Nāyaṁ deho deha-bhājāṁ nṛ-loke kaṣṭān kāmān arhate viḍ-bhujāṁ ye* (*Bhāg.* 5.5.1). People are working so hard simply for bodily comforts, without education regarding the spirit soul. Thus they are living in a very risky civilization, for it is a fact that the spirit soul has to transmigrate from one body to another (*tathā dehāntara-prāptiḥ*). Without spiritual education, people are kept in dark ignorance and do not know what will happen to them after the annihilation of the present body. They are working blindly, and blind leaders are directing them. *Andhā yathāndhair upanīyamānās te 'pīśa-tantryām uru-dāmni baddhāḥ* (*Bhāg.* 7.5.31). A foolish person does not know that he is completely under the bondage of material nature and that after death material nature will impose upon him a certain type of body, which he will have to accept. He does not know that although in his present body he may be a very important man, he may next get the body of an animal or tree because of his ignorant activities in the modes of material nature. Therefore the Kṛṣṇa consciousness movement is trying to give the true light of spiritual existence to all living entities. This movement is not very difficult to understand, and people must take advantage of it, for it will save them from the risky life of irresponsibility.

TEXT 20

उपतिष्ठस्व पुरुषं भगवन्तं जनार्दनम् ।
सर्वभूतगुहावासं वासुदेवं जगद्गुरुम् ॥२०॥

upatiṣṭhasva puruṣaṁ
bhagavantaṁ janārdanam
sarva-bhūta-guhā-vāsaṁ
vāsudevaṁ jagad-gurum

upatiṣṭhasva—just try to worship; *puruṣam*—the Supreme Person; *bhagavantam*—the Personality of Godhead; *janārdanam*—who can kill all the enemies; *sarva-bhūta-guhā-vāsam*—living within the core of the heart of everyone; *vāsudevam*—Vāsudeva, Kṛṣṇa, who is all-pervading and is the son of Vasudeva; *jagat-gurum*—the spiritual master and teacher of the whole world.

TRANSLATION

My dear Aditi, engage in devotional service to the Supreme Personality of Godhead, who is the master of everything, who can subdue everyone's enemies, and who sits within everyone's heart. Only that Supreme Person—Kṛṣṇa, or Vāsudeva—can bestow all auspicious benedictions upon everyone, for He is the spiritual master of the universe.

PURPORT

With these words, Kaśyapa Muni tried to pacify his wife. Aditi made her appeal to her material husband. Of course, that is nice, but actually a material relative cannot do anything good for anyone. If anything good can be done, it is done by the Supreme Personality of Godhead, Vāsudeva. Therefore, Kaśyapa Muni advised his wife, Aditi, to begin worshiping Lord Vāsudeva, who is situated in everyone's heart. He is the friend of everyone and is known as Janārdana because He can kill all enemies. There are three modes of material nature—goodness, passion and ignorance—and above material nature, transcendental to material nature, is another existence, which is called *śuddha-sattva.* In the material world, the mode of goodness is considered the best, but because of material contamination, even the mode of goodness is sometimes overpowered by the modes of passion and ignorance. But when one transcends the competition between these modes and engages himself in devotional service, he rises above the three modes of material nature. In that transcendental position, one is situated in pure consciousness. *Sattvaṁ viśuddhaṁ vasudeva-śabditam* (*Bhāg.* 4.3.23). Above material nature is the position called *vasudeva,* or freedom from material contamination. Only in that position can one perceive the Supreme Personality of Godhead, Vāsudeva. Thus the *vasudeva* condition fulfills a spiritual necessity. *Vāsudevaḥ sarvam iti sa mahātmā sudurlabhaḥ.* When one realizes Vāsudeva, the Supreme Personality of Godhead, he becomes most exalted.

Paramātmā (Vāsudeva) is situated in everyone's heart, as confirmed in *Bhagavad-gītā.* The Lord says:

teṣāṁ satata-yuktānāṁ
bhajatāṁ prīti-pūrvakam
dadāmi buddhi-yogaṁ taṁ
yena mām upayānti te

"To those who are constantly devoted and who worship Me with love, I give the understanding by which they can come to Me." (Bg. 10.10)

īśvaraḥ sarva-bhūtānāṁ
hṛd-deśe 'rjuna tiṣṭhati

"The Supreme Lord is situated in everyone's heart, O Arjuna." (Bg. 18.61)

bhoktāraṁ yajña-tapasāṁ
sarva-loka-maheśvaram

suhṛdaṁ sarva-bhūtānāṁ
jñātvā māṁ śāntim ṛcchati

"The sages, knowing Me as the ultimate purpose of all sacrifices and austerities, the Supreme Lord of all planets and demigods and the benefactor and well-wisher of all living entities, attain peace from the pangs of material miseries." (Bg. 5.29)

Whenever one is perplexed, let him take shelter of the lotus feet of Vāsudeva, Kṛṣṇa, who will give the devotee intelligence to help him surpass all difficulties and return home, back to Godhead. Kaśyapa Muni advised his wife to seek shelter at the lotus feet of Vāsudeva, Kṛṣṇa, so that all her problems would be very easily solved. Thus Kaśyapa Muni was an ideal spiritual master. He was not so foolish that he would present himself as an exalted personality, as good as God. He was actually a bona fide *guru* because he advised his wife to seek shelter at the lotus feet of Vāsudeva. One who trains his subordinate or disciple to worship Vāsudeva is the truly bona fide spiritual master. The word *jagad-gurum* is very important in this regard. Kaśyapa Muni did not falsely declare himself to be *jagad-guru*, although he actually was *jagad-guru* because he advocated the cause of Vāsudeva. Actually, Vāsudeva is *jagad-guru*, as clearly stated here (*vāsudevaṁ jagad-gurum*). One who teaches the instructions of Vāsudeva, *Bhagavad-gītā*, is as good as *vāsudevaṁ jagad-gurum*. But when one who does not teach this instruction—as it is—declares himself *jagad-guru*, he simply cheats the public. Kṛṣṇa is *jagad-guru*, and one who teaches the instruction of Kṛṣṇa as it is, on behalf of Kṛṣṇa, may be accepted as *jagad-guru*. One who manufactures his own theories cannot be accepted; he becomes *jagad-guru* falsely.

TEXT 21

स विधास्यति ते कामान्हरिर्दीनानुकम्पनः ।
अमोघा भगवद्भक्तिर्नेतरेति मतिर्मम ॥२१॥

sa vidhāsyati te kāmān
harir dīnānukampanaḥ
amoghā bhagavad-bhaktir
netareti matir mama

saḥ—he (Vāsudeva); *vidhāsyati*—will undoubtedly fulfill; *te*—your; *kāmān*—desires; *hariḥ*—the Supreme Personality of Godhead; *dīna*—unto the poor; *anukampanaḥ*—very merciful; *amoghā*—infallible; *bhagavat-bhaktiḥ*—devotional service unto the Supreme Personality of Godhead; *na*—not; *itarā*—anything but *bhagavad-bhakti; iti*—thus; *matiḥ*—opinion; *mama*—my.

TRANSLATION

The Supreme Personality of Godhead, who is very merciful to the poor, will fulfill all of your desires, for devotional service unto Him is infallible. Any method other than devotional service is useless. That is my opinion.

PURPORT

There are three kinds of men, who are called *akāma, mokṣa-kāma* and *sarva-kāma.* One who tries to get liberation from this material world is called *mokṣa-kāma,* one who wants to enjoy this material world to its fullest extent is called *sarva-kāma,* and one who has fulfilled all his desires and has no further material desires is called *akāma.* A *bhakta* has no desire. *Sarvopādhi-vinirmuktaṁ tat-paratvena nirmalam.* He is purified and free from material desires. The *mokṣa-kāmī* wants to achieve liberation by merging into the existence of the Supreme Brahman, and because of this desire to merge into the existence of the Lord, he is not yet pure. And since those who want liberation are impure, what to speak of the *karmīs,* who have so many desires to fulfill? Nonetheless, the *śāstra* says:

akāmaḥ sarva-kāmo vā
mokṣa-kāma udāra-dhīḥ
tīvreṇa bhakti-yogena
yajeta puruṣaṁ param

"Whether one desires everything or nothing or desires to merge into the existence of the Lord, he is intelligent only if he worships Lord Kṛṣṇa, the Supreme Personality of Godhead, by rendering transcendental loving service." (*Bhāg.* 2.3.10)

Kaśyapa Muni saw that his wife, Aditi, had some material desires for the welfare of her sons, but still he advised her to render devotional service to the Supreme Personality of Godhead. In other words, everyone, regardless of whether he is a *karmī, jñānī, yogī* or *bhakta*, should invariably take shelter of the lotus feet of Vāsudeva and render transcendental loving service unto Him so that all his desires will be duly fulfilled. Kṛṣṇa is *dīna-anukampana:* He is very merciful to everyone. Therefore if one wants to fulfill his material desires, Kṛṣṇa helps him. Of course, sometimes if a devotee is very sincere, the Lord, as a special favor to him, refuses to fulfill his material desires and directly blesses him with pure, unalloyed devotional service. It is said in *Caitanya-caritāmṛta* (*Madhya* 22.38–39):

kṛṣṇa kahe,—'āmā bhaje, māge viṣaya-sukha
amṛta chāḍi' viṣa māge,—ei baḍa mūrkha

āmi—vijña, ei mūrkhe 'viṣaya' kene diba?
sva-caraṇāmṛta diyā 'viṣaya' bhulāiba

"Kṛṣṇa says, 'If one engages in My transcendental loving service but at the same time wants the opulence of material enjoyment, he is very, very foolish. Indeed, he is just like a person who gives up ambrosia to drink poison. Since I am very intelligent, why should I give this fool material prosperity? Instead I shall induce him to take the nectar of the shelter of My lotus feet and make him forget illusory material enjoyment.' " If a devotee maintains some material desire and at the same time very sincerely desires to engage at the lotus feet of Kṛṣṇa, Kṛṣṇa may directly give him unalloyed devotional service and take away all his material desires and possessions. This is the Lord's special favor to devotees. Otherwise, if one takes to Kṛṣṇa's devotional service but still has material desires to fulfill, he may become free from all material desires, as Dhruva Mahārāja did, but this may take some time. However, if a very sincere devotee wants only Kṛṣṇa's lotus feet, Kṛṣṇa directly gives him the position of *śuddha-bhakti,* unalloyed devotional service.

TEXT 22

श्रीअदितिरुवाच
केनाहं विधिना ब्रह्मन्नुपस्थास्ये जगत्पतिम् ।
यथा मे सत्यसङ्कल्पो विदध्यात् स मनोरथम् ॥२२॥

śrī-aditir uvāca
kenāhaṁ vidhinā brahmann
upasthāsye jagat-patim
yathā me satya-saṅkalpo
vidadhyāt sa manoratham

śrī-aditiḥ uvāca—Śrīmatī Aditi began to pray; *kena*—by which; *aham*—I; *vidhinā*—by regulative principles; *brahman*—O *brāhmaṇa; upasthāsye*—can please; *jagat-patim*—the Lord of the universe, Jagannātha; *yathā*—by which; *me*—my; *satya-saṅkalpaḥ*—desire may actually be fulfilled; *vidadhyāt*—may fulfill; *saḥ*—He (the Supreme Lord); *manoratham*—ambitions or desires.

TRANSLATION

Śrīmatī Aditi said: O brāhmaṇa, tell me the regulative principles by which I may worship the supreme master of the world so that the Lord will be pleased with me and fulfill all my desires.

PURPORT

It is said, "Man proposes, God disposes." Thus a person may desire many things, but unless these desires are fulfilled by the Supreme Personality of Godhead, they cannot be fulfilled. Fulfillment of desire is called *satya-saṅkalpa.* Here the word *satya-saṅkalpa* is very important. Aditi placed herself at the mercy of her husband so that he would give her directions by which to worship the Supreme Personality of Godhead so that all her desires would be fulfilled. A disciple must first decide that he should worship the Supreme Lord, and then the spiritual master will give the disciple correct directions. One cannot dictate to the spiritual master, just as a patient cannot demand that his physician prescribe a certain type of medicine. Here is the beginning of worship of the Supreme Personality of Godhead. As confirmed in *Bhagavad-gītā* (7.16):

catur-vidhā bhajante māṁ
janāḥ sukṛtino 'rjuna
ārto jijñāsur arthārthī
jñānī ca bharatarṣabha

"O best among the Bhāratas, four kinds of pious men render devotional service unto Me—the distressed, the desirer of wealth, the inquisitive, and he who is searching for knowledge of the Absolute." Aditi was *ārta*, a person in distress. She was very much aggrieved because her sons, the demigods, were bereft of everything. Thus she wanted to take shelter of the Supreme Personality of Godhead under the direction of her husband, Kaśyapa Muni.

TEXT 23

आदिश त्वं द्विजश्रेष्ठ विधिं तदुपधावनम् ।
आशु तुष्यति मे देवः सीदन्त्याः सह पुत्रकैः ॥२३॥

ādiśa tvaṁ dvija-śreṣṭha
vidhiṁ tad-upadhāvanam
āśu tuṣyati me devaḥ
sīdantyāḥ saha putrakaiḥ

ādiśa—just instruct me; *tvam*—O my husband; *dvija-śreṣṭha*—O best of the *brāhmaṇas; vidhim*—the regulative principles; *tat*—the Lord; *upadhāvanam*—the process of worshiping; *āśu*—very soon; *tuṣyati*—becomes satisfied; *me*—unto me; *devaḥ*—the Lord; *sīdantyāḥ*—now lamenting; *saha*—with; *putrakaiḥ*—all my sons, the demigods.

TRANSLATION

O best of the brāhmaṇas, kindly instruct me in the perfect method of worshiping the Supreme Personality of Godhead in devotional service, by which the Lord may very soon be pleased with me and save me, along with my sons, from this most dangerous condition.

PURPORT

Sometimes less intelligent men ask whether one has to approach a *guru* to be instructed in devotional service for spiritual advancement. The answer is given here—indeed, not only here, but also in *Bhagavad-gītā*, where Arjuna accepted Kṛṣṇa as his *guru* (*śiṣyas te 'haṁ śādhi māṁ tvāṁ prapannam*). The *Vedas* also instruct, *tad-vijñānārthaṁ sa gurum evābhigacchet:* one must accept a *guru* for proper direction if one is seriously inclined toward advancement in spiritual life. The Lord says that one must worship the *ācārya*, who is the representative of the Supreme Personality of Godhead (*ācāryaṁ māṁ vijānīyāt*). One should definitely understand this. In *Caitanya-caritāmṛta* it is said that the *guru* is the manifestation of the Supreme Personality of Godhead. Therefore, according to all the evidence given by the *śāstra* and by the practical behavior of devotees, one must accept a *guru*. Aditi accepted her husband as her *guru*, so that he would direct her how to advance in spiritual consciousness, devotional service, by worshiping the Supreme Lord.

TEXT 24

श्रीकश्यप उवाच

एतन्मे भगवान्पृष्टः प्रजाकामस्य पद्मजः ।
यदाह ते प्रवक्ष्यामि व्रतं केशवतोषणम् ॥२४॥

śrī-kaśyapa uvāca
etan me bhagavān pṛṣṭaḥ
prajā-kāmasya padmajaḥ
yad āha te pravakṣyāmi
vrataṁ keśava-toṣaṇam

śrī-kaśyapaḥ uvāca—Kaśyapa Muni said; *etat*—this; *me*—by me; *bhagavān*—the most powerful; *pṛṣṭaḥ*—when he was requested; *prajā-kāmasya*—desiring offspring; *padma-jaḥ*—Lord Brahmā, who was born of a lotus flower; *yat*—whatever; *āha*—he said; *te*—unto you; *pravakṣyāmi*—I shall explain; *vratam*—in the form of worship; *keśava-toṣaṇam*—by which Keśava, the Supreme Personality of Godhead, is satisfied.

TRANSLATION

Śrī Kaśyapa Muni said: When I desired offspring, I placed inquiries before Lord Brahmā, who is born from a lotus flower. Now I shall explain to you the same process Lord Brahmā instructed me, by which Keśava, the Supreme Personality of Godhead, is satisfied.

PURPORT

Here the process of devotional service is further explained. Kaśyapa Muni wanted to instruct Aditi in the same process recommended to him by Brahmā for satisfying the Supreme Personality of Godhead. This is valuable. The *guru* does not manufacture a new process to instruct the disciple. The disciple receives from the *guru* an authorized process received by the *guru* from his *guru*. This is called the system of disciplic succession (*evaṁ paramparā-prāptam imaṁ rājarṣayo viduḥ*). This is the bona fide Vedic system of receiving the process of devotional service, by which the Supreme Personality of Godhead is pleased. Therefore, to approach a bona fide *guru*, or spiritual master, is essential. The bona fide spiritual master is he who has received the mercy of his *guru*, who in turn is bona fide because he has received the mercy of his *guru*. This is called the *paramparā* system. Unless one follows this *paramparā* system, the *mantra* one receives will be chanted for no purpose. Nowadays there are so many rascal *gurus* who manufacture their *mantras* as a process for material advancement, not spiritual advancement. Still, the *mantra* cannot be successful if it is manufactured. *Mantras* and the process of devotional service have special power, provided they are received from the authorized person.

TEXT 25

फाल्गुनस्यामले पक्षे द्वादशाहं पयोव्रतम् ।
अर्चयेदरविन्दाक्षं भक्त्या परमयान्वितः ॥२५॥

phālgunasyāmale pakṣe
dvādaśāhaṁ payo-vratam
arcayed aravindākṣaṁ
bhaktyā paramayānvitaḥ

phālgunasya—of the month of Phālguna (February and March); *amale*—during the bright; *pakṣe*—fortnight; *dvādaśa-aham*—for twelve days, ending with Dvādaśī, the day after Ekādaśī; *payaḥ-vratam*—accepting the vow of taking only milk; *arcayet*—one should worship; *aravinda-akṣam*—the lotus-eyed Supreme Personality of Godhead; *bhaktyā*—with devotion; *paramayā*—unalloyed; *anvitaḥ*—surcharged.

TRANSLATION

In the bright fortnight of the month of Phālguna [February and March], for twelve days ending with Dvādaśī, one should observe the vow of subsisting only on milk and should worship the lotus-eyed Supreme Personality of Godhead with all devotion.

PURPORT

Worshiping the Supreme Lord Viṣṇu with devotion means following *arcana-mārga.*

śravaṇaṁ kīrtanaṁ viṣṇoḥ
smaraṇaṁ pāda-sevanam
arcanaṁ vandanaṁ dāsyaṁ
sakhyam ātma-nivedanam

One should install the Deity of Lord Viṣṇu or Kṛṣṇa and worship Him nicely by dressing Him, decorating Him with flower garlands, and offering Him all kinds of fruits, flowers and cooked food, nicely prepared with ghee, sugar and grains. One should also offer a flame, incense and so on, while ringing a bell, as prescribed. This is called worship of the Lord. Here it is recommended that one observe the vow of subsisting only by drinking milk. This is called *payo-vrata.* As we generally perform devotional service on Ekādaśī by not eating grains, it is generally recommended that on Dvādaśī one not consume anything but milk. *Payo-vrata* and *arcana* devotional service to the Supreme Lord should be performed with a pure devotional attitude (*bhaktyā*). Without *bhakti,* one cannot worship the Supreme Personality of Godhead. *Bhaktyā mām abhijānāti yāvān yaś cāsmi tattvataḥ.* If one wants to know the Supreme Personality of Godhead and be directly connected with Him, knowing what He wants to eat and how He is satisfied, one must take to the process of *bhakti.* As recommended here also, *bhaktyā paramayānvitaḥ:* one should be surcharged with unalloyed devotional service.

TEXT 26

सिनीवाल्यां मृदालिप्य स्नायात् क्रोडविदीर्णया ।
यदि लभ्येत वै स्रोतस्येतं मन्त्रमुदीरयेत् ॥२६॥

sinīvālyāṁ mṛdālipya
snāyāt kroḍa-vidīrṇayā
yadi labhyeta vai srotasy
etaṁ mantram udīrayet

sinīvālyām—on the dark-moon day; *mṛdā*—with dirt; *ālipya*—smearing the body; *snāyāt*—one should bathe; *kroḍa-vidīrṇayā*—dug up by the tusk of a boar; *yadi*—if; *labhyeta*—it is available; *vai*—indeed; *srotasi*—in a flowing river; *etam mantram*—this *mantra;* *udīrayet*—one should chant.

TRANSLATION

If dirt dug up by a boar is available, on the day of the dark moon one should smear this dirt on his body and then bathe in a flowing river. While bathing, one should chant the following mantra.

TEXT 27

त्वं देव्यादिवराहेण रसायाः स्थानमिच्छता ।
उद्धृतासि नमस्तुभ्यं पाप्मानं मे प्रणाशय ॥२७॥

tvaṁ devy ādi-varāheṇa
rasāyāḥ sthānam icchatā
uddhṛtāsi namas tubhyaṁ
pāpmānaṁ me praṇāśaya

tvam—you; *devi*—O mother earth; *ādi-varāheṇa*—by the Supreme Personality of Godhead in the form of a boar; *rasāyāḥ*—from the bottom of the universe; *sthānam*—a place; *icchatā*—desiring; *uddhṛtā asi*—you have been raised; *namaḥ tubhyam*—I offer my respectful obeisances unto you; *pāpmānam*—all sinful activities and their reactions; *me*—of me; *praṇāśaya*—please undo.

TRANSLATION

O mother earth, you were raised by the Supreme Personality of Godhead in the form of a boar because of your desiring to have a

place to stay. I pray that you kindly vanquish all the reactions of my sinful life. I offer my respectful obeisances unto you.

TEXT 28

निर्वर्तितात्मनियमो देवमर्चेत् समाहितः ।
अर्चायां स्थण्डिले सूर्ये जले वह्नौ गुरावपि ॥२८॥

nirvartitātma-niyamo
devam arcet samāhitaḥ
arcāyāṁ sthaṇḍile sūrye
jale vahnau gurāv api

nirvartita—finished; *ātma-niyamaḥ*—the daily duties of washing, chanting other *mantras* and so on, according to one's practice; *devam*—the Supreme Personality of Godhead; *arcet*—one should worship; *samāhitaḥ*—with full attention; *arcāyām*—unto the Deities; *sthaṇḍile*—unto the altar; *sūrye*—unto the sun; *jale*—unto the water; *vahnau*—unto the fire; *gurau*—unto the spiritual master; *api*—indeed.

TRANSLATION

Thereafter, one should perform his daily spiritual duties and then, with great attention, offer worship to the Deity of the Supreme Personality of Godhead, and also to the altar, the sun, water, fire and the spiritual master.

TEXT 29

नमस्तुभ्यं भगवते पुरुषाय महीयसे ।
सर्वभूतनिवासाय वासुदेवाय साक्षिणे ॥२९॥

namas tubhyaṁ bhagavate
puruṣāya mahīyase
sarva-bhūta-nivāsāya
vāsudevāya sākṣiṇe

namaḥ tubhyam—I offer my respectful obeisances unto You; *bhagavate*—unto the Supreme Personality of Godhead; *puruṣāya*—the

Supreme Person; *mahīyase*—the best of all personalities; *sarva-bhūta-nivāsāya*—the person who lives in everyone's heart; *vāsudevāya*—the Lord who lives everywhere; *sākṣiṇe*—the witness of everything.

TRANSLATION

O Supreme Personality of Godhead, greatest of all, who lives in everyone's heart and in whom everyone lives, O witness of everything, O Vāsudeva, supreme and all-pervading person, I offer my respectful obeisances unto You.

TEXT 30

नमोऽव्यक्ताय सूक्ष्माय प्रधानपुरुषाय च ।
चतुर्विंशद्गुणज्ञाय गुणसंख्यानहेतवे ॥३०॥

namo 'vyaktāya sūkṣmāya
pradhāna-puruṣāya ca
catur-viṁśad-guṇa-jñāya
guṇa-saṅkhyāna-hetave

namaḥ—I offer my respectful obeisances unto You; *avyaktāya*—who are never seen by material eyes; *sūkṣmāya*—transcendental; *pradhāna-puruṣāya*—the Supreme Person; *ca*—also; *catuḥ-viṁśat*—twenty-four; *guṇa-jñāya*—the knower of the elements; *guṇa-saṅkhyāna*—of the *sāṅkhya-yoga* system; *hetave*—the original cause.

TRANSLATION

I offer my respectful obeisances unto You, the Supreme Person. Being very subtle, You are never visible to material eyes. You are the knower of the twenty-four elements, and You are the inaugurator of the sāṅkhya-yoga system.

PURPORT

Catur-viṁśad-guṇa, the twenty-four elements, are the five gross elements (earth, water, fire, air and ether), the three subtle elements (mind, intelligence and false ego), the ten senses (five for working and five for acquiring knowledge), the five sense objects, and contaminated consciousness. These are the subject matter of *sāṅkhya-yoga*, which was inaugurated by Lord Kapiladeva. This *sāṅkhya-yoga* was again propounded by another Kapila, but he was an atheist, and his system is not accepted as bona fide.

TEXT 31

नमो द्विशीर्ष्णे त्रिपदे चतुःशृङ्गाय तन्तवे ।
सप्तहस्ताय यज्ञाय त्रयीविद्यात्मने नमः ॥३१॥

namo dvi-śīrṣṇe tri-pade
catuḥ-śṛṅgāya tantave
sapta-hastāya yajñāya
trayī-vidyātmane namaḥ

namaḥ—I offer my respectful obeisances unto You; *dvi-śīrṣṇe*—who have two heads; *tri-pade*—who have three legs; *catuḥ-śṛṅgāya*—who have four horns; *tantave*—who expand; *sapta-hastāya*—who have seven hands; *yajñāya*—unto the *yajña-puruṣa*, the supreme enjoyer; *trayī*—the three modes of Vedic ritualistic ceremonies; *vidyā-ātmane*—the Personality of Godhead, the embodiment of all knowledge; *namaḥ*—I offer my respectful obeisances unto You.

TRANSLATION

I offer my respectful obeisances unto You, the Supreme Personality of Godhead, who have two heads [prāyaṇīya and udāyanīya], three legs [savana-traya], four horns [the four Vedas] and seven hands [the seven chandas, such as Gāyatrī]. I offer my obeisances unto You, whose heart and soul are the three Vedic rituals [karma-kāṇḍa, jñāna-kāṇḍa and upāsanā-kāṇḍa] and who expand these rituals in the form of sacrifice.

TEXT 32

नमः शिवाय रुद्राय नमः शक्तिधराय च ।
सर्वविद्याधिपतये भूतानां पतये नमः ॥३२॥

namaḥ śivāya rudrāya
namaḥ śakti-dharāya ca
sarva-vidyādhipataye
bhūtānāṁ pataye namaḥ

namaḥ—I offer my respectful obeisances unto You; *śivāya*—the incarnation named Lord Śiva; *rudrāya*—the expansion named Rudra; *namaḥ*—obeisances; *śakti-dharāya*—the reservoir of all potencies; *ca*—and; *sarva-vidyā-adhipataye*—the reservoir of all knowledge; *bhūtānām*—of the living entities; *pataye*—the supreme master; *namaḥ*—I offer my respectful obeisances unto You.

TRANSLATION

I offer my respectful obeisances unto You, Lord Śiva, or Rudra, who are the reservoir of all potencies, the reservoir of all knowledge, and the master of everyone.

PURPORT

It is the system for one to offer obeisances unto the expansion or incarnation of the Lord. Lord Śiva is the incarnation of ignorance, one of the material modes of nature.

TEXT 33

नमो हिरण्यगर्भाय प्राणाय जगदात्मने ।
योगैश्वर्यशरीराय नमस्ते योगहेतवे ॥३३॥

namo hiraṇyagarbhāya
prāṇāya jagad-ātmane
yogaiśvarya-śarīrāya
namas te yoga-hetave

namaḥ—I offer my respectful obeisances unto You; *hiraṇyagarbhāya*—situated as the four-headed Hiraṇyagarbha, Brahmā; *prāṇāya*—the source of everyone's life; *jagat-ātmane*—the Supersoul of the entire universe; *yoga-aiśvarya-śarīrāya*—whose body is full of opulences and mystic power; *namaḥ te*—I offer my respectful obeisances unto You; *yoga-hetave*—the original master of all mystic power.

TRANSLATION

I offer my respectful obeisances unto You, who are situated as Hiraṇyagarbha, the source of life, the Supersoul of every living entity. Your body is the source of the opulence of all mystic power. I offer my respectful obeisances unto You.

TEXT 34

नमस्त आदिदेवाय साक्षिभूताय ते नमः ।
नारायणाय ऋषये नराय हरये नमः ॥३४॥

namas ta ādi-devāya
sākṣi-bhūtāya te namaḥ
nārāyaṇāya ṛṣaye
narāya haraye namaḥ

namaḥ te—I offer my respectful obeisances unto You; *ādi-devāya*—who are the original Personality of Godhead; *sākṣi-bhūtāya*—the witness of everything within the heart of everyone; *te*—unto You; *namaḥ*—I offer my respectful obeisances; *nārāyaṇāya*—who take the incarnation of Nārāyaṇa; *ṛṣaye*—the sage; *narāya*—the incarnation of a human being; *haraye*—unto the Supreme Personality of Godhead; *namaḥ*—I offer my respectful obeisances.

TRANSLATION

I offer my respectful obeisances unto You, who are the original Personality of Godhead, the witness in everyone's heart, and the incarnation of Nara-Nārāyaṇa Ṛṣi in the form of a human being. O Personality of Godhead, I offer my respectful obeisances unto You.

TEXT 35

नमो मरकतश्यामवपुषेऽधिगतश्रिये ।
केशवाय नमस्तुभ्यं नमस्ते पीतवाससे ॥३५॥

namo marakata-śyāma-
vapuṣe 'dhigata-śriye
keśavāya namas tubhyaṁ
namas te pīta-vāsase

namaḥ—I offer my respectful obeisances unto You; *marakata-śyāma-vapuṣe*—whose bodily hue is blackish like the *marakata* gem; *adhigata-śriye*—under whose control is mother Lakṣmī, the goddess of fortune; *keśavāya*—Lord Keśava, who killed the Keśī demon; *namaḥ tubhyam*—I offer my respectful obeisances unto You; *namaḥ te*—again I offer my respectful obeisances unto You; *pīta-vāsase*—whose garment is yellow.

TRANSLATION

My Lord, I offer my respectful obeisances unto You, who are dressed in yellow garments, whose bodily hue resembles the marakata gem, and who have full control over the goddess of fortune. O my Lord Keśava, I offer my respectful obeisances unto You.

TEXT 36

त्वं सर्ववरदः पुंसां वरेण्य वरदर्षभ ।
अतस्ते श्रेयसे धीराः पादरेणुमुपासते ।।३६।।

tvaṁ sarva-varadaḥ puṁsāṁ
vareṇya varadarṣabha
atas te śreyase dhīrāḥ
pāda-reṇum upāsate

tvam—You; *sarva-vara-daḥ*—who can give all kinds of benedictions; *puṁsām*—to all living entities; *vareṇya*—O most worshipable; *vara-darṣabha*—O most powerful of all givers of benediction; *ataḥ*—for this reason; *te*—Your; *śreyase*—the source of all auspiciousness; *dhīrāḥ*—the most sober; *pāda-reṇum upāsate*—worship the dust of the lotus feet.

TRANSLATION

O most exalted and worshipable Lord, best of those who bestow benediction, You can fulfill the desires of everyone, and therefore

those who are sober, for their own welfare, worship the dust of Your lotus feet.

TEXT 37

अन्ववर्तन्त यं देवाः श्रीश्च तत्पादपद्मयोः ।
स्पृहयन्त इवामोदं भगवान्मे प्रसीदताम् ॥३७॥

anvavartanta yaṁ devāḥ
śrīś ca tat-pāda-padmayoḥ
spṛhayanta ivāmodaṁ
bhagavān me prasīdatām

anvavartanta—engaged in devotional service; *yam*—unto whom; *devāḥ*—all the demigods; *śrīḥ ca*—and the goddess of fortune; *tat-pāda-padmayoḥ*—of the lotus feet of His Lordship; *spṛhayantaḥ*—desiring; *iva*—exactly; *āmodam*—celestial bliss; *bhagavān*—the Supreme Personality of Godhead; *me*—upon me; *prasīdatām*—may be pleased.

TRANSLATION

All the demigods, as well as the goddess of fortune, engage in the service of His lotus feet. Indeed, they respect the fragrance of those lotus feet. May the Supreme Personality of Godhead be pleased with me.

TEXT 38

एतैर्मन्त्रैर्हृषीकेशमावाहनपुरस्कृतम् ।
अर्चयेच्छ्रद्धया युक्तः पाद्योपस्पर्शनादिभिः ॥३८॥

etair mantrair hṛṣīkeśam
āvāhana-puraskṛtam
arcayec chraddhayā yuktaḥ
pādyopasparśanādibhiḥ

etaiḥ mantraiḥ—by chanting all these *mantras; hṛṣīkeśam*—unto the Supreme Personality of Godhead, the master of all senses; *āvāhana*—calling; *puraskṛtam*—honoring Him in all respects; *arcayet*—one should worship; *śraddhayā*—with faith and devotion; *yuktaḥ*—engaged; *pādya-upasparśana-ādibhiḥ*—with the paraphernalia of worship (*pādya, arghya,* etc.).

TRANSLATION

Kaśyapa Muni continued: By chanting all these mantras, welcoming the Supreme Personality of Godhead with faith and devotion, and offering Him items of worship [such as pādya and arghya], one should worship Keśava, Hṛṣīkeśa, Kṛṣṇa, the Supreme Personality of Godhead.

TEXT 39

अर्चित्वा गन्धमाल्याद्यैः पयसा स्नपयेद् विभुम्।
वस्त्रोपवीताभरणपाद्योपस्पर्शनैस्ततः ।
गन्धधूपादिभिश्चार्चेद् द्वादशाक्षरविद्यया ॥३९॥

arcitvā gandha-mālyādyaiḥ
payasā snapayed vibhum
vastropavītābharaṇa-
pādyopasparśanais tataḥ
gandha-dhūpādibhiś cārced
dvādaśākṣara-vidyayā

arcitvā—worshiping in this way; *gandha-mālya-ādyaiḥ*—with incense, flower garlands, etc.; *payasā*—with milk; *snapayet*—should bathe; *vibhum*—the Lord; *vastra*—dress; *upavīta*—sacred thread; *ābharaṇa*—ornaments; *pādya*—water for washing the lotus feet; *upasparśanaiḥ*—touching; *tataḥ*—thereafter; *gandha*—fragrance; *dhūpa*—incense; *ādibhiḥ*—with all of these; *ca*—and; *arcet*—should worship; *dvādaśa-akṣara-vidyayā*—with the *mantra* of twelve syllables.

TRANSLATION

In the beginning, the devotee should chant the dvādaśākṣara-mantra and offer flower garlands, incense and so on. After worshiping the Lord in this way, one should bathe the Lord with

milk and dress Him with proper garments, a sacred thread, and ornaments. After offering water to wash the Lord's feet, one should again worship the Lord with fragrant flowers, incense and other paraphernalia.

PURPORT

The *dvādaśākṣara-mantra* is *oṁ namo bhagavate vāsudevāya.* While worshiping the Deity, one should ring a bell with his left hand and offer *pādya, arghya, vastra, gandha, mālā, ābharaṇa, bhūṣaṇa* and so on. In this way, one should bathe the Lord with milk, dress Him and again worship Him with all paraphernalia.

TEXT 40

श्रृतं पयसि नैवेद्यं शाल्यन्नं विभवे सति ।
ससर्पिः सगुडं दत्त्वा जुहुयान्मूलविद्यया ॥४०॥

śṛtaṁ payasi naivedyaṁ
śāly-annaṁ vibhave sati
sasarpiḥ saguḍaṁ dattvā
juhuyān mūla-vidyayā

śṛtam—cooked; *payasi*—in milk; *naivedyam*—offering to the Deity; *śāli-annam*—fine rice; *vibhave*—if available; *sati*—in this way; *sa-sarpiḥ*—with ghee (clarified butter); *sa-guḍam*—with molasses; *dattvā*—offering Him; *juhuyāt*—should offer oblations in the fire; *mūla-vidyayā*—with chanting of the same *dvādaśākṣara-mantra.*

TRANSLATION

If one can afford to, one should offer the Deity fine rice boiled in milk with clarified butter and molasses. While chanting the same original mantra, one should offer all this to the fire.

TEXT 41

निवेदितं तद्भक्ताय दद्याद् भुञ्जीत वा स्वयम् ।
दत्त्वाचमनमर्चित्वा ताम्बूलं च निवेदयेत् ॥४१॥

niveditaṁ tad-bhaktāya
dadyād bhuñjīta vā svayam
dattvācamanam arcitvā
tāmbūlaṁ ca nivedayet

niveditam—this offering of *prasāda; tat-bhaktāya*—unto His devotee; *dadyāt*—should be offered; *bhuñjīta*—one should take; *vā*—either; *svayam*—personally; *dattvā ācamanam*—giving water to wash the hands and mouth; *arcitvā*—in this way worshiping the Deity; *tāmbūlam*—betel nuts with spices; *ca*—also; *nivedayet*—one should offer.

TRANSLATION

One should offer all the prasāda to a Vaiṣṇava or offer him some of the prasāda and then take some oneself. After this, one should offer the Deity ācamana and then betel nut and then again worship the Lord.

TEXT 42

जपेदष्टोत्तरशतं स्तुवीत स्तुतिभिः प्रभुम् ।
कृत्वा प्रदक्षिणं भूमौ प्रणमेद् दण्डवन्मुदा ॥४२॥

japed aṣṭottara-śataṁ
stuvīta stutibhiḥ prabhum
kṛtvā pradakṣiṇaṁ bhūmau
praṇamed daṇḍavan mudā

japet—should silently murmur; *aṣṭottara-śatam*—108 times; *stuvīta*—should offer prayers; *stutibhiḥ*—by various prayers of glorification; *prabhum*—unto the Lord; *kṛtvā*—thereafter doing; *pradakṣiṇam*—circumambulation; *bhūmau*—on the ground; *praṇamet*—should offer obeisances; *daṇḍavat*—straight, with the whole body; *mudā*—with great satisfaction.

TRANSLATION

Thereafter, one should silently murmur the mantra 108 times and offer prayers to the Lord for His glorification. Then one

should circumambulate the Lord and finally, with great delight and satisfaction, offer obeisances, falling straight like a rod [daṇḍavat].

TEXT 43

कृत्वा शिरसि तच्छेषां देवमुद्वासयेत् ततः ।
द्वयवरान्भोजयेद् विप्रान्पायसेन यथोचितम् ॥४३॥

kṛtvā śirasi tac-cheṣāṁ
devam udvāsayet tataḥ
dvy-avarān bhojayed viprān
pāyasena yathocitam

kṛtvā—taking; *śirasi*—on the head; *tat-śeṣām*—all the remnants (the water and flowers offered to the Deity); *devam*—unto the Deity; *udvāsayet*—should be thrown into a sacred place; *tataḥ*—thereafter; *dvi-avarān*—a minimum of two; *bhojayet*—should feed; *viprān*—*brāhmaṇas*; *pāyasena*—with sweet rice; *yathā-ucitam*—as each deserves.

TRANSLATION

After touching to one's head all the flowers and water offered to the Deity, one should throw them into a sacred place. Then one should feed at least two brāhmaṇas with sweet rice.

TEXTS 44–45

भुञ्जीत तैरनुज्ञातः सेष्टः शेषं सभाजितैः ।
ब्रह्मचार्यथ तद्रात्र्यां श्वोभूते प्रथमेऽहनि ॥४४॥
स्नातः शुचिर्यथोक्तेन विधिना सुसमाहितः ।
पयसा स्नापयित्वार्चेद् यावद्व्रतसमापनम् ॥४५॥

bhuñjīta tair anujñātaḥ
seṣṭaḥ śeṣaṁ sabhājitaiḥ
brahmacāry atha tad-rātryāṁ
śvo bhūte prathame 'hani

snātaḥ śucir yathoktena
vidhinā susamāhitaḥ
payasā snāpayitvārced
yāvad vrata-samāpanam

bhuñjīta—should take the *prasāda; taiḥ*—by the *brāhmaṇas; anujñātaḥ*—being permitted; *sa-iṣṭaḥ*—with friends and relatives; *śeṣam*—the remnants; *sabhājitaiḥ*—properly honored; *brahmacārī*—observance of celibacy; *atha*—of course; *tat-rātryām*—at night; *śvaḥ bhūte*—at the end of the night, when the morning comes; *prathame ahani*—on the first day; *snātaḥ*—bathing; *śuciḥ*—becoming purified; *yathā-uktena*—as stated before; *vidhinā*—by following the regulative principles; *su-samāhitaḥ*—with great attention; *payasā*—with milk; *snāpayitvā*—bathing the Deity; *arcet*—should offer worship; *yāvat*—as long as; *vrata-samāpanam*—the period of worship is not over.

TRANSLATION

One should perfectly honor the respectable brāhmaṇas one has fed, and then, after taking their permission, one should take prasāda with his friends and relatives. For that night, one should observe strict celibacy, and the next morning, after bathing again, with purity and attention one should bathe the Deity of Viṣṇu with milk and worship Him according to the methods formerly stated in detail.

TEXT 46

पयोभक्षो व्रतमिदं चरेद् विष्णवर्चनादृतः ।
पूर्ववज्जुहुयादग्निं ब्राह्मणांश्चापि भोजयेत् ॥४६॥

payo-bhakṣo vratam idaṁ
cared viṣṇv-arcanādṛtaḥ
pūrvavaj juhuyād agniṁ
brāhmaṇāṁś cāpi bhojayet

payaḥ-bhakṣaḥ—one who drinks milk only; *vratam idam*—this process of worshiping with a vow; *caret*—one should execute; *viṣṇu-arcana-ādṛtaḥ*—worshiping Lord Viṣṇu with great faith and devotion;

pūrva-vat—as prescribed previously; *juhuyāt*—one should offer oblations; *agnim*—into the fire; *brāhmaṇān*—unto the *brāhmaṇas; ca api*—as well as; *bhojayet*—should feed.

TRANSLATION

Worshiping Lord Viṣṇu with great faith and devotion and living only by drinking milk, one should follow this vow. One should also offer oblations to the fire and feed the brāhmaṇas as mentioned before.

TEXT 47

एवं त्वहरहः कुर्याद् द्वादशाहं पयोव्रतम् ।
हरेराराधनं होममर्हणं द्विजतर्पणम् ॥४७॥

evaṁ tv ahar ahaḥ kuryād
dvādaśāhaṁ payo-vratam
harer ārādhanaṁ homam
arhaṇaṁ dvija-tarpaṇam

evam—in this way; *tu*—indeed; *ahaḥ ahaḥ*—day after day; *kuryāt*—should execute; *dvādaśa-aham*—until twelve days; *payaḥ-vratam*—the observance of the *vrata* known as *payo-vrata; hareḥ ārādhanam*—worshiping the Supreme Personality of Godhead; *homam*—by executing a fire sacrifice; *arhaṇam*—worshiping the Deity; *dvija-tarpaṇam*—and satisfying the *brāhmaṇas* by feeding them.

TRANSLATION

In this way, until twelve days have passed, one should observe this payo-vrata, worshiping the Lord every day, executing the routine duties, performing sacrifices and feeding the brāhmaṇas.

TEXT 48

प्रतिपद्दिनमारभ्य यावच्छुक्लत्रयोदशीम् ।
ब्रह्मचर्यमधःस्वप्नं स्नानं त्रिषवणं चरेत् ॥४८॥

pratipad-dinam ārabhya
yāvac chukla-trayodaśīm
brahmacaryam adhaḥ-svapnaṁ
snānaṁ tri-ṣavaṇaṁ caret

pratipat-dinam—on the day of *pratipat; ārabhya*—beginning; *yāvat*—until; *śukla*—of the bright fortnight; *trayodaśīm*—the thirteenth day of the moon (the second day after Ekādaśī); *brahmacaryam*—observing complete celibacy; *adhaḥ-svapnam*—lying down on the floor; *snānam*—bathing; *tri-savanam*—three times (morning, evening and noon); *caret*—one should execute.

TRANSLATION

From pratipat until the thirteenth day of the next bright moon [śukla-trayodaśī], one should observe complete celibacy, sleep on the floor, bathe three times a day and thus execute the vow.

TEXT 49

वर्जयेदसदालापं भोगानुच्चावचांस्तथा ।
अहिंस्रः सर्वभूतानां वासुदेवपरायणः ॥४९॥

varjayed asad-ālāpaṁ
bhogān uccāvacāṁs tathā
ahiṁsraḥ sarva-bhūtānāṁ
vāsudeva-parāyaṇaḥ

varjayet—one should give up; *asat-ālāpam*—unnecessary talk on material subject matters; *bhogān*—sense gratification; *ucca-avacān*—superior or inferior; *tathā*—as well as; *ahiṁsraḥ*—without being envious; *sarva-bhūtānām*—of all living entities; *vāsudeva-parāyaṇaḥ*—simply being a devotee of Lord Vāsudeva.

TRANSLATION

During this period, one should not unnecessarily talk of material subjects or topics of sense gratification, one should be com-

pletely free from envy of all living entities, and one should be a pure and simple devotee of Lord Vāsudeva.

TEXT 50

त्रयोदश्यामथो विष्णोः स्नपनं पञ्चकैर्विभोः ।
कारयेच्छास्त्रदृष्टेन विधिना विधिकोविदैः ॥५०॥

trayodaśyām atho viṣṇoḥ
snapanaṁ pañcakair vibhoḥ
kārayec chāstra-dṛṣṭena
vidhinā vidhi-kovidaiḥ

trayodaśyām—on the thirteenth day of the moon; *atho*—thereafter; *viṣṇoḥ*—of Lord Viṣṇu; *snapanam*—bathing; *pañcakaiḥ*—by *pañcāmṛta,* five substances; *vibhoḥ*—the Lord; *kārayet*—one should execute; *śāstra-dṛṣṭena*—enjoined in the scripture; *vidhinā*—under regulative principles; *vidhi-kovidaiḥ*—assisted by the priests who know the regulative principles.

TRANSLATION

Thereafter, following the directions of the śāstra with help from brāhmaṇas who know the śāstra, on the thirteenth day of the moon one should bathe Lord Viṣṇu with five substances [milk, yogurt, ghee, sugar and honey].

TEXTS 51–52

पूजां च महतीं कुर्याद् वित्तशाठ्यविवर्जितः ।
चरुं निरूप्य पयसि शिपिविष्टाय विष्णवे ॥५१॥
सूक्तेन तेन पुरुषं यजेत सुसमाहितः ।
नैवेद्यं चातिगुणवद् दद्यात्पुरुषतुष्टिदम् ॥५२॥

pūjāṁ ca mahatīṁ kuryād
vitta-śāṭhya-vivarjitaḥ
caruṁ nirūpya payasi
śipiviṣṭāya viṣṇave

sūktena tena puruṣaṁ
yajeta susamāhitaḥ
naivedyaṁ cātiguṇavad
dadyāt puruṣa-tuṣṭidam

pūjām—worship; *ca*—also; *mahatīm*—very gorgeous; *kuryāt*—should do; *vitta-śāṭhya*—miserly mentality (not spending sufficient money); *vivarjitaḥ*—giving up; *carum*—grains offered in the *yajña; nirūpya*—seeing properly; *payasi*—with milk; *śipiviṣṭāya*—unto the Supersoul, who is situated in the heart of every living entity; *viṣṇave*—unto Lord Viṣṇu; *sūktena*—by chanting the Vedic *mantra* known as *Puruṣa-sūkta; tena*—by that; *puruṣam*—the Supreme Personality of Godhead; *yajeta*—one should worship; *su-samāhitaḥ*—with great attention; *naivedyam*—food offered to the Deity; *ca*—and; *ati-guṇa-vat*—prepared very gorgeously with all varieties of taste; *dadyāt*—should offer; *puruṣa-tuṣṭi-dam*—everything extremely pleasing to the Supreme Personality of Godhead.

TRANSLATION

Giving up the miserly habit of not spending money, one should arrange for the gorgeous worship of the Supreme Personality of Godhead, Viṣṇu, who is situated in the heart of every living entity. With great attention, one must prepare an oblation of grains boiled in ghee and milk and must chant the Puruṣa-sūkta mantra. The offerings of food should be of varieties of tastes. In this way, one should worship the Supreme Personality of Godhead.

TEXT 53

आचार्यं ज्ञानसम्पन्नं वस्त्राभरणधेनुभिः ।
तोषयेदृत्विजश्चैव तद्विद्ध्याराधनं हरेः ॥५३॥

ācāryaṁ jñāna-sampannaṁ
vastrābharaṇa-dhenubhiḥ
toṣayed ṛtvijaś caiva
tad viddhy ārādhanaṁ hareḥ

ācāryam—the spiritual master; *jñāna-sampannam*—very advanced in spiritual knowledge; *vastra-ābharaṇa-dhenubhiḥ*—with clothing, ornaments and many cows; *toṣayet*—should satisfy; *ṛtvijaḥ*—the priests recommended by the spiritual master; *ca eva*—as well as; *tat viddhi*—try to understand that; *ārādhanam*—worship; *hareḥ*—of the Supreme Personality of Godhead.

TRANSLATION

One should satisfy the spiritual master [ācārya], who is very learned in Vedic literature, and should satisfy his assistant priests [known as hotā, udgātā, adhvaryu and brahma]. One should please them by offering them clothing, ornaments and cows. This is the ceremony called viṣṇu-ārādhana, or worship of Lord Viṣṇu.

TEXT 54

भोजयेत् तान् गुणवता सदन्नेन शुचिस्मिते ।
अन्यांश्च ब्राह्मणाञ्छक्त्या ये च तत्र समागताः ॥५४॥

bhojayet tān guṇavatā
sad-annena śuci-smite
anyāṁś ca brāhmaṇāñ chaktyā
ye ca tatra samāgatāḥ

bhojayet—should distribute *prasāda; tān*—unto all of them; *guṇavatā*—by rich foods; *sat-annena*—with food prepared with ghee and milk, which is supposed to be very pure; *śuci-smite*—O most pious lady; *anyān ca*—others also; *brāhmaṇān*—*brāhmaṇas; śaktyā*—as far as possible; *ye*—all of them who; *ca*—also; *tatra*—there (at the ceremonies); *samāgatāḥ*—assembled.

TRANSLATION

O most auspicious lady, one should perform all the ceremonies under the direction of learned ācāryas and should satisfy them and their priests. By distributing prasāda, one should also satisfy the brāhmaṇas and others who have assembled.

TEXT 55

दक्षिणां गुरवे दद्यादृत्विग्भ्यश्च यथार्हतः ।
अन्नाद्येनाश्वपाकांश्च प्रीणयेत्समुपागतान् ॥५५॥

dakṣiṇāṁ gurave dadyād
ṛtvigbhyaś ca yathārhataḥ
annādyenāśva-pākāṁś ca
prīṇayet samupāgatān

dakṣiṇām—some contribution of money or gold; *gurave*—unto the spiritual master; *dadyāt*—one should give; *ṛtvigbhyaḥ ca*—and to the priests engaged by the spiritual master; *yathā-arhataḥ*—as far as possible; *anna-adyena*—by distributing *prasāda; āśva-pākān*—even to the *caṇḍālas,* persons habituated to eating the flesh of dogs; *ca*—also; *prīṇayet*—one should please; *samupāgatān*—because they have assembled there for the ceremony.

TRANSLATION

One should satisfy the spiritual master and assistant priests by giving them cloth, ornaments, cows and also some monetary contribution. And by distributing prasāda one should satisfy everyone assembled, including even the lowest of men, the caṇḍālas [eaters of dog flesh].

PURPORT

In the Vedic system, *prasāda* is distributed, as recommended here, without discrimination as to who may take the *prasāda.* Regardless of whether one be a *brāhmaṇa, śūdra, vaiśya, kṣatriya,* or even the lowest of men, a *caṇḍāla,* he should be welcome to accept *prasāda.* However, when the *caṇḍālas,* the lower class or poorer class, are taking *prasāda,* this does not mean that they have become Nārāyaṇa or Viṣṇu. Nārāyaṇa is situated in everyone's heart, but this does not mean Nārāyaṇa is a *caṇḍāla* or poor man. The Māyāvāda philosophy of accepting a poor man as Nārāyaṇa is the most envious and atheistic movement in Vedic culture. This mentality should be completely given up. Everyone should be given the opportunity to take *prasāda,* but this does not mean that everyone has the right to become Nārāyaṇa.

TEXT 56

भुक्तवत्सु च सर्वेषु दीनान्धकृपणादिषु ।
विष्णोस्तत्प्रीणनं विद्वान्भुञ्जीत सह बन्धुभिः ॥५६॥

bhuktavatsu ca sarveṣu
dīnāndha-kṛpaṇādiṣu
viṣṇos tat prīṇanaṁ vidvān
bhuñjīta saha bandhubhiḥ

bhuktavatsu—after feeding; *ca*—also; *sarveṣu*—everyone present there; *dīna*—very poor; *andha*—blind; *kṛpaṇa*—those who are not *brāhmaṇas; ādiṣu*—and so on; *viṣṇoḥ*—of Lord Viṣṇu, who is situated in everyone's heart; *tat*—that (*prasāda*); *prīṇanam*—pleasing; *vidvān*—one who understands this philosophy; *bhuñjīta*—should take *prasāda* himself; *saha*—with; *bandhubhiḥ*—friends and relatives.

TRANSLATION

One should distribute viṣṇu-prasāda to everyone, including the poor man, the blind man, the nondevotee and the non-brāhmaṇa. Knowing that Lord Viṣṇu is very pleased when everyone is sumptuously fed with viṣṇu-prasāda, the performer of yajña should then take prasāda with his friends and relatives.

TEXT 57

नृत्यवादित्रगीतैश्च स्तुतिभिः स्वस्तिवाचकैः ।
कारयेत्तत्कथाभिश्च पूजां भगवतोऽन्वहम् ॥५७॥

nṛtya-vāditra-gītaiś ca
stutibhiḥ svasti-vācakaiḥ
kārayet tat-kathābhiś ca
pūjāṁ bhagavato 'nvaham

nṛtya—by dancing; *vāditra*—by beating the drum; *gītaiḥ*—and by singing; *ca*—also; *stutibhiḥ*—by chanting auspicious *mantras; svasti-vācakaiḥ*—by offering prayers; *kārayet*—should execute; *tat-kathābhiḥ*—by reciting the *Bhāgavatam, Bhagavad-gītā* and similar literature; *ca*—also; *pūjām*—worship; *bhagavataḥ*—of the Supreme Personality of Godhead, Viṣṇu; *anvaham*—every day (from *pratipat* to *trayodaśī*).

TRANSLATION

Every day from pratipat to trayodaśī, one should continue the ceremony, to the accompaniment of dancing, singing, the beating of a drum, the chanting of prayers and all-auspicious mantras, and recitation of Śrīmad-Bhāgavatam. In this way, one should worship the Supreme Personality of Godhead.

TEXT 58

एतत्पयोव्रतं नाम पुरुषाराधनं परम् ।
पितामहेनाभिहितं मया ते समुदाहृतम् ॥५८॥

etat payo-vrataṁ nāma
puruṣārādhanaṁ param
pitāmahenābhihitaṁ
mayā te samudāhṛtam

etat—this; *payaḥ-vratam*—ceremony known as *payo-vrata; nāma*—by that name; *puruṣa-ārādhanam*—the process of worshiping the Supreme Personality of Godhead; *param*—the best; *pitāmahena*—by my grandfather, Lord Brahmā; *abhihitam*—stated; *mayā*—by me; *te*—unto you; *samudāhṛtam*—described in all details.

TRANSLATION

This is the religious ritualistic ceremony known as payo-vrata, by which one may worship the Supreme Personality of Godhead. I received this information from Brahmā, my grandfather, and now I have described it to you in all details.

TEXT 59

त्वं चानेन महाभागे सम्यक्चीर्णेन केशवम् ।
आत्मना शुद्धभावेन नियतात्मा भजाव्ययम् ॥५९॥

tvaṁ cānena mahā-bhāge
samyak cīrṇena keśavam
ātmanā śuddha-bhāvena
niyatātmā bhajāvyayam

tvam ca—you also; *anena*—by this process; *mahā-bhāge*—O greatly fortunate one; *samyak cīrṇena*—executed properly; *keśavam*—unto Lord Keśava; *ātmanā*—by oneself; *śuddha-bhāvena*—in a pure state of mind; *niyata-ātmā*—controlling oneself; *bhaja*—go on worshiping; *avyayam*—the Supreme Personality of Godhead, who is inexhaustible.

TRANSLATION

O most fortunate lady, establishing your mind in a good spirit, execute this process of payo-vrata and thus worship the Supreme Personality of Godhead, Keśava, who is inexhaustible.

TEXT 60

अयं वै सर्वयज्ञाख्यः सर्वव्रतमिति स्मृतम् ।
तपःसारमिदं भद्रे दानं चेश्वरतर्पणम् ॥६०॥

ayaṁ vai sarva-yajñākhyaḥ
sarva-vratam iti smṛtam
tapaḥ-sāram idaṁ bhadre
dānaṁ ceśvara-tarpaṇam

ayam—this; *vai*—indeed; *sarva-yajña*—all kinds of religious rituals and sacrifices; *ākhyaḥ*—called; *sarva-vratam*—all religious ceremonies; *iti*—thus; *smṛtam*—understood; *tapaḥ-sāram*—the essence of all austerities; *idam*—this; *bhadre*—O good lady; *dānam*—acts of charity; *ca*—and; *īśvara*—the Supreme Personality of Godhead; *tarpaṇam*—the process of pleasing.

TRANSLATION

This payo-vrata is also known as sarva-yajña. In other words, by performing this sacrifice one can perform all other sacrifices automatically. This is also acknowledged to be the best of all ritualistic

ceremonies. O gentle lady, it is the essence of all austerities, and it is the process of giving charity and pleasing the supreme controller.

PURPORT

Ārādhanānāṁ sarveṣāṁ viṣṇor ārādhanaṁ param. This is a statement made by Lord Śiva to Pārvatī. Worshiping Lord Viṣṇu is the supreme process of worship. And how Lord Viṣṇu is worshiped in this *payo-vrata* ceremony has now been fully described. The ultimate goal of life is to please Lord Viṣṇu by *varṇāśrama-dharma.* The Vedic principles of four *varṇas* and four *āśramas* are meant for worship of Viṣṇu (*viṣṇur ārādhyate puṁsāṁ nānyat tat-toṣa-kāraṇam*). The Kṛṣṇa consciousness movement is also *viṣṇu-ārādhanam,* or worship of Lord Viṣṇu, according to the age. The *payo-vrata* method of *viṣṇu-ārādhanam* was enunciated long, long ago by Kaśyapa Muni to his wife, Aditi, in the heavenly planets, and the same process is bona fide on earth even now. Especially for this age of Kali, the process accepted by the Kṛṣṇa consciousness movement is to open hundreds and thousands of Viṣṇu temples (temples of Rādhā-Kṛṣṇa, Jagannātha, Balarāma, Sītā-Rāma, Gaura-Nitāi and so on). Performing prescribed worship in such temples of Viṣṇu and thus worshiping the Lord is as good as performing the *payo-vrata* ceremony recommended here. The *payo-vrata* ceremony is performed from the first to the thirteenth day of the bright fortnight of the moon, but in our Kṛṣṇa consciousness movement Lord Viṣṇu is worshiped in every temple according to a schedule of twenty-four hours of engagement in performing *kīrtana,* chanting the Hare Kṛṣṇa *mahā-mantra,* offering palatable food to Lord Viṣṇu and distributing this food to Vaiṣṇavas and others. These are authorized activities, and if the members of the Kṛṣṇa consciousness movement stick to these principles, they will achieve the same result one gains by observing the *payo-vrata* ceremony. Thus the essence of all auspicious activities, such as performing *yajña,* giving in charity, observing *vratas,* and undergoing austerities, is included in the Kṛṣṇa consciousness movement. The members of this movement should immediately and sincerely follow the processes already recommended. Of course, sacrifice is meant to please Lord Viṣṇu. *Yajñaiḥ saṅkīrtana-prāyair yajanti hi sumedhasaḥ:* in Kali-yuga, those who are intelligent perform the *saṅkīrtana-yajña.* One should follow this process conscientiously.

TEXT 61

त एव नियमाः साक्षात्त एव च यमोत्तमाः ।
तपो दानं व्रतं यज्ञो येन तुष्यत्यधोक्षजः ॥६१॥

ta eva niyamāḥ sākṣāt
ta eva ca yamottamāḥ
tapo dānaṁ vrataṁ yajño
yena tuṣyaty adhokṣajaḥ

te—that is; *eva*—indeed; *niyamāḥ*—all regulative principles; *sākṣāt*—directly; *te*—that is; *eva*—indeed; *ca*—also; *yama-uttamāḥ*—the best process of controlling the senses; *tapaḥ*—austerities; *dānam*—charity; *vratam*—observing vows; *yajñaḥ*—sacrifice; *yena*—by which process; *tuṣyati*—is very pleased; *adhokṣajaḥ*—the Supreme Lord, who is not perceived by material senses.

TRANSLATION

This is the best process for pleasing the transcendental Supreme Personality of Godhead, known as Adhokṣaja. It is the best of all regulative principles, the best austerity, the best process of giving charity, and the best process of sacrifice.

PURPORT

The Supreme Lord says in *Bhagavad-gītā* (18.66):

sarva-dharmān parityajya
māṁ ekaṁ śaraṇaṁ vraja
ahaṁ tvāṁ sarva-pāpebhyo
mokṣayiṣyāmi mā śucaḥ

"Abandon all varieties of religion and just surrender unto Me. I shall deliver you from all sinful reaction. Do not fear." Unless one pleases the Supreme Personality of Godhead according to His demand, no good result will come from any of his actions.

dharmaḥ svanuṣṭhitaḥ puṁsāṁ
viṣvaksena-kathāsu yaḥ

notpādayed yadi ratiṁ
śrama eva hi kevalam

"The occupational activities a man performs according to his own position are only so much useless labor if they do not provoke attraction for the message of the Personality of Godhead." (*Bhāg.* 1.2.8) If one is not interested in satisfying Lord Viṣṇu, Vāsudeva, all his so-called auspicious activities are fruitless. *Moghāśā mogha-karmāṇo mogha-jñānā vicetasaḥ:* because he is bewildered, he is baffled in his hopes, baffled in his activities, and baffled in his knowledge. In this regard, Śrīla Viśvanātha Cakravartī remarks, *napuṁsakam anapuṁsakenety-ādinaikatvam.* One cannot equate the potent and the impotent. Among modern Māyāvādīs it has become fashionable to say that whatever one does or whatever path one follows is all right. But these are all foolish statements. Here it is forcefully affirmed that this is the only method for success in life. *Īśvara-tarpaṇaṁ vinā sarvam eva viphalam.* Unless Lord Viṣṇu is satisfied, all of one's pious activities, ritualistic ceremonies and *yajñas* are simply for show and have no value. Unfortunately, foolish people do not know the secret of success. *Na te viduḥ svārtha-gatiṁ hi viṣṇum.* They do not know that real self-interest ends in pleasing Lord Viṣṇu.

TEXT 62

तस्मादेतद्व्रतं भद्रे प्रयता श्रद्धयाचर ।
भगवान्परितुष्टस्ते वरानाशु विधास्यति ॥६२॥

tasmād etad vrataṁ bhadre
prayatā śraddhayācara
bhagavān parituṣṭas te
varān āśu vidhāsyati

tasmāt—therefore; *etat*—this; *vratam*—observance of a *vrata* ceremony; *bhadre*—my dear gentle lady; *prayatā*—by observing rules and regulations; *śraddhayā*—with faith; *ācara*—execute; *bhagavān*—the Supreme Personality of Godhead; *parituṣṭaḥ*—being very satisfied; *te*—unto you; *varān*—benedictions; *āśu*—very soon; *vidhāsyati*—will bestow.

TRANSLATION

Therefore, my dear gentle lady, follow this ritualistic vow, strictly observing the regulative principles. By this process, the Supreme Person will very soon be pleased with you and will satisfy all your desires.

Thus end the Bhaktivedanta purports of the Eighth Canto, Sixteenth Chapter, of the Śrīmad-Bhāgavatam, *entitled "Executing the Payo-vrata Process of Worship."*

Appendixes

The Author

His Divine Grace A. C. Bhaktivedanta Swami Prabhupāda appeared in this world in 1896 in Calcutta, India. He first met his spiritual master, Śrīla Bhaktisiddhānta Sarasvatī Gosvāmī, in Calcutta in 1922. Bhaktisiddhānta Sarasvatī, a prominent devotional scholar and the founder of sixty-four Gauḍīya Maṭhas (Vedic institutes), liked this educated young man and convinced him to dedicate his life to teaching Vedic knowledge. Śrīla Prabhupāda became his student, and eleven years later (1933) at Allahabad he became his formally initiated disciple.

At their first meeting, in 1922, Śrīla Bhaktisiddhānta Sarasvatī Ṭhākura requested Śrīla Prabhupāda to broadcast Vedic knowledge through the English language. In the years that followed, Śrīla Prabhupāda wrote a commentary on the *Bhagavad-gītā*, assisted the Gauḍīya Maṭha in its work and, in 1944, without assistance, started an English fortnightly magazine, edited it, typed the manuscripts and checked the galley proofs. He even distributed the individual copies freely and struggled to maintain the publication. Once begun, the magazine never stopped; it is now being continued by his disciples in the West.

Recognizing Śrīla Prabhupāda's philosophical learning and devotion, the Gauḍīya Vaiṣṇava Society honored him in 1947 with the title "Bhaktivedanta." In 1950, at the age of fifty-four, Śrīla Prabhupāda retired from married life, and four years later he adopted the *vānaprastha* (retired) order to devote more time to his studies and writing. Śrīla Prabhupāda traveled to the holy city of Vṛndāvana, where he lived in very humble circumstances in the historic medieval temple of Rādhā-Dāmodara. There he engaged for several years in deep study and writing. He accepted the renounced order of life (*sannyāsa*) in 1959. At Rādhā-Dāmodara, Śrīla Prabhupāda began work on his life's masterpiece: a multivolume translation and commentary on the eighteen thousand verse *Śrīmad-Bhāgavatam* (*Bhāgavata Purāṇa*). He also wrote *Easy Journey to Other Planets.*

After publishing three volumes of *Bhāgavatam*, Śrīla Prabhupāda came to the United States, in 1965, to fulfill the mission of his spiritual master. Since that time, His Divine Grace has written over forty volumes of authoritative translations, commentaries and summary studies of the philosophical and religious classics of India.

In 1965, when he first arrived by freighter in New York City, Śrīla Prabhupāda was practically penniless. It was after almost a year of great difficulty that he established the International Society for Krishna Consciousness in July of 1966. Under his careful guidance, the Society has grown within a decade to a worldwide confederation of almost one hundred *āśramas*, schools, temples, institutes and farm communities.

In 1968, Śrīla Prabhupāda created New Vṛndāvana, an experimental Vedic community in the hills of West Virginia. Inspired by the success of New Vṛndāvana, now a thriving farm community of more than one thousand acres, his students have since founded several similar communities in the United States and abroad.

In 1972, His Divine Grace introduced the Vedic system of primary and secondary education in the West by founding the Gurukula school in Dallas, Texas. The school began with 3 children in 1972, and by the beginning of 1975 the enrollment had grown to 150.

Śrīla Prabhupāda has also inspired the construction of a large international center at Śrīdhāma Māyāpur in West Bengal, India, which is also the site for a planned Institute of Vedic Studies. A similar project is the magnificent Kṛṣṇa-Balarāma Temple and International Guest House in Vṛndāvana, India. These are centers where Westerners can live to gain firsthand experience of Vedic culture.

Śrīla Prabhupāda's most significant contribution, however, is his books. Highly respected by the academic community for their authoritativeness, depth and clarity, they are used as standard textbooks in numerous college courses. His writings have been translated into eleven languages. The Bhaktivedanta Book Trust, established in 1972 exclusively to publish the works of His Divine Grace, has thus become the world's largest publisher of books in the field of Indian religion and philosophy. Its latest project is the publishing of Śrīla Prabhupāda's most recent work: a seventeen-volume translation and commentary—completed by Śrīla Prabhupāda in only eighteen months—on the Bengali religious classic *Śrī Caitanya-caritāmṛta.*

In the past ten years, in spite of his advanced age, Śrīla Prabhupāda has circled the globe twelve times on lecture tours that have taken him to six continents. In spite of such a vigorous schedule, Śrīla Prabhupāda continues to write prolifically. His writings constitute a veritable library of Vedic philosophy, religion, literature and culture.

References

The purports of *Śrīmad-Bhāgavatam* are all confirmed by standard Vedic authorities. The following authentic scriptures are specifically cited in this volume:

Aitareya Upaniṣad, 139

Bhagavad-gītā, 23, 24, 67, 69, 70, 71, 96, 100, 101, 104–105, 105, 107, 108, 113, 113–114, 124, 135, 136, 137, 139, 145, 156, 176, 177, 180, 216, 220–221, 221, 225, 227, 227–228, 231–232, 232, 259

Bhāgavata-candra-candrikā, 107

Bhakti-rasāmṛta-sindhu, 108–109, 112

Brahma-saṁhitā, 100, 115

Brahma-yāmala, 112

Caitanya-caritāmṛta, 24, 135, 230, 233

Chāndogya Upaniṣad, 108

Manu-saṁhitā, 8

Śrīmad-Bhāgavatam, 48–49, 81, 103, 113, 125, 133, 174, 213, 225, 227, 229, 259–260

Śvetāśvatara Upaniṣad, 131

Vedānta-sūtra, 107

Viṣṇu Purāṇa, 109

Glossary

A

Ācamana—purification by sipping water and chanting the names of the Lord.
Ācārya—a spiritual master who teaches by example.
Acit—without life or consciousness.
Ārati—a ceremony for greeting the Lord with offerings of food, lamps, fans, flowers and incense.
Arcanā—the devotional process of Deity worship.
Artha—economic development.
Asat—not eternal.
Āśrama—(1) the four spiritual orders of life: celibate student, householder, retired life and renounced life. (2) the residence of a saintly person.
Asuras—atheistic demons.
Avatāra—a descent of the Supreme Lord.

B

Bhagavad-gītā—the basic directions for spiritual life spoken by the Lord Himself.
Bhakta—a devotee.
Bhakti-yoga—linking with the Supreme Lord by devotional service.
Brahmacarya—celibate student life; the first order of Vedic spiritual life.
Brahman—the Absolute Truth; especially the impersonal aspect of the Absolute.
Brāhmaṇa—one wise in the *Vedas* who can guide society; the first Vedic social order.
Brahmāstra—a nuclear weapon produced by chanting *mantras.*

C

Chandas—the different meters of Vedic hymns.
Cit—alive and conscious.

D

Dharma—eternal occupational duty; religious principles.
Dvādaśī—the twelfth day after the full or new moon.

E

Ekādaśī—a special fast day for increased remembrance of Kṛṣṇa, which comes on the eleventh day of both the waxing and waning moon.

G

Goloka (Kṛṣṇaloka)—the highest spiritual planet, containing Kṛṣṇa's personal abodes, Dvārakā, Mathurā and Vṛndāvana.
Gopīs—Kṛṣṇa's cowherd girl friends, His most confidential servitors.
Gṛhastha—regulated householder life; the second order of Vedic spiritual life.
Guru—a spiritual master.

H

Hare Kṛṣṇa mantra—*See: Mahā-mantra*

J

Jagat—the material universe.
Jīva-tattva—the living entities, atomic parts of the Lord.
Jñāna-kāṇḍa—the portion of the *Vedas* containing knowledge of Brahman, spirit.
Jñānī—one who cultivates knowledge by empirical speculation.

K

Kali-yuga (Age of Kali)—the present age, characterized by quarrel; it is last in the cycle of four and began five thousand years ago.
Kāma—lust.
Karatālas—hand cymbals used in *kīrtana.*
Karma—fruitive action, for which there is always reaction, good or bad.
Karma-kāṇḍa—a section of the *Vedas* prescribing fruitive activities for elevation to a higher material position.
Karmī—a person satisfied with working hard for flickering sense gratification.

Kīrtana—chanting the glories of the Supreme Lord.
Kṛṣṇaloka—*See:* Goloka
Kṣatriyas—a warrior or administrator; the second Vedic social order.

M

Mahā-mantra—the great chanting for deliverance:
Hare Kṛṣṇa, Hare Kṛṣṇa, Kṛṣṇa Kṛṣṇa, Hare Hare
Hare Rāma, Hare Rāma, Rāma Rāma, Hare Hare.
Mantra—a sound vibration that can deliver the mind from illusion.
Manvantara—the duration of each Manu's reign (306,720,000 years); used as a standard division of history.
Mathurā—Lord Kṛṣṇa's abode, surrounding Vṛndāvana, where He took birth and later returned to after performing His Vṛndāvana pastimes.
Māyā—illusion; forgetfulness of one's relationship with Kṛṣṇa.
Māyāvādīs—impersonal philosophers who say that the Lord cannot have a transcendental body.
Mokṣa—liberation.
Mṛdaṅga—a clay drum used for congregational chanting.

P

Paramparā—the chain of spiritual masters in disciplic succession.
Prajāpatis—the populators of the universe.
Prasāda—food spiritualized by being offered to the Lord.

R

Rāsa—the nonmaterial taste of a personal relationship with the Supreme Lord.
Ṛṣi—a sage.

S

Sac-cid-ānanda-vigraha—the Lord's transcendental form, which is eternal, full of knowledge and bliss.
Saṅkīrtana—public chanting of the names of God, the approved *yoga* process for this age.
Sannyāsa—renounced life; the fourth order of Vedic spiritual life.
Śāstras—revealed scriptures.

Sat—eternal.
Smṛti scriptures—supplementary explanations of the *Vedas.*
Śravaṇaṁ kīrtanaṁ viṣṇoḥ—the devotional processes of hearing and chanting about Lord Viṣṇu.
Śruti scriptures—the original Vedic literatures: the four *Vedas* and the *Upaniṣads.*
Śūdra—a laborer; the fourth of the Vedic social orders.
Svāmī—one who controls his mind and senses; title of one in the renounced order of life.

T

Tapasya—austerity; accepting some voluntary inconvenience for a higher purpose.
Tilaka—auspicious clay marks that sanctify a devotee's body as a temple of the Lord.

U

Upāsanā-kāṇḍa—a section of the *Vedas* prescribing worship of demigods.

V

Vaikuṇṭha—the spiritual world.
Vaiṣṇava—a devotee of Lord Viṣṇu, Kṛṣṇa.
Vaiśyas—farmers and merchants; the third Vedic social order.
Vānaprastha—one who has retired from family life; the third order of Vedic spiritual life.
Varṇa—the four occupational divisions of society: the intellectual class, the administrative class, the mercantile and agricultural class, and the laborer class.
Varṇāśrama—the Vedic system of four social and four spiritual orders.
Vedas—the original revealed scriptures, first spoken by the Lord Himself.
Viṣṇu, Lord—Kṛṣṇa's first expansion for the creation and maintenance of the material universes.
Viṣṇu-tattva—the original Personality of Godhead's primary expansions, each of whom is equally God.

Vṛndāvana—Kṛṣṇa's personal abode, where He fully manifests His quality of sweetness.

Vyāsadeva—Kṛṣṇa's incarnation, at the end of Dvāpara-yuga, for compiling the *Vedas*.

Y

Yajña—sacrifice; work done for the satisfaction of Lord Viṣṇu.

Yoga-siddhis—mystic powers.

Yogī—a transcendentalist who, in one way or another, is striving for union with the Supreme.

Yugas—ages in the life of a universe, occurring in a repeated cycle of four.

Sanskrit Pronunciation Guide

Vowels

अ a आ ā इ i ई ī उ u ऊ ū ऋ ṛ ॠ ṝ
ऌ ḷ ए e ऐ ai ओ o औ au
ं ṁ *(anusvāra)* ः ḥ *(visarga)*

Consonants

Gutturals:	क ka	ख kha	ग ga	घ gha	ङ ṅa
Palatals:	च ca	छ cha	ज ja	झ jha	ञ ña
Cerebrals:	ट ṭa	ठ ṭha	ड ḍa	ढ ḍha	ण ṇa
Dentals:	त ta	थ tha	द da	ध dha	न na
Labials:	प pa	फ pha	ब ba	भ bha	म ma
Semivowels:	य ya	र ra	ल la	व va	
Sibilants:	श śa	ष ṣa	स sa		
Aspirate:	ह ha	ऽ ' *(avagraha)* – the apostrophe			

The vowels above should be pronounced as follows:

a – like the *a* in org*a*n or the *u* in b*u*t.
ā – like the *a* in f*a*r but held twice as long as short *a*.
i – like the *i* in p*i*n.
ī – like the *i* in p*i*que but held twice as long as short *i*.
u – like the *u* in p*u*sh.
ū – like the *u* in r*u*le but held twice as long as short *u*.

ṛ – like the *ri* in *ri*m.
ṝ – like *ree* in *ree*d.
ḷ – like *l* followed by *ṛ* (*lṛ*).
e – like the *e* in th*e*y.
ai – like the *ai* in *ai*sle.
o – like the *o* in g*o*.
au – like the *ow* in h*ow*.
ṁ (*anusvāra*) – a resonant nasal like the *n* in the French word *bon*.
ḥ (*visarga*) – a final *h*-sound: *aḥ* is pronounced like *aha; iḥ* like *ihi*.

The consonants are pronounced as follows:

k – as in *k*ite
kh – as in Ec*kh*art
g – as in *g*ive
gh – as in di*g-h*ard
ṅ – as in si*ng*
c – as in *ch*air
ch – as in staun*ch-h*eart
j – as in *j*oy
jh – as in he*dgeh*og
ñ – as in ca*ny*on
ṭ – as in *t*ub
ṭh – as in ligh*t-h*eart
ḍ – as in *d*ove
ḍha- as in re*d-h*ot
ṇ – as r*na* (prepare to say the *r* and say *na*).

Cerebrals are pronounced with tongue to roof of mouth, but the following dentals are pronounced with tongue against teeth:

t – as in *t*ub but with tongue against teeth.
th – as in ligh*t-h*eart but with tongue against teeth.
d – as in *d*ove but with tongue against teeth.
dh – as in re*d-h*ot but with tongue against teeth.
n – as in *n*ut but with tongue between teeth.
p – as in *p*ine
ph – as in u*ph*ill (not *f*)
b – as in *b*ird
bh – as in ru*b-h*ard
m – as in *m*other
y – as in *y*es
r – as in *r*un
l – as in *l*ight
v – as in *v*ine
ś (palatal) – as in the *s* in the German word *sprechen*
ṣ (cerebral) – as the *sh* in *sh*ine
s – as in *s*un
h – as in *h*ome

There is no strong accentuation of syllables in Sanskrit, only a flowing of short and long (twice as long as the short) syllables.

Index of Sanskrit Verses

This index constitutes a complete listing of the first and third lines of each of the Sanskrit poetry verses of this volume of *Śrīmad-Bhāgavatam*, arranged in English alphabetical order. The first column gives the Sanskrit transliteration, and the second and third columns, respectively, list the chapter-verse reference and page number for each verse.

A

O

P

T

U

V

General Index

Numerals in boldface type indicate references to translations of the verses of *Śrīmad-Bhāgavatam.*

A

Absolute Truth
devotional service reveals, 109
Lord as, **101**, 102, 135
as one and different, 102
pāñcarātrikī-vidhi reveals, 112
philosophers cannot find, 180
surrender reveals, 113
Vaiśeṣika philosophers misunderstand, 108
See also: Supreme Lord
Ācārya. See: Spiritual master, all entries
Ācāryaṁ māṁ vijānīyāt
quoted, 233
Acintya-bhedābheda
Absolute Truth as, 102
Lord as, 105
Activities
in base modes of nature, 112
fruitful vs. futile, 260
of the Lord. *See:* Incarnations of the Supreme Lord; Supreme Lord, *appropriate entries*
Lord's pleasure as measure of, 259–260
material vs. spiritual, **23–24**, **25–26**
time controls, **68**, 69, **70**
See also: Karma
Adbhuta, **159**, **160**
Aditi
as *ārta,* 232
as demigods' mother, **210**, 222
as householder, **212**, 213
Aditi
Kaśyapa advised, on devotional service, **226**, 228, **229**
Kaśyapa begged by, for instructions, **231**, **232**
Kaśyapa begged by, for protection, **222**, **223**
Kaśyapa instructed, on *payo-vrata,* **235–256**
Kaśyapa queried, **212**, **214**, **215**, 217
Kaśyapa reassured by, about household, **218**, **219**
lamentation of, **210**, **211**, **117**, **222**
as materially attached, **212**, **214**
quoted on household life, **218**
quoted on worshiping the Lord, **231**
as Vāmana's mother, **151**
Age of Kali. *See:* Kali-yuga
Agni as demigod warrior, **41**, **92**
Ahaituky apratihatā
quoted, 105
Aham ādir hi devānāṁ
quoted, 102
Ahaṁ sarvasya prabhavo
quoted, 102, 180
Ahaṁ tvāṁ sarva-pāpebhyo
verse quoted, 259
Ahaṅkāra itīyaṁ me
verse quoted, 101, 107
Aikāntikī harer bhaktir
verse quoted, 112
Air, Lord compared to, **114**, 115
Airāvata
Bali attacked, **51**

H

I

N

T

DATE DUE

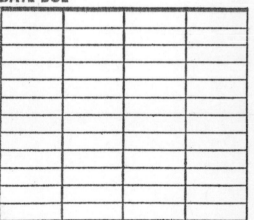